THE BEST SHORT PLAYS *1971*

Chilton Book Company
RADNOR, PA.

THE
BEST
SHORT
PLAYS *1971*

edited and with an introduction by

STANLEY RICHARDS

The Margaret Mayorga Series

ANALYTICS

Copyright © 1971 by Stanley Richards
First Edition
All rights reserved
Published in Radnor, Pa., by Chilton Book Company
and simultaneously in Ontario, Canada,
by Thomas Nelson & Sons, Ltd.

Second Printing, June 1974

ISBN: 0-8019-5587-4
Library of Congress Catalog Card Number 38-8006
Designed by Adrianne Onderdonk Dudden
Manufactured in the United States of America

for Joan White and

Paul Slocumb-Rolley

BOOKS AND PLAYS *by Stanley Richards*

BOOKS:

The Best Short Plays 1970
The Best Short Plays 1969
The Best Short Plays 1968
Best Mystery and Suspense Plays of the Modern Theatre
Best Plays of the Sixties
Modern Short Comedies from Broadway and London
Best Short Plays of the World Theatre: 1958–1967
Canada on Stage

PLAYS:

Through a Glass, Darkly
August Heat
Sun Deck
Tunnel of Love
Journey to Bahia
O Distant Land
Mood Piece
Mr. Bell's Creation
The Proud Age
Once to Every Boy
Half-Hour, Please
Know Your Neighbor
Gin and Bitterness
The Hills of Bataan
District of Columbia

CONTENTS

INTRODUCTION

According to a well-weathered aphorism, it is only the dead actor who does not rejoice in telling a theatrical anecdote. Anthony Quayle is no exception. Co-star of the international success, *Sleuth,* he often enjoys regaling backstage visitors with a particular favorite: "One day, an old and rather shabby-looking Victorian actor, who was touring the British countryside with his troupe of players, came upon a run-down pub by the side of the road and decided to partake of some healthy imbibing. After several drinks, and while leaning against the bar, he noticed a woman dressed in a very tantalizing outfit wearing a lot of flashy make-up standing next to him and who obviously was a prostitute. He asked the bartender to bring a stout mug of ale for him and a gin for the lady. As they were just about to take the drinks, the actor stood up straight and tall and made a toast: 'I drink to the two oldest professions in the world—both of them ruined by amateurs!' "

Mr. Quayle's droll little tale has more than a modicum of truth when one considers the state of today's Broadway theatre with its steadily decreasing volume of production, its emphasis on musicals and comedies, and its cavalier indifference to serious drama. It is a situation that recurrently is attributed to two major factors—soaring production costs and the desertion of the theatre by our established and more talented playwrights, thus creating a paucity of significant and worthy plays.

While it is simple enough to agree with the economic reference, it is difficult to assimilate the theory that our professional dramatists have yielded our stages to the less experienced, the less talented, and, by inference, the amateur. In truth, very few of our leading contemporary dramatists have been usurped by death, television or Hollywood. Most are very well indeed, vibrantly alive and working at their craft, though, admittedly, they are finding it increasingly difficult to have their works staged, especially serious plays. Although the present state of affairs has generated a good deal of discussion and theorizing, few have pinpointed one of its more fundamental causes: the producer.

In the past decade or so, there has emerged a new breed of impressario, many of them theatrically inexperienced, creatively inept, and more concerned with swelling their personal coffers than with enriching our theatre. Since a play also is a reflection of a producer's taste—after all, he chooses the play and sets its production wheels in motion—he is giving the public what *he* wants or what he *thinks* the public wants. More often than not, his superimposed judgment boomerangs because he has fatally underestimated the intelligence and demands of audiences.

To a large measure, this accounts for the comparatively few serious plays produced during the Broadway season and for the involuntary absence of many of our distinguished dramatists. If, then, the legitimate theatre, as related in Mr. Quayle's timeless anecdote, has been diminished by "amateurs," the fault, dear Brutus, is not so much in our playwrights, but in our managements. They must assume the brunt of responsibility for the existent mediocrity and the unfortunate deprivation of serious works in the Broadway theatre.

The producers of yesteryear were of an entirely different ilk. Though some were fierce, almost despotic in their pursuit of perfection, they were keen showmen with a passionate devotion to the theatre. They had perception, an innate sense of what would or would not work theatrically and were cognizant of the fact that good theatre only eventuates when the dramatic effect is inherent in the writing. They developed playwrights as well as stars, directors and designers, for theirs was a theatre of continuity, offering to its artists exceptional opportunities for creative growth and achievement.

Plays require careful and dedicated nurturing in order

to reach proper fulfillment on stage, just as the playwright (regardless of his stature) benefits from perceptive guidance in the delicate process of effectively transmuting his work from the impersonal manuscript page to the viability of the theatre. As Jean Anouilh has said, "Completing the writing of a play is only the beginning. Come the rehearsals, which often revise the play itself. It must be fitted to the production. Perhaps the stage is too big, or perhaps too small. Or there are insufficient means . . . new lines, new incidents occur to me as we are working, or the perfect actor is unavailable and another must do. All this spurs theatrical ingenuity."

With perhaps a handful of exceptions, few present-day producers (and, alas, some directors) have the capability of offering this essential creative ministering to a play or else rush headlong into rehearsal as soon as the capital is raised regardless of the condition of the script because of a theatre booked for a specific date, the sudden availability of a star or theatre party commitments.

Since the opening night jurors are on hand to evaluate the finished product rather than whatever potentials the play may have had, when an abortive work fails it is the author who generally is censured, frequently discouraging him from further work in the theatre. Countless promising talents have trod this disheartening path and consequently moved on to other fields.

Yet, hope is brightest when it dawns from fears, and the League of New York Theatres has just announced a new and revolutionary plan designed to revitalize the Broadway theatre. Referred to as the "Middle Theatre Contract," plays now may be staged in one of twelve "limited gross" Broadway houses on considerably modified budgets through concessions from the various craft unions and guilds. With reduced production and operating costs, ticket prices will be substantially lowered and, hopefully, will win back a considerable segment of the theatre-going public that has been priced out of the inflated market, as well as attracting young people to the legitimate theatre. Most significant of all, however, the plan is expected to motivate a resurgence of serious drama in an area that, in spite of recent creative lapses, still remains the theatrical center of the nation. Correlatively, it also could give rise to a new crop of courageous and imaginative producers.

STANLEY RICHARDS
New York, New York
March, 1971

Barry Hines

BILLY'S LAST STAND

Barry Hines

When *Billy's Last Stand* opened on June 30, 1970, at the Royal Court's Theatre Upstairs, London, it was hailed in the British press as a "triumph" that is both "tender and touching," its author, Barry Hines, "obviously a master of the small, closely observed subject."

The drama critic for *The Financial Times* reported: "Barry Hines' play can be interpreted in whichever way one pleases: an instinctive revolt against the pressure of modern life; the struggle for freedom, the destructive power of capitalist methods—or simply a story told with the intensity and detail of D. H. Lawrence at his best, each small movement significant in its day to day routine. Dramatically, the effect is gripping. . . ." Other reviewers concurred: "An engrossing and affecting study of good and evil in terms of coal-shoveling in Yorkshire. The mood is very much that of the D. H. Lawrence plays in its exact and loving care for realism; and the theme is as straightforward as in any morality play about a man whose soul is being bargained for. It is a beautifully told tale. . . ."

Milton Shulman of the *London Evening Standard* provided the copestone in his summation of the work: "As a neat exercise in oblique, shadowed writing, Mr. Hines reveals a considerable literary touch. One feels creeping beneath the surface of the obvious action something more sinister, more significant and more universal."

Originally produced on B.B.C. Television, *Billy's Last Stand* was adapted for the stage by Mr. Hines, and its premiere at the Octagon Theatre in Bolton was a notable success. It was then brought to London (with Ian McKellen and John Barrett as, respectively, Darkly and Billy), where it immediately became a sellout at the Royal Court's experimental playhouse in Sloane Square.

The initial version of the play contained a good deal of regional dialect that might have proven somewhat difficult for American audiences. Consequently, the editor suggested to the author that the dialect be modified, to which he readily consented: "The dialect in this area is very complicated and really convoluted, it changes from village to village within the radius of a few miles. I've modified it and I don't think it loses anything in translation."

The locale of the play is a mining village in South Yorkshire, England. "In these villages," explains Mr. Hines, "the household coal is not bagged before delivery but is transported straight from the pit by lorry and tipped loose outside people's houses. Billy earns his living by moving this coal into their coal houses and cellars."

Billy's milieu and profession are thoroughly familiar to Barry Hines for he was born in 1939 in the mining village of Hoyland Common near Barnsley, where his father worked in the mines. While attending grammar school, he was selected for the England Grammar Schools' soccer team. From there it was perhaps a natural, though temporary, step to play football for Barnsley while also working variously as an apprentice mining surveyor, a laborer mending hydraulic pit props, and as an assistant in a blacksmith's shop. Following this interlude, he entered Loughborough Training College where he studied physical education, then went south to London to teach in a comprehensive school for two years. Now he is once more back in his native heath, living in Barnsley with his wife and two children.

Mr. Hines' first novel, *The Blinder,* was published in 1966. Shortly thereafter, he won a bursary from the B.B.C. which enabled him to spend several months on Elba, where he completed his second novel, *A Kestrel for A Knave,* published in 1968. Warmly received, the novel was sold to films, and the author was signed to work on the screenplay with the director, Kenneth Loach. Subsequently titled *Kes,* it was acclaimed in Britain as the "sleeper" of the year and as an official entry at the 1970 Cannes Film Festival was cited as "the best British film of the past several years." The feature was selected for showing at the eighth annual New York Film Festival at Lincoln Center and in January was named runner-up as the best movie of 1970 in the annual poll conducted by the National Board of Review of Motion Pictures.

In addition to his books and plays, Barry Hines has

written many poems and short stories and presently is working on a new novel. *Billy's Last Stand,* his initial play to reach the London stage, appears in print for the first time in *The Best Short Plays 1971.*

Characters:

BILLY

DARKLY

BARMAN

STARK

MEN IN BAR

Scene One

A mining village in South Yorkshire, England.

A man standing at a heap of coal tipped onto the pavement outside a garden gate. The coal fills the pavement. He works in shirt sleeves and cap. Very shabbily dressed. He whistles as he fills a barrow, wheels it up the garden path then tips the contents into the coal shed, empties it and returns, resumes loading. Another man appears who stops and watches. He is tall and slovenly in a big black overcoat.

Silence, except for the scrape of the shovel on the ground and the tumble of the coal into the barrow.

BILLY: *(Stops shoveling and straightens up)* Anything I can do for you?

DARKLY: No.

BILLY: I'm not in your way, am I?

DARKLY: No.

BILLY: Thought you p'raps wanted to come up t'path.

DARKLY: No.

BILLY: Well, what's it you want then?

DARKLY: Nothing. Just watching.

BILLY: Watching what?

DARKLY: You get them coals in.

BILLY: What for?

DARKLY: 'Cos I feel like it.

BILLY: It's a pity you've nothing else to do with your time; it's not a bloody sideshow, you know.

DARKLY: Making hard work of the job, aren't you?

BILLY: Well, it's a hard job, isn't it?

DARKLY: Ar, but you're making it harder still for yourself.

BILLY: In what way?

DARKLY: You're not using your head at all.

BILLY: How can I use my head to get a ton o'coal in? It's not a number five shovel I've got on my shoulders, you know.

DARKLY: Well, for a start you're putting too much in your barrow. Better to put less in, even if it means a few more trips. Conserves energy, less chance o' strains.

BILLY: Anything else?

DARKLY: Ar, you're not using your legs at all when you're shoveling.

BILLY: You don't shovel with your legs.

DARKLY: That's where you're wrong; that's where your power comes from.

BILLY: How's that then?

DARKLY: Well, by bending your legs that mobilizes your large muscle groups and takes all t'strain off your back.

BILLY: O' yes.

DARKLY: You see, the way you're shoveling your back's taking all the weight. Use your legs; conserves energy; less chance o' strains.

BILLY: Who's told you that, then?

DARKLY: I've read it in books.

BILLY: I didn't know there were any books on getting coals in.

DARKLY: There isn't. I've read it in mechanics books, basic principles o'lifting they call it.

BILLY: So, you think you know more about it than me, then, do you?

DARKLY: No. I'm just trying to gi' you a bit of advice, that's all.

BILLY: Well, sod off then and advise somebody else. Who do you think you are standing there in your bloody great overcoat? Get 'em in yourself if you're not satisfied.

(*Darkly begins to unbutton his coat*)

BILLY: Hey, what you doing?

DARKLY: I'm goin' to show you how it's done.

BILLY: Tha's no need to bother, I can get 'em in myself.

DARKLY: (*Buttoning his coat*) You want to make your mind up.

BILLY: Well, what do you expect when you come up, stand there like Clem, then start telling me what to do? Who are you—one o' them time and motionless men?

DARKLY: I'm trying to help you.

BILLY: Well, go and help somebody else. I wa' doing all right till you came interfering.

DARKLY: No need to get nasty.

BILLY: I'm not getting nasty, I just want to get on wi' this job, that's all. I've a living to earn if you haven't. (*He starts to shovel again*)

DARKLY: How much do they pay you?

BILLY: Look, bugger off, and mind your own business, can't you? They'll not pay me *anything* at this rate.

DARKLY: Why don't you let me gi' you a hand? We'll get 'em in twice as sharp then.

BILLY: I don't want a hand. I'd sooner work on my own. I've always worked on my own. (*He starts to shovel again*)

DARKLY: How much do they pay you?

BILLY: (*Straightening up*) Look, I'm warning you. Hey! She's looking through t'curtains; you'll be losing me trade if you're not careful. (*He starts to shovel vigorously*)

DARKLY: We wouldn't want that, would we?

(*Billy continues shoveling for a minute, then stops in midstroke and straightens up as if he has suddenly thought of something*)

BILLY: How do you mean, we?

DARKLY: What?

BILLY: You said *we*. What you got to do wi' it?

DARKLY: I'm thinking o' coming into partnership wi' you.

BILLY: (*Pause*) You're thinking o' *what*?

DARKLY: Forming a partnership.

BILLY: A partnership getting coals in? You must be mad!

DARKLY: Far from it. I've put a lot o' thought into this matter and after careful deliberation . . . very careful deliberation, mind you . . . I've decided to make this offer.

BILLY: *What* offer?

DARKLY: Offer of a partnership. I'm going to take you under my wing and turn this business into a paying proposition.

BILLY: What you talking about, business? I only get coals in.

DARKLY: Well, that's a business, in't it?

BILLY: Is it buggery, it's getting coals in.

DARKLY: Well, what is it then if it isn't a business?

BILLY: (*Pause*) I don't know. I've never thought about it before.

DARKLY: Now's your chance to start then. You're self-employed, aren't you?

BILLY: 'Course I am.

DARKLY: An' you make your living getting coals in, don't you?

BILLY: (*Pause*) Ar.

DARKLY: Well then, what is it if it isn't a business? (*Pause*) Go on, tell me.

BILLY: I suppose it is if you look at it that way—but I think you're making a big thing out of nothing.

DARKLY: That's exactly what I *am* going to do. I'm going to make this job pay. I'm going to reorganize an inefficient business and put it onto a firm financial footing.

BILLY: Hey! Now just hang on a minute. I don't know who you are or what you want, but t'way you're talking you're either pissed or barmy—or both.

DARKLY: Just watch who you're calling barmy!

BILLY: Well, you must be to come up wi' such a bloody daft idea.

DARKLY: What's daft about it?

BILLY: Whoever heard of a partnership on a job like this?

DARKLY: Well, what's wrong wi' that?

BILLY: It's bloody daft.

DARKLY: Why is it?

BILLY: 'Cos it is.

DARKLY: Why? (*Pause*) Go on, tell me.

BILLY: (*Pause*) 'Cos it is.

DARKLY: You don't know, do you? Well, just listen here and . . .

BILLY: You listen here; let's get this straight once and for all. I'm holding this shovel, and I'm getting these coals in. Right?

DARKLY: Right.

BILLY: They've employed *me* to do t' job, and they're paying *me* when it's done. Right?

DARKLY: Right.

BILLY: I've got a job—you haven't. I'm working and you're watching; and you're offering me a partnership in *my* job. Right?

DARKLY: Right.

BILLY: You generous bugger; you'd better sod off before I offer you a crack o'er th' head wi' this shovel!

DARKLY: Hey up! Just be careful who you're threatening. I could always go into direct competition, you know.

BILLY: You can please yourself, it's nothing to do with me.

DARKLY: You'll not be bothered, then, if I come and take half o' your orders?

BILLY: I'd have to put up wi' it, wouldn't I? (*Pause*) I'd make a living somehow.

DARKLY: But what's t' sense in it when we could be working together? What did he say? United we stand, divided we fall.

BILLY: Who?

DARKLY: Abraham Lincoln.

BILLY: Bugger him. I'm working on my own, my own boss in my own time. I scrape a living and I'm satisfied.

DARKLY: You could be doing a lot better though, I know.

BILLY: How do you?

DARKLY: Because I've kept my eyes open and I know that you're the only bloke who does this kind o' work in t' village.

BILLY: So what?

DARKLY: And I know you don't bother overmuch. I've

seen coal lying around for days in one place an' another an' it's
finished up wi' t' lads getting it in.

BILLY: Anything else you know?

DARKLY: I know that you could be earning a lot more
than you are doing.

BILLY: I daresay I could, but I'm not killing myself wi'
an extra two or three ton a day for t' sake o' ten or fifteen bob.

DARKLY: So they pay you five bob a ton, do they?

BILLY: Ar. Any objections?

DARKLY: None at all. Do you know we could really get
this job organized, working together we could really make some
coal crack.

BILLY: I'm making enough crack as it is. I earn enough
for what I want, so what's the point in earning more if I've got
enough already?

DARKLY: You might be managing now, but what about
t'future? I shouldn't think your labor expectancy's much over
five years at most.

BILLY: How do you mean, labor expectancy? You make
it sound as though I'm having a bairn.

DARKLY: What I mean is, I think your working days are
numbered. (*Pause*) Five years at most, I should say.

BILLY: Get away! I'm as fit as a young bull.

DARKLY: You're not getting any younger, though.

BILLY: I know I'm not, but there's plenty o' work left
in me yet.

DARKLY: Ar, but your strength's diminishing, an' it'll ooze
away till you won't be able to shift a spoonful o' coal, ne'er mind
a ton.

BILLY: I don't like to think so far in front.

DARKLY: No, but it'll come 'round just the same. We've
to look at this thing constructively, utilize our powers and make
some money while we've the chance.

BILLY: (*Pause; thinks*) I'll tell you what I'll do.

DARKLY: What?

BILLY: I'll see you some other time. I can't be stood
around like this. I've some work to do.

DARKLY: What other time?

BILLY: Oh, any time. I'm not going anywhere, I'll be about.

DARKLY: I'll come into the Royal and see you then.

BILLY: How do you know I go in there?

DARKLY: I've seen you. I'll see you in there then?

BILLY: You might do.

(*Billy resumes shoveling. Darkly watches for a minute, then walks away. Billy continues shoveling, then straightens up and stands looking after Darkly*)

Scene Two

Bar of the Royal, shabby but comfortable with a coal fire. A few men are scattered around the tables on stools; all are drinking pints. Darkly is standing at the bar. The atmosphere is friendly and the men are talking in their normal speaking voices, laughing out loud quite often. Billy walks in, exchanging greetings as he crosses to the bar. The Barman takes a glass.

BARMAN: Usual, Billy?

BILLY: Ar.

DARKLY: Make it a pint.

(*The Barman hesitates, as if waiting to receive confirmation of the new order. Billy makes no indication one way or the other so the Barman commences to draw the pint. Billy watches him, takes the glass from the bar, drinks, so that he can carry the glass comfortably. Then he walks away and sits at an empty table. Darkly pays for the drink, picks up his own glass and follows him. He sits down with Billy*)

BILLY: You've come then?

DARKLY: I said I would, didn't I?

BILLY: (*Pause*) I thought you might o' packed t' job up.

DARKLY: Why should I?

BILLY: Don't know, just thought you might o' packed it up, that's all.

DARKLY: No. When I say I'm going to do a thing, then I'm going to do it; an' while we're at it, where've you been for t'last three days? I've looked all o'er for you.

BILLY: Oh, 'round about.

DARKLY: Where? I know you haven't been working, an' you haven't been in here 'cos I've called in every night.

BILLY: What's it got to do wi' you where I've been; you're like a bloody vulture hovering 'round. It fair puts me on edge, all this watching and waiting.

DARKLY: Don't start getting agitated.

BILLY: Don't you start telling me what to do then.

DARKLY: All right, all right, let it drop. I wa' just getting worried about you, that's all.

BILLY: Worried, my arse! Why should you be worried about me?

DARKLY: Well, I wouldn't want anything to happen to my partner, would I?

BILLY: Who said anything about being your partner? I never . . .

DARKLY: Just listen t' what I've got to say, will you, before you proceed.

BILLY: Go on then, you might let me alone a bit then.

DARKLY: Right. (*Pulling his chair up closer and leaning over towards Billy across the table*) I've got this thing all worked out an' I know there's money to be made; all it needs is a bit of organization. You see, t'way you're working, Billy, it's too haphazard. There's no planning, no organization. It's a miracle that you get any work at all.

BILLY: An' what will *you* do that'll be so bloody marvelous?

DARKLY: (*Shuffling his chair even closer to the table and leaning across to Billy*) First of all, we've got to build up a clientele of regular customers.

BILLY: A what?

DARKLY: A clientele.

BILLY: What's that?

DARKLY: It's a—you know, a—a group, a group! Have you got any regulars?

BILLY: One or two, nothing definite though.

DARKLY: Well, that's t'first thing we've got to do; build this nucleus o' regulars, let 'em know that they can rely on us.

BILLY: We'll gi' 'em t'office number, they can gi' us a ring when we're wanted.

DARKLY: No, be serious.

BILLY: I'm trying to be.

DARKLY: We've got to have a timetable, work to a schedule. If folks know that we're reliable they'll tell others about us.

BILLY: Then what?

DARKLY: We've got to go 'round shops, pubs, houses, canvassing.

BILLY: What do you mean? Begging for work?

DARKLY: It's not begging, it's just offering our services. You've got to make contacts somehow when you're running a business.

BILLY: Well, I'm not goin' 'round wi' my cap in my hand. All t'work I've done folks have come up to me, asked *me* if I'd do t'job for *them*.

DARKLY: Ar, an' that's why you're in such a state. Folks have never known where to find you. You've got to talk to folks, let 'em see that you're willing.

BILLY: I'm not so willing as to go tramping from door to door. I've still some pride left, even if you haven't.

DARKLY: All right then, but don't start grumbling if you're left shoveling on your own 'cos somebody'll have to organize t'business.

BILLY: There is no business yet.

DARKLY: No, but there can be if only you'd listen! There's plenty o' work, I know that. It just needs brains to organize it. We've to make sure that no customers get away, gi' people dates so that . . .

BILLY: Dates? How do you mean, dates?

DARKLY: Let me finish, will you? Well, if they know that

we're coming on a certain day then they'll not set anybody else on, will they?

BILLY: An' what if we can't make it? It's nearly impossible to stick to a timetable on a job like this.

DARKLY: We'll have to use a bit o' bluff, tell 'em that we'll be round t'first thing in t'morning.

BILLY: Bit o' lying, you mean.

DARKLY: There's bound to be days when we've more on than we can manage, so what else can we do if we want to keep our customers?

BILLY: I don't like t'sound o' this lot. It's dishonest, it's too cunning.

DARKLY: You've *got* to be cunning if you're running a business.

BILLY: You don't have to be dishonest about it though.

DARKLY: We're not being dishonest.

BILLY: I've never swindled anybody in my life.

DARKLY: We're not going to swindle anybody.

BILLY: An' I'm not starting now.

DARKLY: We're not starting now; we're just going to employ a bit of method, that's all, use our brains to make a decent living.

BILLY: (*Pause*) Why pick on me? Why don't you go an' organize somebody else? There are all them folks in t'world an' you've to come and sort me out.

DARKLY: Well, most folks have got themselves organized; there's not many left who live from hand-to-mouth like you do.

BILLY: An' so you felt sorry for me and thought you'd come and save me from starvation, did you?

DARKLY: No, I just saw a good chance for both of us to make some money like everybody else seems to be doing.

BILLY: Save me from starvation an' I've only been on my own since I wa' fourteen. I don't know how I managed to live all them years wi' out you.

DARKLY: Ar, but it's getting harder and harder working on and off like you do, things are changing, closing in. There's no room left any more for casual workers.

BILLY: Ar, things are closing in as you say; *you're* closing in on me. I don't want you, but here you are pestering my life out. I don't doubt that what you say is true, but I don't know as I want it. It might mean more money, but what else will it mean?

DARKLY: It'll mean you'll work regular hours like everybody else. You'll have a decent wage—tax free an' all if we're crafty—you'll be able to buy a few decent clothes, more cigs, more beer.

BILLY: Anything else?

DARKLY: Ar, plenty. You'll be able to get into lodgings if you've a mind, living like a king wi' t'grub on t'table an' all you've to do is come in and scoff it.

BILLY: Sounds like a regular carry-on, don't it?

DARKLY: Well, what's wrong wi' that?

BILLY: Nothing if you're a regular bloke.

DARKLY: Don't you want a regular carry-on then?

BILLY: No, why should I?

DARKLY: Why should you? I've never heard such a ridiculous question in all my life.

BILLY: Go on, answer it then.

DARKLY: Well 'cos you should, that's why. You're just irresponsible, it's nothing but sheer irresponsibility.

BILLY: Call it what you want, name don't matter to me; it's life behind it that I like.

DARKLY: Just think though what we could do; we could build up a fleet o' barrows, different models for different jobs. What do you think to that then, eh? A fleet o' barrows.

BILLY: In black.

DARKLY: Ar, in black—black's distinctive.

BILLY: Matches coal an' all, won't show t'muck, then.

DARKLY: We'll have a stack o' shovels, shining in racks all different sizes. Just think, selecting your shovel in a morning, testing it for size an' weight, judging which'll be t'best for t'job.

BILLY: (*Pause*) A fleet o' barrows and shiny shovels. (*Pause*) Hey! You've forgotten something.

DARKLY: What?

BILLY: Names!

DARKLY: What names?

BILLY: Names on t'sides o' t'barrows. Billy an' . . . Billy an' what?

DARKLY: Darkly.

BILLY: Billy and Darkly Ltd. (*Slight pause*) Coal Shifters.

DARKLY: Not coal *shifters,* we can't have coal SHIFT-ERS.

BILLY: Why can't we? It's what we'll be doing, isn't it—shifting coal?

DARKLY: I know, but it's not dignified enough, needs more style. (*Pause*) Coal . . .

BILLY: Coal getters in.

DARKLY: No! Coal . . . coal removers. That's it, coal removers! Billy and Darkly, coal removers. I like it.

BILLY: You make it sound like Pickfords. Where the bloody hell we going to remove it to? Most we'll ever go is ten yards. Coal removers. It sounds barmy.

DARKLY: It's better than coal shifters. There's no elegance about it, no class. It'll put folks off just to say it. Billy and Darkly, coal shifters. Ugh!

BILLY: I've got another idea an' all.

DARKLY: What?

BILLY: We'll paint t'names in silver. That's real class, in't it?

DARKLY: In silver. (*Pause*) You're right, silver and black. Billy and Darkly in silver and black.

BILLY: Don't miss it, folks! Now showing, the fabulous, the one and only, Billy and Darkly in silver and black! (*Laughs, highly amused with himself*) Sounds like a bloody music hall turn.

DARKLY: You can't put Billy, it'll have to be your other name.

BILLY: My other name? (*Pause*) You're not serious, are you?

DARKLY: 'Course, I'm serious.

BILLY: I thought you wa' acting.

DARKLY: Acting?

BILLY: Well, I wa'. I think it's funny.

DARKLY: I can't see anything funny about it!

BILLY: I can.

DARKLY: What?

BILLY: Everything. Shovels, barrows, names . . . everything.

DARKLY: What's wrong wi' it?

BILLY: Nothing except it kills me just to think about it. Billy and Darkly, coal removers.

DARKLY: Not Billy.

BILLY: Not Darkly either. You can forget it.

DARKLY: (*Pause*) Do you want another drink?

BILLY: Ar, I'll force myself.

(*Darkly goes to the bar for two fresh drinks, returns*)

DARKLY: Well, what do you think o' my plans?

BILLY: I don't know what to think.

DARKLY: Does it make sense what I've said so far?

BILLY: Ar, too much sense for my liking.

DARKLY: How can you have too much sense?

BILLY: It puts me about, makes me wonder what to do for t'best. I wa' satisfied till you came putting fresh ideas into my head.

DARKLY: Nothing wrong wi' fresh ideas.

BILLY: No, but I wa' happy enough as I wa' before. I'd nothing to bother about, and I lived.

DARKLY: You don't call that living, do you? Never knowing where your next meal's coming from, living wi' out system, or organization.

BILLY: I didn't need any system, there wa' nothing to organize. It's just a simple carry-on.

DARKLY: An' look where it's got you.

BILLY: I didn't want to go anywhere.

DARKLY: You've stagnated, that's your trouble, you're rooted down.

BILLY: We'll all be rooted down one day, so what's it matter? A long way down.

DARKLY: That's why you've got to make an effort before it's too late.

BILLY: That's where you're wrong, old lad. That's exactly why you don't have to make an effort 'cos it just don't matter in t'end. I can remember my mother standing at our door watching t'woman next door scuffling about shaking rugs and scrubbing t'flags. She turned on my mother—who wasn't right bothered about housework at t'best o'times—and said, "Have you done then?" sharp-like. My mother said nothing for a minute, then responded, "I've finished early, I'm off up to t'graveyard to visit all them clean folks in there." (*Pause*) She used to get herself talked about, my mother, but she's in there wi' t'rest of 'em now. They're all-in-together-girls and nobody cares.

DARKLY: If you're going to go 'round thinking that life's not worth living . . .

BILLY: It all depends on how you live it, anyway. What have you made of yours then?

DARKLY: A lot more than you.

BILLY: Like hell you have! You've no more than I have except a few more brains—and they've done you no good so it makes no odds.

DARKLY: Done me no good! Do you know, wi' a bit o' luck I'd a been a rich man by now. I've had some brilliant ideas.

BILLY: They've come to naught, though.

DARKLY: How do you know?

BILLY: You wouldn't be sitting here wasting your time wi' me if they had.

DARKLY: It's only a matter o' time before . . .

(*He is interrupted by Billy who begins to sing*)

BILLY: "Tell me the old, old story." (*Pause*) Do you know, I've heard that tale a thousand times. Wherever you go there's always a bloke who thinks it's going to be his turn next. (*Pause*) It might be, but in a different way to what he thinks.

DARKLY: Is that all you think about?

BILLY: No, but it's that certain you can't ignore it.

DARKLY: There's no need to keep harping on about it, though.

BILLY: Nobody's forcing you to stop and listen.

DARKLY: I know they're not.

BILLY: What you stopping for then?

DARKLY: It's not out o' love, I can tell you! I'd be off like a shot if I wasn't here on business.

BILLY: I'll tell you what, I'll think about it. If you want to go I'll see you some other time.

DARKLY: Nay! I'm in no hurry.

BILLY: No, I didn't think you were. You'll not go till you get what you want, will you?

DARKLY: Anybody'd think I wa' trying to pinch something off you.

BILLY: That's what it feels like.

DARKLY: I'm trying to gi' you something, not take it away.

BILLY: It's just a feeling I've got, I can't explain it right.

DARKLY: It's 'cos it's something new, that's all.

BILLY: Might be.

DARKLY: Gi' it a try for a couple o' months. (*Pause*) If you don't like it we'll separate, an' things'll be just like they were before.

BILLY: That's where you're wrong, old lad. Once you've made a change, things can never be t'same as they were before.

DARKLY: (*Pause*) What do you say then?

BILLY: I'm not keen.

DARKLY: A month?

BILLY: A month's a long time.

DARKLY: A month's no time at all. Anyway, it'll be a change for you working wi' somebody else, bring you out a bit.

BILLY: I don't know as I want to be brought out.

DARKLY: It's not good for a man to be on his own all along.

BILLY: Makes life a lot easier.

DARKLY: In what way?

BILLY: Oh, little things. Who else but me could go about dressed like this for instance?

DARKLY: Who'd want to?

BILLY: Folks let me alone 'cos they know it's me, Billy. They laugh but they don't interfere.

DARKLY: There's no wonder.

BILLY: They'll tolerate my rags as long as I'm a ragman, but they'll expect 'em to be burned if I play another part.

DARKLY: You do say some rum things. I reckon it's turned your head being on your own so much.

BILLY: There's a lot thinks that, but it's me that's got t'laugh on them. I made my own choice, I'm independent, an' I enjoy doing what I do. How many folks can say that?

DARKLY: You enjoy getting coals in?

BILLY: I enjoy it as much as I could ever enjoy any job.

DARKLY: What do you like about it?

BILLY: Well . . . it satisfies me. Sometimes, when I've finished a load, I think eee I could shift that lot again. It's like wanting a second helping o' pudding.

DARKLY: Enjoy it, do you?

BILLY: Wouldn't do anything else.

DARKLY: You'd enjoy it a lot more if you were making it pay.

BILLY: Couldn't do anything else.

DARKLY: (Pause) Did you hear what I said?

BILLY: I'm my own boss.

DARKLY: I say!

BILLY: What?

DARKLY: I wa' saying you'll enjoy it a lot more if you're making it pay. Mixing business wi' pleasure as t'saying goes. (Pause) Well, what about it? (Pause) I'm waiting for an answer, you know.

BILLY: I know you are.

DARKLY: Well?

BILLY: I'm thinking. It's a big thing realizing that your whole way o' life's goin' to alter; it's a thought you can't grasp at one go.

DARKLY: There'll hardly be any difference. You'll still be doing t'same job.

BILLY: I'll be saddled for t'first time in my life.

DARKLY: Saddled?

BILLY: That's what it amounts to, in't it? It seems to happen to everybody at some time or another, and there don't seem to be a lot you can do about it once you've been singled out.

DARKLY: (*Pause*) What about it then?

BILLY: I wonder if there are any loners left?

DARKLY: (*Pause*) Is it on then?

BILLY: If it hadn't o' been you, it'd been somebody wi' something else, I suppose. (*Pause*) Might o' been a woman.

DARKLY: Well?

BILLY: Else working *for* somebody.

DARKLY: Is it a deal then?

BILLY: On one condition.

DARKLY: What?

BILLY: If it don't work, we pack it in an' you never bother me again.

DARKLY: Right.

BILLY: (*Pause*) I'll gi' it a try then. I might as well get you off my back now as have you pestering me for evermore.

DARKLY: We'll drink on it.

BILLY: Ar, get 'em in.

Scene Three

Three months later.

Billy is shoveling coal as at the beginning of Scene One, only this time slowly, making hard work of it. He takes frequent rests, straightening up and rubbing the small of his back.

BILLY: I'll have to ease up or else I'm goin' to find myself laid up wi' this blasted back. (*Groans*) An' we've all that work on. (*Starts to shovel again*) There's no rest for t'wicked . . . there's no rest for anybody, come to that.

(*He loads the barrow slowly with difficulty, emitting occasional groans. He throws down his shovel and sits on*

the edge of the pavement, head in hands, miserable.
Darkly walks on quickly, halts, looking down at Billy)

DARKLY: You've no time to be resting, we've two more
loads to shift today!

BILLY: I know. I know.

DARKLY: Get cracking then.

BILLY: I know exactly how much coal we've got to shift.
I know it lump by lump as if every one wa' my worst enemy.
(*He continues to sit*)

DARKLY: What's up with you?

BILLY: You bloody well know what's up wi' me!

DARKLY: Your back again? (*Pause*) Does it ache?

BILLY: Ar, it aches. I ache, I ache all o'er. I'm tired an'
I'm bloody well fed up!

DARKLY: You don't know when you're well off.

BILLY: How can I be well off wi' a back like I've got?

DARKLY: It's your own fault. You've been warned. It wa'
t' first thing I said to you. Can you remember?

BILLY: Remember? I'll never forget it.

DARKLY: Use your legs, I kept telling you, but you took
no notice.

BILLY: I reckon I've slipped a disk.

DARKLY: Get away with you, you've just strained it.

BILLY: It's more than a strain.

DARKLY: There isn't such a thing as a slipped disk. Doctors say so.

BILLY: I might have a few days off.

DARKLY: You what! You can't.

BILLY: Who says?

DARKLY: We've too much work on.

BILLY: Bugger t'work.

DARKLY: We've work arranged for t'rest o' t'week at least.

BILLY: Bugger it.

DARKLY: What about t'business?

BILLY: Bugger t'business.

DARKLY: Just when we're making it pay?

BILLY: If I don't lay off I'll be off for good.

DARKLY: Get away with you.

BILLY: I'm telling you!

DARKLY: It'd be t'worst thing you could do, that, have a rest.

BILLY: Why?

DARKLY: It'd all stiffen up. You'd never get started again.

BILLY: (*Pause*) Who's told you that?

DARKLY: It's a well-known fact.

BILLY: It's not well-known to me.

DARKLY: Do you ever read medical books?

BILLY: No.

DARKLY: Well, you can't expect to know then, can you?

BILLY: Where've you seen any medical books?

DARKLY: In t'library, where do you think?

BILLY: What do you want to be reading them for?

DARKLY: For interest. Looking things up.

BILLY: What things?

DARKLY: Ne'er mind what things! Anyway, I'm telling you.

BILLY: (*Rubbing his back*) It's bad though.

DARKLY: It'll be all right in a day or two.

BILLY: It's all right you talking, there's no danger o' you straining your back, is there? You only come on t'scene to show me where t'next load is when I'm sweeping up after t'last 'un.

DARKLY: Well, somebody's got to do t'organizing.

BILLY: You an' your organizing!

DARKLY: You do it then! Let's see what sort of a job you make of it.

BILLY: You know very well that I won't do it.

DARKLY: Stop moaning then.

BILLY: I told you in t'first place that I wasn't goin' 'round begging.

DARKLY: No, but you're willing enough to pinch t'money off o' t'beggar.

BILLY: (*Springs up; faces Darkly in an aggressive man-*

ner) Pinch money! Me pinch money! I'll bloody flatten you in a minute. Work I'm doin' an' you've the cheek to stand there an' say I'm pinching money!

DARKLY: Calm down, will you! I think we're both getting a bit tired.

BILLY: (*Pause*) Let's have a rest then.

DARKLY: We've all that work on.

BILLY: It'll wait.

DARKLY: You can't run a business like that!

BILLY: Do you call this a business?

DARKLY: What do you call it then?

BILLY: Slave labor, an' all for an extra couple o' bob a day.

DARKLY: It's not only that, we've t'good will o't'firm to think about. We've to go out of our way to please folks, even if it does mean a bit of extra work.

BILLY: Well, if we don't ease up a bit there's going to be no business left. I'll be worn to a frazzle an' then t'job 'll be a bad 'un, won't it?

DARKLY: (*Pause*) Look, Billy, we might as well face it, you're going to have to get used to this change o'pace, 'cos it's going to be regular.

BILLY: Jesus wept! Still, it's all right for you, you can organize sixty to the dozen; it's *me* that's doing t'donkey work.

DARKLY: Nay, Billy!

BILLY: I'm like t'colliers, strong in t'back and weak in t'head.

DARKLY: You're not t'only one that gets tired, you know.

BILLY: Don't tell me that you do?

DARKLY: 'Course, I do! Mental fatigue, that's what I get.

BILLY: Well, give your brain a rest then and get some shoveling done.

DARKLY: An' who's going to arrange t'work for us to shovel?

BILLY: You, I suppose.

DARKLY: I can't do both.

BILLY: Don't arrange as much then.

DARKLY: I've got to. On a job like this we've to grab as much as we can get.

BILLY: Even if it kills us.

DARKLY: Kills us! You always bring death into it. Why don't you look on t'bright side for a change?

BILLY: What bright side?

DARKLY: Well, you're better off now than you've ever been.

BILLY: I am that!

DARKLY: You've more money . . .

BILLY: Ar. There's only one trouble. I'm always too tired to spend it.

DARKLY: You'll be saving it then. That's better still. (*Pause*) You'll be grateful to me one o' these days.

BILLY: That's one thing I'll never be. Don't think that I'm happy wi' this carry-on 'cos I'm not. In fact, I'm ready for pulling out any time. You've had well o'er your month now.

DARKLY: You can't pull out, just like that.

BILLY: Can't I? You'll see what I can do.

DARKLY: An' ruin t'business . . .

BILLY: That's all you think about, t'business, t'business.

DARKLY: . . . just when it's getting on its feet.

BILLY: Ar, an' trampling me down in t'process! I wa' a fool, a bloody fool!

DARKLY: It was t'best move you ever made. You're earning *twice* as much now.

BILLY: But a lot's gone. A lot o' *me*'s gone, a lot o' what I wa'. I'm not happy any more.

DARKLY: You ought to be.

BILLY: But I'm not. When I had nothing, I never bothered like I do now.

DARKLY: You'd no security, though.

BILLY: An' I'd no worry.

DARKLY: Your money's building your security for you.

BILLY: An' it's building my worries an' all.

DARKLY: You talk t'opposite way 'round to everybody else.

BILLY: But I act t'same. I never used to, but I do now.

DARKLY: Nothing wrong wi' that, is there?

BILLY: There is! There is! It means that I'm not t'same bloke any more. I'm nothing but a bloody fool now! What do I do first time I get a bit o'money in my pocket? I rush out an' buy myself a few extras. Luxuries they call 'em, but before I know where I am, they've become necessities an' I'm on t'scrounge for something else.

DARKLY: It's all part o'modern living, Billy lad.

BILLY: What, being in a turmoil all along? Worrying about growing old, about saving, your mind sharpened to a razor's edge through constant contact wi' cash, cash, cash! (*He bangs his fist into his open palm three times*)

DARKLY: Anybody wi' any sense saves for a rainy day.

BILLY: I never did, an' t'fine ones always come 'round again. (*Pause*) I think I'll make a break.

DARKLY: You can't, we're committed.

BILLY: You might be.

DARKLY: I am, an' you are an' all. You don't think you can pull out now, do you?

BILLY: That's what I'm frightened of. I've got to make a break now or else I'll never do it.

DARKLY: It's too late, it's far too late. Do you think you could go back to living wi' nothing but coppers in your pocket again?

BILLY: I can try.

DARKLY: Do you think that you can go back to counting every penny when you feel like a drink?

BILLY: (*Pause*) It'll be hard, I'll admit.

DARKLY: There's no turning back now, Billy lad, it's too late. You've tasted money an' what went before'll never be good enough again.

BILLY: I've been touched, right enough, but there still might be time.

DARKLY: It's no good! Just think o' t' working side of it.

BILLY: How do you mean?

DARKLY: Way t' business works.

BILLY: What about it?

DARKLY: It's worked all right up to now, I'd say.

BILLY: We've not done so bad.

DARKLY: We've managed all we've took on so far.

BILLY: Even though it has meant working in t'dark—something I never did before.

DARKLY: An' why have we had to work in t'dark?

BILLY: 'Cos we've had too much work on.

DARKLY: Not too much, overtime we'll call it.

BILLY: Call it what you want, it's still too much!

DARKLY: An' who went out of his way to arrange all that work?

BILLY: You, running after folks—something I never used to do.

DARKLY: No, they used to run after you. But they'll never run after you again.

BILLY: Why won't they?

DARKLY: Use your common sense! Do you think that folks'll go racing t'streets chasing you when they've got used to door-to-door service?

BILLY: They'll have no option if there's nobody else.

DARKLY: Who says there'll be nobody else?

BILLY: Who will there be?

DARKLY: Me.

BILLY: You!

DARKLY: What's wrong wi' that? Do you think I'll chuck t'job as easy as that when we've brought it so far?

BILLY: You couldn't shift an eyeful on your own.

DARKLY: Who says I'll be on my own?

BILLY: Who else will there be?

DARKLY: You never know. I'll bet there'll be plenty o' likely lads willing to step in if you pack up.

BILLY: (*Pause*) So, you'd work against me, would you?

DARKLY: If I had to.

BILLY: You bloodsucking bugger!

DARKLY: It's no good being like that . . .

BILLY: If it hadn't o' been for me, you'd never have got a look in 'round here. Folks used to stop me an' say, "Who's

that funny looking sod you've got working with you, Billy?"
"It's an apprentice I've taken on," I used to say, "A local lad
making good." An' they used to go away laughing and shaking
their heads. You'd never have got a smell if it hadn't been for
me!

DARKLY: But I've got my foot in t'door now.

BILLY: (*Pause*) *You* against *me*, eh? You wouldn't stand
a dog's chance! Folks know me, they've known me all their
lives.

DARKLY: They know *me* now.

BILLY: Not like me, though.

DARKLY: No, but they know t'way I run this business
and that's all that matters. If I carry on running a business like
this one wi' door-to-door service, do you think that *you'll* get
any orders running the job the way you do? Two against one?
Efficiency against chaos?

BILLY: Ar, but they know me.

DARKLY: An' they'll soon forget you if it causes 'em any
inconvenience.

BILLY: Some'll remember me.

DARKLY: Don't rely on it.

BILLY: (*Pause*) So it's like that, then?

DARKLY: Choice's thine.

BILLY: Bloody Hobson's! My, things have come to a sorry
end.

DARKLY: Sorry end! This is only t'*beginning*, Billy lad.
Business is thriving.

BILLY: But I'm not.

DARKLY: It's only a matter o' readjustment. You've had
things too easy in t'past.

BILLY: But what about my back? I can't carry on wi' it
like this.

DARKLY: I'll tell you what. Go an' have a lay down when
you've finished an' I'll bring you some lotion.

BILLY: What sort o' lotion?

DARKLY: It's recommended, works on anything; bruises,
aches, cuts, anything you can mention. I've even taken it in water
in a morning, after a heavy night's drinking.

BILLY: Sounds rum stuff.

DARKLY: It's miraculous!

BILLY: Doctor's might be better. It's a long time since I wa' there, though.

DARKLY: You want no doctor. This stuff I've got's better than any doctor's.

BILLY: (*Pause*) One thing, it'll not make it any worse.

DARKLY: I'll bring it down, then.

BILLY: Do you know where I live?

DARKLY: One o' them huts down t'allotments, in't it?

BILLY: Ar.

DARKLY: Which one?

BILLY: Just shout when you get near, I'll hear you.

DARKLY: Can't you tell me?

BILLY: What's th' use? It'll be pitch dark anyway. Just shout.

DARKLY: Right, I'll bring it down, then.

Scene Four

Night, very dark. Darkly gropes blindly along a narrow path running between the higgledy-piggledy of the allotments. He is cursing and grumbling to himself.

DARKLY: Of all the bloody stupid places to live! (*Calls*) Billy! Nobody in his right mind'd live in a place like this. (*Calls again*) Billy! (*Stands still, listening*) Billy! Billy! Where are you?

(*A muffled voice is heard*)

BILLY: Hold on.

DARKLY: Where are you?

BILLY: Let me put a light on.

(*A dim light appears in the window of Billy's hut. Darkly moves towards it. Billy opens the door*)

DARKLY: Of all the places to live . . .

BILLY: I must have dozed off waiting for you. I thought you weren't coming.

DARKLY: (*Enters Hut*) Jesus Christ! Do you live in here? You must be mad.

BILLY: (*Closing Door*) Why, what's wrong wi' it?

DARKLY: What's right wi' it? It's not human to live in a place like this . . .

BILLY: Why in't it? I've a bed an' a fire, what more do you want?

DARKLY: It's not fit for a dog to live in.

BILLY: Suits me.

DARKLY: Anything suits you. I can't see why you don't move into lodgings. You can afford it now.

BILLY: Can't be bothered.

DARKLY: Looks like you'll have to be.

BILLY: You're in a grand mood, aren't you? Where've you been? I've been waiting hours.

DARKLY: An' it reeks o' booze.

BILLY: I had to pass time somehow. (*Pause*) How do you mean, I'll have to be bothered?

DARKLY: That's why I'm late.

BILLY: (*Puzzled pause*) What do you mean? Have you been drinking an' all?

DARKLY: Just shut up, and I'll tell you.

BILLY: Sit down then, we might as well talk sitting down as standing up. (*Pause; they sit*) Here, we might as well finish this off while we're at it. Seems a shame to waste it when it's so expensive.

(*He scrounges around, looking under the bedclothes, then under the bed and comes up with a tin mug, pours two drinks and passes one across to Darkly. Darkly drinks his and reaches across again for the bottle*)

DARKLY: I need this tonight.

BILLY: Where've you been then? Boozing?

DARKLY: Ar, but not for pleasure, I can tell you. (*Pause*) You know when I left you after that last load?

BILLY: Ar.

DARKLY: Well, I wa' walking up Pitt Street pleased as punch 'cos we'd finished, when I saw this bloke.

BILLY: What bloke?

DARKLY: This bloke getting coals in outside the grocer's. It stopped me dead in my tracks.

BILLY: Who was it?

DARKLY: Got any more o' that left?

BILLY: Here. (*Passes the bottle*) Go on.

DARKLY: (*Drinks*) I couldn't believe my eyes, a complete stranger shoveling like a maniac.

BILLY: Did you say anything to him?

DARKLY: I'm just coming to that. I went up to him an' I said, "Hey! What do you think you're doing?" He looked up at me an' he said, "What's it look like, you silly bugger?" Then he carried on shoveling. I said, "You can't get coals in 'round here; me and my mate do that in this village." He looked up again an' said, "Who says I can't? Do you have to have a license or something?" Then he carried on shoveling again.

BILLY: Who was it? Did you know him?

DARKLY: No, I've told you, he wa' a complete stranger.

BILLY: What did you say then?

DARKLY: I asked him who he was an' where he came from, but he only told me to mind my own business and bugger off. I could see I wa' going to get nowhere standing there arguing, so . . .

BILLY: So what did you do?

DARKLY: Well, he was working in t'light from t'shop window and I knew it wa' knocking on, so I asked him to come for a drink when he'd finished.

BILLY: An' did he come?

DARKLY: He came all right. That's where I've been all this time, in t'bloody Ship arguing wi' him.

BILLY: Did you find out who he is?

DARKLY: They call him Stark. He's a drifter, moves about working anywhere.

BILLY: We've nothing to bother about then, if he's a drifter he'll be off in a crack.

DARKLY: That's the trouble. He says he'll stop here as long as there's any work for him to do.

BILLY: He'll not get much work 'round here. Not coal shifting, anyhow.

DARKLY: Why won't he?

BILLY: We've got it all tied up, haven't we? (*Pause*) Well, we have, haven't we?

DARKLY: Ar, 'course we have.

BILLY: We've nothing to bother about then.

DARKLY: (*Pause*) He went on about undercutting.

BILLY: (*Pause*) Do you mean getting 'em in for less than us?

DARKLY: That's it.

BILLY: I never thought o' that. (*Pause*) Still, there's plenty of work an' he'll soon get fed up. They always do, that type. Pass me that bottle back. (*Pause*) What's up, are you deaf? (*He tries to stretch across for the bottle, but flops back again*) Oooooo! my back. Have you brought that lotion? (*Pause*) I say, have you brought that stuff you were on about?

DARKLY: It's here.

(*Darkly takes a bottle from his pocket and places it on the table*)

BILLY: What you looking so miserable about, as though t'end o' t'world is nigh, as they say on t'sandwich boards.

DARKLY: It might be unless we do something about it.

BILLY: Get away with you, hey! This is rum looking stuff. (*Picks up bottle and inspects it*) Are you sure it'll work?

DARKLY: 'Course I am. Shake it up, it'll look better then. (*Billy shakes the bottle*)

BILLY: (*Trying to find the best position for applying the lotion*) I don't know how I'm going to manage this, my arms are not long enough.

DARKLY: Lay down, I'll do it for you.

(*Darkly shakes the bottle, pulls out the cork, pours some liquid into his palm, replaces the bottle on the table, then slaps the liquid on Billy's back*)

BILLY: (*Jumping*) Oooo! It's freezing! Stop it, it's bloody freezing!

DARKLY: Shut your mouth, it'll soon warm up. (*He massages Billy's back*)

BILLY: That's grand; it's a long time since anybody rubbed my back for me like that.

DARKLY: I'm not surprised, wi' t'color of it.

BILLY: Too much soap an' water weakens it, any old collier'd tell you that. (*Pause*) Anything left in that bottle?

DARKLY: No.

BILLY: Pity.

DARKLY: Here, have some o' this.

(*Darkly produces another bottle, pours out two mugs*)

BILLY: Good old Darkly lad, you've done something that's pleased me at last. Where've you got this from?

DARKLY: Bought it. I thought if I could get yon Starky pissed he might listen to me an' then bugger off.

BILLY: Did he?

DARKLY: Did he buggery! He just sat there guzzling without turning a hair. I finished up threatening him, but it was useless.

BILLY: Then what did you do?

DARKLY: I could see I wa' wasting my time an' money, so I came away. (*Pause*) I'll have him though.

BILLY: You must have been keen to get rid of him, buying him this stuff. It's a grand feeling, a drop o' lotion on your back an' a drop in your belly.

DARKLY: (*Giving Billy's back a slap*) I think that'll do you.

BILLY: Nay, you haven't been at it two minutes.

DARKLY: I'm not a bloody masseur, you know.

BILLY: A what?

DARKLY: A masseur.

BILLY: What's that?

DARKLY: A bloke who massages.

BILLY: I didn't know you knew any French.

DARKLY: You'd be surprised at t'things I know.

BILLY: Did you go to one o' them Grammar Schools, then?

DARKLY: No, I could have done. But I never went to school much, I used to get bad heads and have attacks. My mother used to keep me at home a lot. Still get 'em sometimes.

BILLY: Why what's up wi' you?

DARKLY: It's a kind of mental strain. I have to be eased up when they come on.

BILLY: Eased up?

DARKLY: I go away for electrical treatment.

BILLY: You sound in a bad way.

DARKLY: It's only sometimes, when I get worked up.

BILLY: How do you mean, worked up?

DARKLY: It's hard to say. I go all tense, screw up inside as though I'm going to burst. I have to scream to let some of it go.

BILLY: Jesus!

DARKLY: If it hadn't been for that, I'd have been made now!

BILLY: Steady on, old lad.

DARKLY: And just when I get started, this Starky comes interfering!

BILLY: Bugger him. Here, this'll calm you down better than any electrical treatment.

DARKLY: Are you tryin' to be funny?

BILLY: 'Course I'm not. Here, gi' my back another rub, will you?

DARKLY: I'm not your servant, you know.

BILLY: No, but you're my partner. You don't want your labor force reducing by half, do you?

DARKLY: I suppose not. Turn o'er then.

BILLY: (*Pause*) I can't remember my back ever being as bad as this in all my years on this job.

DARKLY: That'll be some, won't it? When did you start?

BILLY: I don't know, but I can remember working hard in t' pit one day and thinking, if the King don't work why should I?

DARKLY: You daft bugger.

BILLY: What's daft about that?

DARKLY: Well, what's shifting coals if it's not working?

BILLY: Ar, but I was working for myself, that's different. I wasn't employed. And there's a big difference in work and being employed.

DARKLY: I don't know what you're on about.

BILLY: I can't explain it right, it's just t'way I feel. (*Pause*) Looking back, I've had some good times getting coals in.

DARKLY: You're easily satisfied.

BILLY: I'll show you something, something I've never shown to anybody else.

DARKLY: What is it?

BILLY: Look! (*He uncovers a heap of coal in the corner*)

DARKLY: (*Pause*) What about it? They're only lumps of coal.

BILLY: They might be to you, but there's a lot o' memories in that little lot for me. They're all souvenirs o'loads I've got in over t'years.

DARKLY: They're only lumps o' coal.

BILLY: What's it matter what they are? Some folks save stamps, don't they, but nobody says they're only stamps.

DARKLY: I know! But whoever heard o' saving lumps o' coal?

BILLY: Me, I did. Everyone o' them lumps brings back a memory. I spend hours looking o'er 'em, remembering.

DARKLY: I've never heard anything as bloody ridiculous in my life!

BILLY: (*Pause: he handles the pieces, reminiscing*) Look at this one, for example. I can remember t'load this one came out of as if it wa' yesterday. It was outside a cellar, you know, where all you have to do is to slide t'coal down. They're about t'easiest there are, loads like that, but they're maddening an' all, what wi' t'hole always getting blocked up so that you're forever broddling about wi' t'shovel. It spoils your rhythm, an' what should be a lovely clean job finishes up into a lot o'poking an' sweating 'round t'hole. (*Pause*) Well, this load wasn't like that, t'hole was big an' well shaped, an' all I had to do was keep shoveling, an' they went in as smooth as glass. I worked non-stop until it had all gone an' then I stood up panting and heaving, feeling fair satisfied with myself.

DARKLY: It's a funny way o' feeling satisfied.

BILLY: I enjoyed it so much that I saved this piece, just

this piece. (*He replaces it, picks up another lump*) You see this, this was when I nearly had my hand bitten off wi' a bloody great Alsatian down at t' vicarage. He gave me a pound to keep my mouth shut, said t'dog was like a son to him an' he couldn't stand it if it wa' destroyed.

DARKLY: (*Picks up another lump*) What's this one then?

BILLY: It's funny you should pick on that, it's one o' my favorites. It's from a load I shifted one summer's day towards t'end of a spell o' fine weather when a storm wa' due. (*Pause*) I can feel it now, fair close it was, gray an' heavy, waiting. I didn't want to take t' job on, but it was an old woman up in t'bunga-lows an' she was frightened of it getting saturated or swept away or something. Anyway, I made a start an' talk about sweat, it was boiling an' what wi' these clouds pressing down, it felt just like being down t'pit again. I really tried wi' that load an' I finished just before it started.

DARKLY: (*Pause*) I can't see anything special about that.

BILLY: Hold on, I haven't finished yet. All that wa' left was t'coal dust on t' causeway. Well, I've always enjoyed that part o' t' job . . .

DARKLY: What, cleaning up?

BILLY: Ar, I like swilling water o'er it, then brushing it away wi' a big stiff brush. Anyway, I didn't have to bother 'cos t'first drops came down just then, big as blackclocks, they were, curling up into furry balls when they hit t'dust. Then t'heavens opened an' all t'wet joined up on t'ground, an' t'dust turned to sludge, runnin' into gutters, 'til t'causeway wa' shining wet as if nothing had ever been there.

DARKLY: An' where were you while all this wa' goin' on?

BILLY: Stood watching. Once it started I couldn't get away. I had to stand an' watch it all come clean.

DARKLY: You must have been drenched.

BILLY: I was. T'old woman kept knocking on t'window telling me to come in, but I didn't take no notice. I just stood and watched it all wash away.

DARKLY: You must have been crazy to get wet through for that.

BILLY: Why? It didn't hurt me. I came home and got changed. It's nothing to get wet.

(*He replaces cover on the stack of coal*)

DARKLY: *Nothing* matters to you, does it? (*He starts to pace the hut*)

BILLY: Oh! Stop worrying! (*Pause*) Here. (*Shoves the bottle across to Darkly*) This'll shift your troubles, it's shifting mine grand.

DARKLY: It didn't shift *him*.

BILLY: I'm almost back t' my old carefree state.

DARKLY: We've *got* to do something!

BILLY: What for? He'll soon get stalled.

DARKLY: We can't risk it!

BILLY: There is no risk; it's two to one, he hasn't got a chance.

DARKLY: He's not going to get a chance!

BILLY: There's nothing we can do about it.

DARKLY: There is.

BILLY: What?

DARKLY: Make him leave.

BILLY: How?

DARKLY: Gi' him a good thumping! It's t'only way he'll learn any sense.

BILLY: You're thinking o' thumping a bloke just 'cos he's after a few days' work?

DARKLY: *Our* work.

BILLY: How do you mean, our work? We don't own this place.

DARKLY: No, but we've got to! We've got to discourage blokes like him. We can't afford to let him stay.

BILLY: He'll soon get fed up.

DARKLY: An' what if he don't?

BILLY: It'll be us against him.

DARKLY: There isn't enough work for three!

BILLY: There'll have to be. You reckon to be a business man, don't you?

DARKLY: I *am* a business man.

BILLY: This'll be a real test for you, then, thinking up ways of outdoing him.

DARKLY: I've thought o' one.

BILLY: Is that t'best you can do?

DARKLY: (*Pause*) What's up, are you frightened?

BILLY: What you talking about? Just because I won't belt a bloke who wants to earn a living. If that's being frightened, I'm glad I'm not brave.

DARKLY: He's costing you money.

BILLY: So what, he's got to live.

DARKLY: But not out of our pockets!

BILLY: They're as liable as anybody else's.

DARKLY: (*Pause*) He can go an' earn his money somewhere else!

BILLY: He will do in a day or two, if he's left alone.

DARKLY: We've got to get rid of him *now!* I couldn't bear to be working knowing that he wa' pinching money from behind my back.

BILLY: What if he did linger? It wouldn't be t'first time I've been short o' money. It'd be like old times again.

DARKLY: Is that all you can think about at a time like this?

BILLY: You're making a mountain out of a molehill. (*Pause*) Hey! Can you imagine a mountain o' coal an' a giant asking you to shift it for him? You'd need a number five shovel for that lot, wouldn't you? (*He laughs to himself*)

DARKLY: Give up arsing about; you're getting on my nerves!

BILLY: An' you're getting on mine! Give me that bottle! (*Snatches it*) I never used to touch this stuff. (*Pause*) God knows where I'll end up!

DARKLY: I can tell you without asking Him. In t'workhouse, if you're not careful.

BILLY: More likely in t'nuthouse.

DARKLY: You shouldn't call 'em that!

BILLY: Why? That's what they are, in't it?

DARKLY: No, it in't! They're mental institutions.

BILLY: What's it matter what they call 'em, t'folks inside are nuts.

DARKLY: Not all of 'em, some only need treatment, an' you don't have to be insane to receive treatment.

BILLY: Oh shut your mouth! I'll call 'em what I want.

DARKLY: That's typical of you, you pig-headed bugger! I wish you'd use brains for a change instead o' always being so bloody awkward! *You* decide what to do about Starky then!

BILLY: I'm doing nothing about him.

DARKLY: Well, I *am*.

BILLY: What can you do on your own?

DARKLY: I'll think o' something.

BILLY: What? You can't thump him, 'cos according to what you've said, he might finish up thumping *you*.

DARKLY: Well, if I can't fight him, there's only one thing for it.

BILLY: What?

DARKLY: Join him!

BILLY: (*Pause*) How do you mean?

DARKLY: Join up wi' him, work wi' him, what do you think?

BILLY: You wouldn't do a thing like that, would you?

DARKLY: Wouldn't I?

BILLY: He's a stranger. You don't know him.

DARKLY: What difference does that make?

BILLY: (*Pause*) I thought I reckoned to be your partner.

DARKLY: That's what *I* thought, but if you won't co-operate, I'll have to team up wi' somebody who will!

BILLY: There's reasons, though.

DARKLY: A partner's a partner as far as I'm concerned; somebody you can rely on.

BILLY: You could get us both locked up for what you're thinking of!

DARKLY: It's something we've got to risk. (*Pause*) Anyway, if I did get locked up, it'd be no worse than some o' them places I've been in.

BILLY: *What* places?

DARKLY: Ne'er mind!

BILLY: What places? Do you mean jail?

DARKLY: I said *forget it!*

BILLY: All right, but you're risking jail for nothing.

DARKLY: I'm risking nothing, 'cos if you won't help, me an' you have finished!

BILLY: Just like that?

DARKLY: If I have to.

BILLY: Some partner you've turned out to be, as soon as a bit o' competition comes on t'scene, you turn tail an' run.

DARKLY: I'm not running far, though. (*Pause*) I've got it all weighed up; there's only work for *two* to make a decent living, an' I'm goin' to be one of 'em!

BILLY: Of all the lousy tricks!

DARKLY: There's no sentiment in business. Folks can't afford it.

BILLY: (*Pause*) You'd better bugger off to your new mate then. . . . Go on, bugger off.

DARKLY: An' what are you goin' to do?

BILLY: I'll manage. Somebody'll set me on.

DARKLY: Who?

BILLY: Folks'll not let me starve.

DARKLY: You won't stand a chance against us two.

BILLY: If *I* don't stand a chance against you two, how come *he'll* stand a chance against us?

DARKLY: He's young and strong an' there's something about him that's frightening.

BILLY: Are you frightened of him, then?

DARKLY: I don't know what I am, but he's not t' sort o' bloke you can lark about with. Anyway, I've decided I've either got to be on his side or else he's got to go. One thing's certain, I'm not working *against* him!

BILLY: I'll bet he's no stronger than me.

DARKLY: No, but he's a sight younger; he'd be a good bloke to latch on to. There'd be prospects workin' wi' him.

BILLY: Go on then, bugger off!

DARKLY: You wouldn't earn a penny, Billy.

BILLY: I'd manage.

DARKLY: What? Wi' a back like yours? Can you imagine trying to keep pace in your condition.

BILLY: I'll rest till it gets right, then I'll show you!

DARKLY: There'd be nothing to show by that time. You'd never get a look in again. (*Pause*) An' there'll always be t'risk that your back'll go again workin' under pressure.

BILLY: A bit o' hard work'll not kill me.

DARKLY: This'll be more than hard work, it'll be one long struggle for orders. Just imagine it, Billy.

BILLY: I am doing.

DARKLY: (*Pause*) Whereas, we'd be able to ease up a bit once we got *rid* o' Starky. Take it easy, till your back's right.

BILLY: (*Pause*) What a bloody choice! It's either starve or fight.

DARKLY: That's it.

BILLY: Whoever'd have thought it.

DARKLY: There's no telling what you've to do to make a living.

BILLY: (*Long pause*) What's your plan?

DARKLY: Wait for him to come out o't'boozer an' then nobble him.

BILLY: Where?

DARKLY: That spare ground up near t'chapel. There's hardly a soul goes past there that time o'night.

BILLY: (*Pause*) He might have gone already.

DARKLY: I doubt it. He didn't seem like a bloke who'd go before closing time.

BILLY: We'll never get away wi' it.

DARKLY: 'Course we will.

BILLY: An' what if we did? It don't mean to say that he'd go away; he might not connect it wi' us at all.

DARKLY: He would. I gave him fair warning.

BILLY: He might be gone tomorrow then.

DARKLY: He'll not.

BILLY: Why, what did he say?

DARKLY: Nothing, he just laughed in my face. I'll learn him to laugh at me, the ignorant pig!

BILLY: Don't you think if we both went an' had a word wi' him, he'd take notice then? Nobody likes threatening wi' two. . .

DARKLY: Do you know what he'd do? Laugh in *both* our faces!

BILLY: He would be asking for trouble then.

DARKLY: He's asking for it now, an' he's going to get it! (*He thumps his closed fist into his open palm*)

BILLY: What if he goes to t'police?

DARKLY: He's not that sort. He's like you in a way, sort o' bloke that you never see in a doctor's or a barber's shop. He'd no more dream o' goin' to t' police than you'd dream o' goin' to t'tailors for a new suit. Do you see what I mean? (*Pause*) He belongs to that sort o' men outside o' things. Something like you, only nasty wi' it.

BILLY: (*Pause*) Sounds a rum bloke.

DARKLY: He is, an' we shan't have to gi' him a chance. Straight in and wallop!

BILLY: There's no need to go mad though.

DARKLY: He needs a good walloping!

BILLY: A bit o' pushing an' threatening's all that's needed.

DARKLY: He wants a good thrashing. Come on, we'd better be off, it must be knocking on now.

BILLY: If there's any thumping needed, I think you'd better do it; my back kills me every time I move my arms.

DARKLY: Send t'boot in then.

BILLY: I never thought anything like this'd come to me.

DARKLY: Get your coat on an' shut up.

BILLY: I'll just finish this bottle off before I go. I'll need it.

DARKLY: Be quick then, an' save me a drop.

(*They drink up, swigging at the bottle in turns, then leave the hut*)

Scene Five

A dark passageway. A few minutes later.

DARKLY: Couldn't be better, no moon. He'll wonder what hit him!

BILLY: What if we get t' wrong bloke?

DARKLY: We shan't. I could tell that cocky walk a mile off.

BILLY: I bet he's gone.

DARKLY: He won't have, it's not half past ten yet. (*Pause; he looks around for somewhere to hide*) Here, this'll do.

BILLY: He'll see us there.

DARKLY: He won't, He'll not be looking.

BILLY: I feel dizzy.

DARKLY: You've had too much to drink.

BILLY: I haven't had enough!

DARKLY: (*Pause*) Sh! There's somebody coming. (*Footsteps. A man passes*) What did I tell you? That bloke never saw us. Neither will Starky.

BILLY: I knew him. It wa' Tommy Derbyshire. I wonder what he'd have thought if he'd seen me cringing in this corner! I feel fair ashamed.

DARKLY: Just remember that your *livelihood*'s at stake. That's all you've got to keep in mind.

BILLY: I've a job on to keep anything in mind, t'way I feel. My head's goin' 'round like cocks and hens.

DARKLY: (*Pause*) He's here! He's here!

(*Footsteps, determined, purposeful; Stark appears, passes the spot where Billy and Darkly are hidden; then Darkly leaps onto his back and knocks him to the ground. Billy hovers around, uncertain, while the combatants struggle furiously on the ground, rolling over and over*)

DARKLY: Billy, damn you, come on!

(*Stark appears to be getting the upper hand and is gradually getting astride Darkly*)

DARKLY: Billy! Billy! Get him, you bloody fool!

(*Billy pauses for an agonizing second, then leaps in desperation onto Stark, rolling him off Darkly and pinning him to the ground. Darkly quickly joins Billy astride Stark and starts punching at random*)

DARKLY: I'll show him! (*He is violently punching away at the struggling body*) I warned you what'd happen, you bloody bastard!

BILLY: That's enough now, he's had enough!

(*The body goes limp, but Darkly takes no notice and continues with his savage attack*)

BILLY: That's enough, I said! What are you trying to do—kill him?!

(*Billy restrains Darkly and they roll off the limp body. As Billy pulls him to his feet, Darkly manages to get a couple of kicks in at the inert form*)

BILLY: You bloody fool! You'll have us both on t'end of a rope! Come on, let's go!

(*Billy drags Darkly away*)

Scene Six

Billy's hut. They hurry inside, closing and bolting the door behind them. Billy flops down on the bed. Darkly sits on the chair lolling his head on the table. They remain in these positions for a couple of minutes, breathing heavily. Darkly then looks up.

DARKLY: Well, we did it. (*Billy does not reply*) I say!

BILLY: What?

DARKLY: I said it worked a treat, didn't it?

BILLY: (*Pause*) What if he's dead?

DARKLY: He'll be on his road home now.

BILLY: You were pounding away like a maniac.

DARKLY: Don't call me a maniac!

BILLY: You shouldn't act like one, then.

DARKLY: I wa' having to do your share an' all, you windy bastard.

BILLY: I did enough.

DARKLY: You never lifted a finger.

BILLY: I did enough, I tell you!

DARKLY: I thought you wa' goin' to let him do me in at one time. (*Billy makes no reply*) What's up wi' you?

BILLY: I feel sick, sick as a dog.

DARKLY: What, wi' drinking?

BILLY: You know what wi'!

DARKLY: Forget it now, it's all o'er.

BILLY: Ar, it's all o'er.

DARKLY: Here! Look what I've got. Bought it special for this celebration. (*He produces a bottle from his inside pocket*)

BILLY: Where've you got that from?

DARKLY: Bought it special from the pub after I'd been home for that lotion.

BILLY: Had it all worked out?

DARKLY: You've got to make plans, Billy lad. Pass your mug o'er. (*He pours himself a drink*)

BILLY: So bloody sure o' yourself!

DARKLY: It worked, didn't it? (*Billy is silent*) Cheer up! Just think, Billy lad, all your worries are over! We can carry on as if nothing had ever happened.

BILLY: No, we can't.

DARKLY: 'Course we can, nothing's changed.

BILLY: Something has changed, *me,* an' it's a change for t'worse.

DARKLY: Stop being morbid! Come on, we're supposed to be celebrating. We've won.

BILLY: What have I got to celebrate? My ruination? 'Cos that's what I am, bloody ruined.

DARKLY: You *would* have been, if we hadn't have done what we did.

BILLY: I don't mean ruined like that. I mean *inside* me, it's all gone. I'm no good to man nor beast now.

DARKLY: You're drunk, that's what's up wi' you.

BILLY: It's you that's drunk. Drunk wi' power!

DARKLY: Drunk wi' power! I like that. Drunk wi' power!

BILLY: It's something you've cared for all your life, isn't it? You've wanted it so much that it's eaten away any bit o' common decency that you ever had.

DARKLY: Steady on, Billy lad! Here, have another drink. (*Pause*) P'raps you'd better not.

BILLY: Don't tell me whether to drink or not! I'm sick, sick to death o' you telling me what to do.

DARKLY: All right! All right! Drink all t'bloody bottle if you want. (*Pause*) I don't know what you're getting so ratty about.

BILLY: 'Course you don't! You don't know anything about feeling, that's why. How can you when you haven't got any? When it comes to feelings, you're *dead,* dead inside.

DARKLY: That's where you're wrong! I've only just *started* to live. (*Pause*) I had to get rid o' Starky or he'd have snuffed me out, he'd have snuffed out that flicker that wa' just beginning to grow. No, you're wrong, Billy lad. If I'm dead, there's a resurrection due any minute 'cos this is only t'start o' my life.

BILLY: An' t'end o' mine.

DARKLY: Get away wi' you!

BILLY: You've drained me like a vampire 'til I'd no strength left to resist. Then tonight, you finally killed me.

DARKLY: That's right, blame me! Everything you've done's been of your own free will.

BILLY: You lying bastard!

DARKLY: What did I do? (*Pause*) Go on, tell me! Hold a gun to your head? Twist your arm up your back?

BILLY: You know very well, you cunning two-faced sod, what you've always done.

DARKLY: What? Go on, tell me!

BILLY: Wheedling and plotting, playing me against him, playing me against everything!

DARKLY: You're making excuses for yourself, blaming me for things that I've never done.

BILLY: I know I am; I'm having to 'cos I'm that bloody ashamed o' myself!

DARKLY: You're makin' a tragedy out o' nothing.

BILLY: There's never been a bigger tragedy in t'history o' man compared wi' mine these last three months.

DARKLY: An' it's all my fault, I suppose?

BILLY: Ar, every rotten bit of it, but I'm through wi' you. I'm startin' on my own again! Do you hear? Startin' on my own!

DARKLY: Startin' on your own! You'll never do that again an' you know it! You rely on me too much now ever to break away. You need *me* to get you work, to earn that extra bit that you've grown used to.

BILLY: I'm finished, I tell you, I'm goin' back to . . .

DARKLY: Goin' back to what? Fish an' chips every night an' savin' up for a glass o' bitter?

BILLY: It's not too late yet.

DARKLY: Goin' back to *what?* Your stupid rotten lumps o' coal!

(*Darkly strides over to the corner where the coal is stacked and whips away the cover*)

BILLY: Put that back an' get away!

DARKLY: A grown man saving lumps o' coal! They'd lock you up if they found out! (*He starts to pick up the lumps of coal*)

BILLY: Put 'em down!

DARKLY: What do you do wi' 'em? Take 'em to bed an' drool o'er 'em like nasty books?

BILLY: You bloody lunatic, put it down before I kill you!

DARKLY: Me a lunatic, that's a good one! A lunatic, me, a lunatic!

BILLY: Put it down, an' get out of here while you've a chance!

DARKLY: He's gettin' mad! He's gettin' mad! He will be when I tell him what I'm going to do.

BILLY: Get out!

DARKLY: I'll tell you what I'm goin' to do. I'm goin' to burn 'em *all!* I'm goin' to sneak down here an' make a bloody great fire an' burn 'em all. All except this one. And do you know what I'm goin' to do wi' this? I'm goin' to smash it to a thousand pieces!

BILLY: You do an' I'll kill you!

DARKLY: You couldn't kill a fly t'state you're in! Look, you've a job to stand up.

(*Billy attempts to rise*)

BILLY: I'll kill you if you smash that!

DARKLY: (*Pause*) Right! Let's see you try! (*He smashes the lump of coal to the ground. Then, Darkly goes berserk and starts flinging the other lumps of coal all around the hut, taking no notice of Billy*) This is what I think o' your souvenirs, you barmy bugger! You're barmy! You're barmy! You're barmy!!

(*Billy groans, stoops to pick up a lump of coal then rises and brings it down on Darkly's head. Darkly staggers, but Billy continues to smash at his head following him all the way down to the floor, where he finally pauses over the crumpled figure. Then he rises slowly, looking down at his victim*)

BILLY: I warned you, but you wouldn't listen, would you? Where's your business now, then? Where's your organization now? It's gone, old lad, all gone an' I'm back where I started, all on my own like I used to be. (*Pause*) It's just goin' to be like old times again now.

Curtain

Howard Sackler
SKIPPY

Howard Sackler

In 1969, Howard Sackler won the American theatre's three foremost honors—the Pulitzer Prize, the New York Drama Critics' Circle Award and the Antoinette Perry (Tony) Award—for his play *The Great White Hope.* A work of enormity in scale and power based on the life and times of Jack Johnson who, in 1908, became the first Negro heavyweight champion of the world, it ran for 556 performances in New York. In 1970, it was made into a film with James Earl Jones repeating his galvanic performance of the beleagured fighter that brought him instant Broadway stardom.

While *The Great White Hope* catapulted Howard Sackler into the vanguard of major American dramatists, the author could hardly be categorized as a "newcomer" to the theatre. Born in New York City in 1929 and educated at Brooklyn College, Mr. Sackler already had the distinction of seeing seven of his earlier plays on stage. Among these: *The Pastime of Monsieur Robert,* produced at the Hampstead Theatre Club, London, and presently scheduled for production by the American Conservatory Theatre, San Francisco; *Uriel Acosta,* for which he won the Maxwell Anderson Award; *The Man Who Stammers* and *The Yellow Loves,* produced by The Poet's Theatre, Cambridge, Massachusetts; and *Mr. Welk and Jersey Jim,* initially presented at the Actors Studio with Zero Mostel, and later at the Arena Stage, Washington.

A man of diversified talent, Mr. Sackler also has functioned as a director for nearly two hundred dramatic recordings (including most of Shakespeare's plays) with such notables as Paul Scofield, Sir Ralph Richardson, Rex Harrison, Dame Edith Evans, Margaret Leighton, Dame Flora Robson, Claire Bloom, Albert Finney, Julie Harris, Jessica Tandy and others.

In 1961, Mr. Sackler wrote the adaptation and also directed the English version of the Czechoslovakian film of *A Midsummer Night's Dream,* and earlier, fashioned the original stories and screenplays for *Killer's Kiss* and *Fear and Desire,* both directed by Stanley Kubrick with whom he also created the documentary *Desert Padre.*

Skippy originally was published in 1970 in *A Few En-*

quiries, a collection of four short plays by Mr. Sackler. Although each play is an entity, he conceived the quartet as a program to be played together as an evening in the theatre. "Perhaps the connections between them are visible only to myself," he has noted, "but seeing them performed as a program on one occasion by the Theatre Company of Boston (as a Sunday night 'staged reading') seemed to confirm that they do strike some chord together."

In his introduction to *A Few Enquiries,* drama critic Martin Gottfried described Howard Sackler as "an artist, speaking in a unique voice without trying to fit into one school of playwriting or another. . . . He uses forms that are proportionate and diverse. Most consequentially—at least for the theatre—he uses the language with care, the structures with confidence, at a time when both language and structure are both suspect and rare. He is disciplined in a period of anarchy, writes for actors in a period of performers. He is his own man, as any artist must be."

A poet as well as a dramatist, Mr. Sackler's poems have been published in *Poetry Magazine, Commentary, The Hudson Review, New Directions Annual* and in a volume entitled *Want My Shepherd.*

The author, his wife, and two children now divide their time between London and the island of Ibiza, Spain.

Characters:

HARRY WEIMAN
MURIEL WEIMAN
A YOUTH
BETTY LEWIS
A POLICEMAN
DETECTIVE SIMONE
A BOY

Scene:

M&H Wines & Liquors. At the back is a narrow wooden staircase which leads to an apartment above. Behind the counter the proprietor, Harry Weiman, an unprepossessing man of about sixty, is guardedly speaking on the telephone.

HARRY: I see . . . I see . . . no, if you first opened in 1923 . . . it's way before that, yeah . . . (*He sighs heavily*) Mount what? . . . I called there yesterday. No luck . . . Most of you keep pretty good records, don't you? . . . I know, but this was such a long time ago . . . (*Footsteps are heard on the staircase; Harry quickly closes a small notebook and slips it into his pocket*) It has to be somewhere, sure . . .

(*Muriel Weiman comes down the stairs. She is a cheerful woman in her fifties*)

HARRY: OK, thank you . . . thanks for the encouragement . . . Goodbye. (*Hangs up*)

MURIEL: You busy, honey?

HARRY: Not if you're a customer.

MURIEL: Some customer! (*He smiles*) I came down in case you were lonesome.

HARRY: Oh, there's plenty to do.

MURIEL: Any business yet?

HARRY: Ordinary . . . (*Examines bill on a spindle*) A pint of Seagram's . . . couple of wine sales.

MURIEL: (*Making a face*) Uh! That cheap wine!

HARRY: It moves.

MURIEL: Don't worry, after lunch we'll pick up.

HARRY: I have plenty to do . . . bills, calls . . .

MURIEL: You're telling me! I could hear that dial going all morning.

HARRY: Had to call up wholesalers.

MURIEL: So many?

HARRY: Yes, for . . . vodka. All of a sudden everybody wants vodka, different brands . . .

MURIEL: In this neighborhood?

HARRY: Why not? It's the style.

MURIEL: Vodka!

HARRY: Sure. So you have to phone around.

MURIEL: How do you like that!

HARRY: I ought to keep after them, still a few labels . . .

MURIEL: All right, sweetheart, I won't hold you up. (*Going toward the staircase*) If you miss me, just yell.

HARRY: (*Smiling*) I miss you already.

MURIEL: (*Stops*) You feel a little cheerfuller today, don't you?

HARRY: Oh, yes.

MURIEL: You do?

HARRY: You cheer me up, so I do.

MURIEL: It's such a big shock, to get over just like that.

HARRY: Two weeks isn't "just like that."

MURIEL: It's a big shock, Harry.

HARRY: Well, she was a very old lady.

MURIEL: May she rest in peace.

HARRY: Eighty-one, it's not like a surprise . . .

MURIEL: Oh! It's always a surprise.

HARRY: I suppose . . . But you know, I think it made it easier, going by the book, sitting around the house a week, and all that. It helps you drain it out of your system.

MURIEL: Listen, whoever made up those rules, they weren't morons.

HARRY: (*Smiles*) They wouldn't have closed up their liquor stores, you mean.

MURIEL: So we lost a few dollars—so what?

HARRY: You didn't mind?

MURIEL: Please! You had to do it right, period!

HARRY: Well, I appreciate that, Muriel . . .

MURIEL: (*Kisses him*) Formalities yet! I'll fix your lunch and you track down your stock. OK?

HARRY: OK, sweetheart.

MURIEL: (*Going upstairs*) Vodka! All right, live and learn.

(*As soon as she is gone, Harry takes out the notebook, crosses out a line, consults another page, and dials*)

HARRY: Hello, is this Mount Ephraim? . . . I'm trying to locate a burial plot . . . no, it's occupied, I'm sorry to say . . . no, but in case it is, could you check, please, it's . . . I did, I called up all of them in Westchester . . . no, I never realized . . . Just you alone? . . . 490! . . . In one year! Tsk, tsk . . . It was May sixth or seventh, nineteen oh eight . . . yes, oh eight. . . .

(*Enter a Puerto Rican Youth. Nervous. A bell jangles at the door when it is opened*)

HARRY: Sure it's a long time, I can't help that . . . the name would be Edward Weiman . . . W-E-I-M-A-N. Edward. . . . Thanks, I'll hold on. (*To the Youth*) With you in a second.

(*The Youth nods, averts his face quickly and studies the racked bottles*)

HARRY: Hello! . . . sixth or seventh, yes . . . No . . . no . . . no . . . that's all? . . . Nothing, huh . . . (*He sighs*) You're positive your records . . . OK. Thanks anyway. (*Hangs up*) Sorry to keep you waiting.

YOUTH: No, I dun' horry.

HARRY: What can I do for you?

YOUTH: (*Pointing aimlessly*) I lighe a buttel some . . .

HARRY: Sherry? Rum?

YOUTH: No, no ron. Eh—(*Pointing high on a shelf*) What is dere . . . op . . .

HARRY: The sauterne?

YOUTH: Allrigh' . . . you tek don.

HARRY: You're a big fellow—can you reach it?

YOUTH: (*Shrugging*) Wale, eef I brek, so . . .

HARRY: I'll get the ladder. (*Moves a ladder from the*

corner to the shelf and climbs up. The Youth moves close to him. Harry touches a bottle) This one?

YOUTH: No, dee odder . . . eh . . .

HARRY: (*Pointing to another*) This?

YOUTH: (*Putting his hand in his pocket*) No meester . . . (*The doorbell jangles and the Youth jerks his hand out of his pocket. Betty Lewis, a woman of fifty, bustles in. She wears a white smock*)

HARRY: Hello, Mrs. Lewis.

BETTY: Good morning! Oh, it's nice and cool in here!

HARRY: Yes—be right with you . . . (*To the Youth*) Did you make up your mind?

YOUTH: (*Pointing*) I tek dot.

HARRY: (*Picking one out*) This? (*The Youth nods; Harry climbs down*) A dollar sixty-nine plus tax.

(*The Youth takes out money as Harry wraps the bottle*)

BETTY: How do you feel today, Mr. Weiman?

HARRY: Can't complain, thanks. (*Takes the money, rings up sale, gives the Youth his change and the bottle*) Much obliged.

(*The Youth grunts and walks out*)

BETTY: Wine, huh?

HARRY: It's all they can afford.

BETTY: We didn't have enough winos around, they had to come join the club.

HARRY: Ah, not many of them.

BETTY: Spanish who are winos?

HARRY: Not so many.

BETTY: Well, here you would know. I didn't like the look of that one, though.

HARRY: Some of them just look tough. I guess because they're dark . . .

BETTY: Bah!

HARRY: Oh, I have to handle them, once in a blue moon.

BETTY: You know what they do in the bakery? They go up to the counter, and with fingers you would not believe, Mr. Weiman, with those fingers they poke the rolls! I really want to scream. (*Harry smiles*) Is your wife upstairs?

HARRY: Yes,

BETTY: MURIEL!

MURIEL: (*From above*) Betty? I'll be right down.

BETTY: Your husband likes the Spanish people!

MURIEL: (*Descending*) The girls he likes.

BETTY: What an idea!

MURIEL: Oh, they make eyes at him all the time—(*To Harry*) don't they!

HARRY: (*To Betty*) You hear?

MURIEL: How's business, Betty?

BETTY: Thank God.

MURIEL: And Jack?

BETTY: Jack.

MURIEL: What?

BETTY: The same. Always a battle.

MURIEL: Oh, Betty. Not again.

BETTY: Muriel, with marriage you put up with this, with that, OK, it's give and take—but this man?

MURIEL: What now?

BETTY: Twenty-two years in the bakery business he does the same schedule day in, day out and it's fine by me, wonderful! Four o'clock he closes the oven, goes home, has his nap, and then he takes his bath, a nice hot bath. Always I have a fresh towel hanging up there, a terrycloth *bathrobe*—understand? The works! For his birthday I even bought him clogs, that's another story. And now, right out of a clear sky, this man will not take his bath anymore! Two days go past, no bath. Three days, still no bath. I'm tired he says. He's tired! You ever see him when he's baking twelve hours, what's *on* him from it? With the flour and the eggs? With the yeast? A man gets into a bed like that?

MURIEL: Maybe he could take a shower.

BETTY: A shower hurts on his eyes, he says!

HARRY: (*Picking up the phone and heading up the stairs with it*) If you ladies could excuse me—

BETTY: I'm pushing him out of his own store!

HARRY: No, I don't mind.

BETTY: We'll go upstairs, Harry . . .

HARRY: Stay, stay. I can do my calls up here.

BETTY: Some sweet man!

MURIEL: One in a million.

BETTY: Who's he calling so much? All morning your number's busy, busy, busy!

MURIEL: It's busy with business.

BETTY: Business is so good?

MURIEL: So-so.

BETTY: He still can't get over it, huh.

MURIEL: Little by little.

BETTY: Muriel, you bury a mother, it's no joke.

MURIEL: He'll snap out of it.

BETTY: It costs plenty nowadays, I bet.

MURIEL: A fortune!

BETTY: The daughters chipped in?

MURIEL: Oh sure.

BETTY: They can spare it!

MURIEL: We could spare it, too.

BETTY: Muriel, she . . . she left him something?

MURIEL: (*Sighs*) Listen, may she rest in peace, that's all.

BETTY: You see? Never should a person expect . . . it's only heartache! When my Uncle Stanley was lying there in *oxygen* . . .

MURIEL: Oh, it's not that. She split up what there was between him and his sisters. I don't begrudge her for . . . Ah!

BETTY: What?

MURIEL: Only say good about the dead.

BETTY: What wasn't good?

MURIEL: I shouldn't talk about it.

BETTY: Are we on the radio or something?

MURIEL: Betty, it was nothing *bad* . . . But she never gave Harry any—I don't know—any *encouragement*. As long as I can remember. He would go to her whenever something big came up, investing, moving somewhere, buying a store—not to borrow, or anything, just for her opinion—and believe me, she was nobody's fool. But he could ask till he was blue in the face there, she'd always give him the same answer, no matter what it was about.

BETTY: What?

MURIEL: Harry, she'd say—with her eyebrows up to here, you know?—if that's what you really want, then good luck.

BETTY: That's all?

MURIEL: That's all. He would eat his heart out.

BETTY: Tsk, tsk! Imagine!

MURIEL: May she rest in peace, but that's what I begrudge her for.

BETTY: Take it from me, you made up for it, Muriel.

MURIEL: I hope so.

BETTY: Twice over! I should get along so lovely with my husband!

(*The Youth enters again, turns immediately to face the racks*)

MURIEL: (*Calling up*) Customer, honey, should I take it?

HARRY: (*From above*) I'll come down.

BETTY: (*Going*) All right, thanks for hearing all my troubles.

MURIEL: Likewise, Betty.

BETTY: See you later.

MURIEL: Regards. . . .

(*Betty shrugs and goes out as Harry descends the stairs carrying the phone and intently talking*)

HARRY: It wouldn't . . . no, I haven't called them yet. . . .

MURIEL: (*To the Youth*) He'll be with you in a jiffy.

(*The Youth grunts in reply. Muriel pats Harry's arm affectionately as she passes him, and goes up the stairs*)

HARRY: Oh, don't bother, I have the number . . . (*He sighs*) . . . don't know, I just don't know . . . Mine? Evergreen three, one, five, eight, eight . . . That's very considerate of you. Thanks . . . (*Hangs up, sees who his customer is and steps in front of the counter, a bit wary*) Don't tell me you polished off that bottle already!

YOUTH: (*Studying the racks*) No . . . I nut drink eet.

HARRY: Anything wrong with it?

YOUTH: (*Still not turning*) Meester . . . you halp me?

HARRY: What do you mean? Would you like to bring it back?

YOUTH: I lighe some money.

HARRY: You would, huh? What else is new?

YOUTH: I lighe feefteen dullar.

HARRY: Are you looking for work here, is that it?

YOUTH: No.

HARRY: Listen, I'm sorry but it's not my policy to hand out money, feller.

YOUTH: (*Still not turning*) Tayn dullar, you geev me?

HARRY: Sorry, feller.

YOUTH: I askeen you . . .

HARRY: Be a good guy, will you, ask somewhere else.

YOUTH: (*Rocking on his heels*) You halp me, meester.

HARRY: (*Walking toward the door*) Do yourself a favor, take a walk!

YOUTH: Meester . . .

HARRY: (*Almost to the door*) Come on . . . (*The Youth whirls around with a knife in his hand*) What the hell are you . . . (*He tries to open the door but the youth blocks him and backs him away from it*)

YOUTH: (*Panting*) All righ' . . .

HARRY: Take it easy, kid!

YOUTH: (*Edging him back, gesturing to the cash register*) Uppen de . . . machin'!

HARRY: If you want your money back . . .

YOUTH: Uppen!

MURIEL: (*From above*) Harry?

(*The Youth brings the knife close to Harry's face*)

HARRY: What is it dear?

MURIEL: Lunch in five minutes!

HARRY: Fine!

YOUTH: (*Lowering his voice, forcing Harry to the register*) Uppen!

HARRY: (*Lowering his voice, his hand creeping under the register*) They'll catch you, you know, they always . . .

(*The Youth sees what he is doing, knocks his hand away and shoves him backward*)

YOUTH: You mek de botton, ha?

HARRY: Look, chico . . .

YOUTH: (*Menacing*) Nut uppen de bux, I cot you! Pliz, meester . . .

(*Harry rings open the register; the Youth shifts the knife to his left hand, gathers up the money and stuffs it into his pocket*)

HARRY: All right, you've got it, go ahead! (*The Youth backs him around the counter to the center of the store*) Look, you've got it, haven't you?

YOUTH: (*Gesturing for him to turn*) You—aroun'!

(*Harry turns, clicking his tongue with dismay. The Youth braces himself, brings up his fist and strikes him on the side of the head, knocking him down. Pocketing the knife the Youth flees. Harry, dazed, shakes his head, then crawls around the counter to the register and presses the button. An alarm bell goes off*)

MURIEL: (*From above*) Harry!

(*Her running footsteps are heard. Harry staggers to the door, opens it, and stumbles out*)

HARRY: Stop thief! Thief!

(*Muriel comes running down the stairs. Harry re-enters, holding his hand to his head*)

MURIEL: Oh my God!

HARRY: It's all right, it's all right—he got away.

MURIEL: (*Flying to him*) Harry!

HARRY: It's all right. . . .

MURIEL: Oh my God, let me look at it!

(*Harry sidesteps her and pulls a switch, shutting off the bell*)

HARRY: Let me call the cops.

MURIEL: Harry . . .

(*He takes his hand from his head and dials the phone*)

MURIEL: Oh, look at your *ear!*

HARRY: (*Touching it*) A little blood . . .

MURIEL: Those dirty rotten hoodlums!

(*Betty runs in*)

MURIEL: Look at this!

HARRY: (*As the two women buzz*) Ssh! Hello, look, I've just been robbed . . . M & H Wines and Liquors, Two thirty-one Fifteenth Avenue . . . yes, I put in the alarm . . . no, just a knife . . . (*As Muriel daubs at his ear*) . . . about twenty-three or-four, skinny . . . a Spanish fellow . . . long black hair, sideburns . . . a gold tooth in front . . . sort of tan jacket, dark pants, some kind of colored plaid shirt . . . yes . . . OK. (*Hangs up*)

BETTY: The Spanish fellow! I knew it!

MURIEL: I'm calling the doctor!

HARRY: No, no.

BETTY: (*Bringing around a chair*) Sit down at least!

MURIEL: (*On the verge of tears*) Look what that hoodlum did to him!

BETTY: It hurts, Mr. Weiman, huh?

HARRY: (*Sitting*) Well, he gave me a wallop—

MURIEL: What did he hit you with?

HARRY: Who knows—his fist—

MURIEL: I'm calling the doctor.

HARRY: (*Putting his hand on the phone*) What! It's a headache, a knock on the head!

BETTY: Better you should, Mr. Weiman.

MURIEL: Oh, Harry!

HARRY: Come on, crybaby, it's all over!

BETTY: Is it fractured?

HARRY: Nah! I've had worse.

MURIEL: (*Daubing at it*) Worse—look at this!

HARRY: Come on, he did pull a knife, he could have . . .

BETTY: Oh my God!

MURIEL: Let me call the . . .

HARRY: Please! A waste of money.

MURIEL: (*To Betty*) You see how a man is?

HARRY: Just get a cold compress . . . a little bandage . . .

BETTY: Put peroxide first!

HARRY: Peroxide, we'll cover it, and—how do they say?—"Life must go on." OK?

MURIEL: Some life—

BETTY: Ha!

HARRY: What can you do?

BETTY: In the next world maybe they'll tell you! (*Going out*) If you want anything, just call.

MURIEL: (*Ascending the stairs*) Thanks, Betty.

HARRY: Yes. Thanks.

(*Exit Betty*)

MURIEL: Sit quiet, darling. I'll be down in a minute.

HARRY: Take your time. (*He consults his notebook and dials*) Hello—is this Mount Tabor? I'm trying to locate a grave; it goes back some time . . . nineteen oh eight . . . Took over from who? . . . But when did *they* start? . . . It could be there, then, would you . . . Oh . . . before nineteen sixteen . . . Well, maybe if I went out Sunday and hunted around . . . (*He sighs*) Thanks . . . (*Urgently, lowering his voice*) Would you answer me something straight, please? It couldn't happen you might go and use some of that old ground, from those years, I mean . . . (*Siren is heard approaching*) You know, dig it up to make some more room . . . Of course it had a stone, what do you think it had? . . . All right . . . (*Siren comes closer and stops*) I will if I can't find it anyplace else. Thanks. (*Hangs up and stands as Policeman enters*) How do you do?

POLICEMAN: You the owner?

HARRY: That's right, officer.

POLICEMAN: (*Pulling out his notebook*) OK . . . What's your name, please.

HARRY: Weiman. Harry Weiman.

POLICEMAN: (*Writing*) W-E-I-?

HARRY: Yes.

MURIEL: (*From above*) That the cops, honey? (*She descends, carrying a cloth, bandages, water in a bowl and peroxide*)

HARRY: Yes, Muriel, the police.

POLICEMAN: Just one of us, lady.

MURIEL: How do you do—sit, sweetheart, you can sit. Did you see his ear?

POLICEMAN: (*As Harry sits*) He clouted you, huh? (*Harry nods*) Gee, that's a nasty one.

HARRY: (*As Muriel proceeds to bathe it*) Nah.

MURIEL: (*As Policeman makes a note*) Tell him he ought to see the doctor!

HARRY: I feel fine!

POLICEMAN: Can never be too safe with the head, you know.

HARRY: It's all right.

POLICEMAN: Well, it's your head, Mr. Weiman. Just hit you once?

MURIEL: (*Holding the cloth to his ear*) It's not enough?

HARRY: Ssh! From behind, with his fist, I think.

POLICEMAN: (*Writing*) I see . . .

MURIEL: He pulled a knife on him!

POLICEMAN: Yes, we got that . . . and how much did he grab, Mr. Weiman?

HARRY: Maybe forty dollars. (*Muriel applies the peroxide*) Fff! You hurt more than he did!

POLICEMAN: Never saw him before?

HARRY: No.

POLICEMAN: (*Writing*) And he escaped on foot.

HARRY: Yes.

POLICEMAN: OK. We got your description—nothing to add?

HARRY: Just that he doesn't speak English so good.

MURIEL: (*Bandaging the ear as the Policeman writes*) I hope if you catch him you really give it to him!

HARRY: (*Feeling the bulky bandage*) Ha! She's out for blood.

MURIEL: Never mind!

POLICEMAN: Anything else? (*Harry shakes his head; the Policeman puts away his notebook*) They put over a general call, he might still be in the neighborhood.

MURIEL: Probably jumped on a subway.

HARRY: He was pretty scared.

MURIEL: Not scared enough!

POLICEMAN: When they get *too* scared, lady, they use whatever's in their hand.

MURIEL: Is that right!

HARRY: But this one was just a kid, an amateur . . .

POLICEMAN: That's the age to watch out for, Mr. Weiman.

HARRY: Oh, I don't know.

POLICEMAN: Face it, most kids got a wild streak anyway, even the straight ones. You think back!

HARRY: (*Lowering his head*) It's a long time ago.

POLICEMAN: I remember, on my old block, we had three cat-killers!

MURIEL: What?

POLICEMAN: (*Demonstrating*) You know. Swing 'em around and let 'em go.

MURIEL: Ugh!

HARRY: They did that on purpose?

POLICEMAN: Sure! One's on Park Avenue now, a chiropodist!

(*The phone rings*)

MURIEL: Imagine!

HARRY: (*Beating her to it*) I'll get it . . . Hello? . . . speaking . . . yes . . . all right . . . Oh, I'll keep trying . . . thanks for your trouble, anyway. Good-bye. (*Hangs up with a sigh*)

MURIEL: (*To the Policeman*) The vodka shortage!

POLICEMAN: Yeah. Well, OK, Mr. Weiman. Let's try and get your Spagnol for you . . .

HARRY: Thanks, officer.

MURIEL: I hope you do!

POLICEMAN: (*Going out*) Take care of that head now!

MURIEL: I'll call the insurance man.

HARRY: No, I'll do it.

MURIEL: It's no trouble, Harry.

HARRY: I can do it.

MURIEL: Does it throb or anything?

HARRY: No, I'm fine.

MURIEL: You're not dizzy?

HARRY: I'm fine, I said.

MURIEL: What's the matter?

HARRY: Nothing. I'm fine.

MURIEL: Let me be concerned, for God's sake!

HARRY: Well. Enough concern for one day.

MURIEL: Harry!

HARRY: Yes?

MURIEL: Did I do something wrong?

HARRY: No, no . . . Is lunch fixed yet?

MURIEL: Harry, are you trying to get rid of me?

HARRY: I'd like to sit alone here for a while, that's all.

MURIEL: (*Hurt*) You could have just said so.

HARRY: Well, I'm saying so—OK?

MURIEL: (*Shrugs*) OK, anything you like. (*Going up*) Holler up when you want your lunch, dear.

HARRY: Yes, thanks. (*As she goes up, he takes out his notebook*) Thanks. (*Dials*) . . . Is this Mount Hermon? . . . Maybe you could help me, I'm looking for a grave . . . no, not for myself, an old one . . . May sixth or seventh, nineteen hundred and eight . . . Weiman, Edward Weiman, W-E-I- . . . Yes, of the date I'm sure . . . Please . . . Evergreen three one five eight eight . . . If it happens to be busy, please keep trying, would you? . . . Thanks. (*Cuts off the call and quickly dials again*) Hello . . . Mount Nebo? I'd like to inquire about a burial plot I thought might be . . . I see . . . What time? . . . Mr. Palace . . . OK . . . No, I'll call back.

> (*Cuts off the call, consults his notebook, begins to dial again, then hangs up and slumps. He touches his injured ear gently, sighs, picks up the phone again, then hangs up as Detective Simone enters*)

SIMONE: You Harry Weiman?

HARRY: Yes.

SIMONE: I'm Detective Simone, from the precinct. I think we nailed the kid who robbed you.

HARRY: No! Already?

SIMONE: Well, this kid ran into Haley's a couple of blocks away, shaking like a leaf with his pants all wet in front— that's what they do sometimes, it's one of the calling-cards. The bartender asked him what was the matter and he just flew out of there like a rabbit. Didn't pay for his drink. The bartender ran after him, and finally the patrolman on the beat nabbed him, over on the Boulevard. He brought him in, and they had your three oh one there.

HARRY: Isn't that amazing!

SIMONE: Oh, we hit a few like that.

HARRY: You're sure it's him though?

SIMONE: Ninety-nine percent. He won't say nothing yet, but we'll have an interpreter down, we'll run a line-up with him . . .

HARRY: Tsk, tsk, tsk.

SIMONE: I see he slugged you, too.

HARRY: Yes, he did.

SIMONE: Well, his hand's all swollen, if that's any consolation.

HARRY: (*Touching his ear*) Just a little knock.

SIMONE: Tell me, how many times have you been robbed?

HARRY: This is the fourth since I'm here. Twelve years.

SIMONE: And you still don't keep a revolver?

HARRY: Oh, no.

SIMONE: You'd get a permit, you know.

HARRY: I know, but I wouldn't like it around—I've got the alarm, I'm insured . . .

SIMONE: Insurance won't help you if you get a real case of the leaps in here.

HARRY: It would help me to shoot him?

SIMONE: I understand being queasy about it, but I tell you, just because you're lucky four times . . .

(*Phone rings*)

HARRY: Excuse me. (*Answers it*) Hello . . . yes, I'm the one . . . yes . . . yes? . . . yes! . . . It's not a mistake, now? . . . That's right! . . . Edward . . . Yes! . . . that's right! That's right! . . . Oh, listen, listen, I don't know how to thank you . . . Really, I thank you, thanks, believe me—please, how do

I get out there? . . . No, I don't have one . . . Elmhurst, right,
I'll take a cab from the station—(*To Simone*) Please excuse
me . . . (*On phone*) Soon! Now! Is it—I mean you have—
er—visiting time this afternoon? . . . Oh I'll make it, I'll get
there . . . Thanks, honest, I can't tell you how—look, let me
bring you a bottle of something, what do you drink? . . . No,
really, I want to . . . Go on, it's nothing, I'm in the business—
no, no, take Canadian Club! OK? . . . No, believe me, it's a
pleasure . . . Thank you, sir. Thank you . . . (*Hangs up and
sits, overcome*)

SIMONE: Anything wrong, Mr. Weiman?

HARRY: No, no.

SIMONE: Sure?

HARRY: (*Controlling himself*) Yes, it's personal. Anything
else you want to . . . ?

SIMONE: No, we'll call you when we're running the
line-up.

HARRY: Fine.

SIMONE: You just pick him out, that's all.

HARRY: Yes? All right.

SIMONE: (*Playfully*) No obstructing justice now!

HARRY: (*Getting up*) Yes, I know.

SIMONE: (*Going out*) And think about that permit!

HARRY: Fine, fine, yes. (*He finds a number in the direc-
tory and dials*)

MURIEL: (*From above*) Lunch is ready, hon!

HARRY: I'm on the phone, one minute— Hello, Mr.
Majeska? This is Mr. Weiman, from the . . . no, a scratch—
tell me, what do you have extra-nice? . . . Good, those, make up
a big bouquet. . . . And listen, some roses too . . . Right now!
Could you? Yes . . . Thanks! (*Hangs up*) Could you come
down, Muriel?

MURIEL: (*Above*) If you want to eat later, I can . . .

HARRY: No, I have to get dressed.

MURIEL: (*Descending*) You have to go to the police
station?

HARRY: Not yet. But they caught him.

MURIEL: They did! Oh, I'm glad.

HARRY: Do I need a shave?

MURIEL: For the police station?

HARRY: (*Feeling his face*) No, I don't need one. (*Running up the stairs*) Stay here, will you, dear?

MURIEL: (*Troubled, looking after him*) Eat something first!

HARRY: (*From above*) Not now!

MURIEL: They'll wait. (*Sound of drawers from above*) Don't knock yourself out. Did you call the insurance man?

HARRY: (*Muffled*) I'll call him later!

(*Betty enters carrying a cake box*)

MURIEL: Betty, guess what—they caught him!

BETTY: No! The Spanish fellow? So quick?

MURIEL: Yop!

BETTY: How do you like that!

MURIEL: New York's Finest, huh?

BETTY: *Good* for him!

MURIEL: That's what I say!

BETTY: Mr. Weiman's lying down?

MURIEL: No, getting dressed.

BETTY: (*Giving her the box*) I brought him some strudel, right now from the oven!

MURIEL: Oh, Betty, that's so sweet.

BETTY: He has to go to the station house, huh?

MURIEL: Not yet, he says. I don't know, he's very mysterious . . .

BETTY: Listen! With one shock after the other . . .

MURIEL: No, he was acting strange all day.

BETTY: Go on!

MURIEL: No, he was . . .

BETTY: Between you and him what should be strange, I ask you!

(*A Boy enters carrying two bouquets wrapped in white paper. In the small one are roses and in the larger, chrysanthemums*)

BETTY: Will you look at those flowers!

MURIEL: (*To the Boy*) You're bringing them here?

BOY: Mr. Weiman called up for them.

MURIEL: (*To Betty*) Something's going on. (*To the Boy*) All right, put them down.

BETTY: (*As he does so*) It can't be so bad, whatever it is.

(*Muriel rings open the register and gives the Boy some change*)

BOY: Thanks, lady. (*He goes out as Muriel broods over the bouquets*)

BETTY: What are you examining! Go put them in water.

MURIEL: (*Hinting*) I'd better wait. You know what I mean?

BETTY: OK, I'm going!

MURIEL: Thanks, Betty!

BETTY: But call up later and tell me—promise? (*Muriel nods*) With me, if I don't find out, I pass out.

(*Exit. Betty Muriel touches the flowers and pokes in the wrapping for a card, then steps away as Harry descends. He is now dressed in a dark suit and wears a tie*)

MURIEL: Oh, my, how nice you look!

HARRY: Yes? Is my tie on right?

MURIEL: (*Touching it*) Perfect! No hat?

HARRY: No, it looked funny with this. (*Points to his bandaged ear*) Oh, the flowers came.

MURIEL: (*Watching him as he examines them*) The boy just delivered them.

HARRY: Fine . . . fine . . . (*He picks up the roses and offers them*) Here, Muriel. These are for you.

MURIEL: (Taking them) Oh, they're beautiful—thank you! (*Kisses him*)

HARRY: Unwrap them, unwrap them . . . (*She does so, watching him*) I know how you like them and . . . I'm sorry I talked to you that way before.

MURIEL: Oh, honey—(*Puts aside the flowers and kisses him*) What you make an occasion over!

HARRY: I wasn't myself before, I really didn't mean to . . .

MURIEL: Who gave it a thought!

HARRY:　Well . . .

MURIEL:　Especially after such a tumult . . .

HARRY:　Well . . . you're OK, Muriel. If I didn't have you . . .

MURIEL:　(*Laughing*) Please, no speeches!

HARRY:　I just want you to know it. (*She watches as he picks up the larger bouquet and moves away from her*) These . . . I'm taking to the cemetery.

MURIEL:　Now?

HARRY:　Yes.

MURIEL:　Harry . . . it's not even two weeks. You'll only aggravate yourself.

HARRY:　No, Muriel . . .

MURIEL:　I'll go up with you on Sunday, if you want.

HARRY:　I'm not going up there.

MURIEL:　Then . . . where are you going?

HARRY:　To a different one. Lebanon.

MURIEL:　I don't understand . . .

HARRY:　Near Elmhurst. Around there.

MURIEL:　But who do you . . . have there, Harry?

HARRY:　My brother. My brother is there.

MURIEL:　What brother?

HARRY:　My brother.

MURIEL:　But Harry . . . you have no brother.

HARRY:　(*Facing her with the flowers in his arms*) Well . . . I never told anyone about this, but . . . fifty-one years ago . . . we were down on Jefferson Street . . . and I had this—brother. Edward, his name was . . . Eddie, may-he-rest-in-peace. We used to call him Skippy though, mostly on account of that comic-strip. He looked, you know . . . with the little cap and all . . . and I was seven years old and he was six, so I would . . . take care of him, you see. And one day I was playing on the stairs there with him, some kind of game on the banisters there, and he leaned way over, and he tried to pull himself back, and I was reaching for him. I got him by the wrist, and then he started to slip or something, and I wasn't strong enough to hold him and he just . . . four flights, right down the shaft. And he was buried, you see, nobody ever mentioned it. I . . . I'd always thought about it and . . . oh, lots of times, you know, over the years, I really wanted to ask my mother where he's buried exactly. I had no idea. Seven years old, what do you remember? But I never did because, well . . . I thought it might upset her too much. So I just went along, kept quiet about it. I figured she might bring it up herself sometime, then maybe I could ask her but . . . Anyway, Tuesday, soon as we got finished with the mourning there, I went to the library and made up a list of all the cemeteries, in the city, in Westchester, Long Island, everywhere, and I just called them, and called them, and called them, and . . .

MURIEL: Oh, Harry.

HARRY: Called them up till I found out where my brother was. So now I'll go out there. I'm sorry for those lies before.

MURIEL: Harry . . . it's true? Harry—(*Moves towards him*)

HARRY: No, no, it's all right now. (*Turning to the door*) I'll be back soon. (*Turning back with an apologetic smile*) Maybe when they pass away, they really are gone. But maybe they're not. Nobody knows. And he was such a little bit of a guy, I mean, if he's still . . . well . . . now he can tell, now maybe he can see it, that I didn't forget him altogether. It's late—I better run.

(*Turns and walks out. Murial turns to the roses on the counter*)

Curtain

Tennessee Williams

I CAN'T IMAGINE
TOMORROW

Tennessee Williams

The life and career of Tennessee Williams (born Thomas Lanier Williams in Columbus, Mississippi, in 1911) have been so thoroughly documented in countless periodicals and books, as well as in critical and biographical studies, that there seems little need for reiteration in the pages of this collection. Merely to list Mr. Williams' plays is sufficient for the evocation of many memorable moments in the theatre, for he has peopled the world's stages with characters so durably vibrant that their presences still stalk the corridors of a playgoer's memory.

It is true, perhaps, that the past decade—with the exception of *The Night of the Iguana*—was not particularly benign to the distinguished dramatist. But then, isn't this the rule rather than the exception in the arts: to topple over what one previously has placed on a pedestal? Yet, Tennessee Williams, recipient of two Pulitzer Prizes and four New York Drama Critics' Circle Awards remains, indisputably, a consummate master of theatre. His plays pulsate with the heart's blood of the drama: passion. When one re-examines Mr. Williams' predominant works, one cannot but be awed by the dazzling skill of a remarkable dramatist whose major plays no longer tend to be merely plays but, somehow, through the process of creative genius, have transcended into haunting realities.

Tennessee Williams is, at his best, an electrifying dramatist because, in the main, he creates people who are the sort who breathe fire into scenes, explosively and woundingly. His dialogue reverberates with a lilting eloquence far from the drab, disjunctive patterns of everyday speech and, above all, he is a master of mood. At times, it is hot, oppressive, simmering with catastrophe as in *A Streetcar Named Desire* and *Cat on a Hot Tin Roof;* at other times, it is sad, autumnal, elegiac as in *The Glass Menagerie* and *The Night of the Iguana.* To achieve it, he utilizes the full complement of theatrical instruments: setting, lighting, music, plus that most intangible of gifts, the genius for making an audience forget that any other world exists except the one on stage.

As Mr. Williams often has stated, his special compassion is for "the people who are not meant to win—the lost, the odd, the strange, the difficult people—fragile people who lack talons for the jungle." The clarion call of many, if not most, of his plays is loneliness. Just as the captured iguana in *The Night of the Iguana* symbolizes the bondage to which the people who populate the play are chained, so do his characters in other of his dramas yearn to break loose, out of the cell of the lonely self, to touch and reach another person. "Hell is yourself," Mr. Williams has said. "When you ignore other people completely, that is hell." The revelation toward which all of his plays aspire is that "moment of self-transcendence, when a person puts himself aside to feel deeply for another person."

The author first won general recognition with the 1945 production of *The Glass Menagerie,* starring Laurette Taylor. Thereafter, he attained world-wide repute with a succession of impressive plays, notably: *A Streetcar Named Desire* (1947); *Summer and Smoke* (1948); *The Rose Tattoo* (1951); *Cat on a Hot Tin Roof* (1955); and *The Night of the Iguana* (1961). Among his other plays, in nonchronological order: *Sweet Bird of Youth; Camino Real; Orpheus Descending; Period of Adjustment; The Milk Train Doesn't Stop Here Anymore; Kingdom of Earth* (known in its Broadway manifestation as *The Seven Descents of Myrtle*); and *In the Bar of a Tokyo Hotel.*

Mr. Williams also has written a number of short plays, including: *27 Wagons Full of Cotton, This Property Is Condemned, The Lady of Larkspur Lotion, The Last of My Solid Gold Watches, Moony's Kid Don't Cry, Suddenly Last Summer, Slapstick Tragedy (The Mutilated and The Gnädiges Fräulein),* and *I Rise in Flame, Cried the Phoenix.* Additionally, he has published several volumes of short stories, a book of poetry and a novella, *The Roman Spring of Mrs. Stone.*

A firm disciplinarian where his work is concerned, the dramatist dedicates four hours of each day—"year in, year out"— to writing and about every two years completes a new play. Before settling down to the actual task of writing, however, he "marinates impressions, characters, experiences."

One of the most poignant and affecting of his recent plays, *I Can't Imagine Tomorrow* was written and published in 1970 in Tennessee Williams' *Dragon Country*—"the country of pain, an uninhabitable country which is inhabited, where there is endured but unendurable pain."

As the first of the Williams plays to "open" on television instead of in the theatre, an audience of millions attended its world premiere (starring Kim Stanley and William Redfield) in December, 1970. Now, with its publication in *The Best Short Plays 1971, I Can't Imagine Tomorrow* appears in an anthology for the first time.

Characters:

ONE, *a woman*
TWO, *a man*

One and Two are, respectively, a woman and a man ap-proaching middle age: each is the only friend of the other. There are no walls to the set, which contains only such pieces of furniture (a sofa, a chair, another chair on the landing of a low flight of stairs, a lamp table and a card table) that are required by the action of the play. There is a doorframe far down stage left. Soft blue evening dusk is the lighting of the play, with soft amber follow spots on the players. The sofa and chairs should be upholstered in satin, pastel-colored, perhaps light rose and turquoise. Beside the chair on the stair landing there might be a large potted palm or fern. The woman, One, stands downstage, near the doorframe, with her arms spread apart as if she were dividing curtains to look out a window. She wears a white satin robe with a wine stain on it. The man, Two, appears before the door-frame; the woman draws back and covers her face with her hands. Two raises an arm as if to knock at a door. This action is repeated two or three times before the woman crosses to the doorframe and makes the gesture of opening the door.

ONE: Oh, it's you.

TWO: Yes, it's me.

ONE: I thought so. (*There is a strangely prolonged silence, during which neither moves*) You have on your ice-cream suit. (*Two laughs at this, embarrassed*) Well, don't just stand there like a delivery boy without anything to deliver.

TWO: You didn't say come in.

ONE: Come in, come in—enter!

TWO: (*Entering*) Thank you. (*There is another strange pause*) As I came up the drive I saw you at the window. Then you closed the curtains.

ONE: What's wrong with that?

TWO: I had to knock and knock before you—opened the door.

ONE: Yes, you nearly broke the door down.

TWO: I wondered if . . .

ONE: If what?

TWO: You didn't want to—to . . .

ONE: Want to what?

TWO: . . . to see me this—this evening.

ONE: I see you every evening. It wouldn't be evening without you and the card game and the news on TV.

TWO: But . . .

ONE: It's not getting any better, is it?

TWO: What?

ONE: I said it's not getting any better, your difficulty in speaking.

TWO: It will. It's—temporary.

ONE: Are you sure? It's been temporary for a long time now. How do you talk to your students at the high school, or do you say nothing to them, just write things on the blackboard?

TWO: No, I . . .

ONE: What?

TWO: I've been meaning to tell you. It's been five days since I've met my high school classes.

ONE: Isn't that strange. I thought so. I thought you'd stopped. What next? Something or nothing?

TWO: There's always . . .

ONE: What?

TWO: Got to be something, as long as . . .

ONE: Yes, as long as we live.

TWO: Today. Today I did go.

ONE: To the clinic?

TWO: Yes. There.

ONE: What did you tell them? What did they tell you?

TWO: I only talked to the girl, the . . .

ONE: Receptionist?

TWO: Yes, she gave me a paper, a . . .

ONE: An application, a . . .

TWO: Questionnaire to . . .

ONE: Fill out?

TWO: I— I had to inform them if I . . .

ONE: Yes?

TWO: Had ever before had . . .

ONE: Psychiatric?

TWO: Treatment, or been— hospitalized.

ONE: And you?

TWO: Wrote no to each question.

ONE: Yes?

TWO: No.

ONE: (*Impatiently*) Yes, I know, you wrote no.

TWO: Then the receptionist told me . . .

ONE: Told you what?

TWO: There wasn't an opening for me now, right now, but—I'd be informed as soon as—one of the . . .

ONE: Doctors?

TWO: Th—*therapists* could— fit me into his— *schedule.*

ONE: Did you tell her you were a teacher and the situation was desperate because you can't talk to your classes?

TWO: She was just the receptionist so I— didn't go into that. But I put on the, the . . .

ONE: Questionnaire?

TWO: That there was only one person that I—could still talk to—a little. I underlined desperately and I underlined urgent.

(*He pauses. Abashed, he turns away slightly*)

ONE: (*Gently*) In this dim light you could pass for one of your students, in your ice-cream suit, just back from the cleaners.

(*She drifts away from him*)

TWO: On the way coming over I passed a lawn, the lawn of a house, and the house was dark and the lawn was filled with white cranes. I guess at least twenty white cranes were stalking about on the lawn.

ONE: Oh? So?

TWO: At first I thought I was seeing things.

ONE: You were, you were seeing white cranes.

TWO: I suppose they were migrating on their way further south.

ONE: Yes, and stopped off on the lawn of the dark house, perhaps to elect a new leader because the old one, the one before, was headed in the wrong direction, a little disoriented or losing altitude, huh? So they stopped off on the lawn of the dark house to change their flight plans or just to feel the cool of the evening grass under their feet before they continued their travels.

TWO: It's only a block from here. Would you like to go over and see them?

ONE: No. Your description of them will have to suffice, but if you would like to go back over and have another look at them, do it, go on. I think they'd accept you in your lovely white suit.

TWO: The maid didn't come today?

ONE: She came but couldn't get in, the door was bolted.

TWO: Why?

ONE: I didn't want her fussing around in the house. She knocked and called, and called and knocked and finally gave up and—went away . . .

TWO: Everything's just like it was yesterday evening. The cards are still on the table. You still have on your white robe with the wine stain on it.

ONE: I've stayed down here since last night. I haven't gone upstairs. I finished the wine and I slept on the sofa. Oh. No supper tonight. None for me. I did go into the kitchen and opened the Frigidaire, but the sight and smell of the contents made me feel sick. So go in the kitchen and make yourself a sandwich or whatever you want while I deal the cards.

TWO: I'll make something for us both.

ONE: No, just for yourself! Do you hear me? And eat it out there, in the kitchen. (*He goes out of the lighted area. She wanders back to the windowframe and draws her hands apart as if dividing curtains*) Dragon Country, the country of pain, is an uninhabitable country which is inhabited, though. Each one crossing through that huge, barren country has his own separate track to follow across it alone. If the inhabitants, the explorers of Dragon Country, looked about them, they'd see other explorers, but in this country of endured but unendurable pain each one is so absorbed, deafened, blinded by his own journey across it, he sees, he looks for, no one else crawling across it with him. It's uphill, up mountain, the climb's very steep: takes you to the top of the bare Sierras. I won't cross into that country where there's no choice anymore. I'll stop at the border of the Sierras, refuse to go any further. —Once I read of an old Eskimo woman who knew that her time was finished and asked to be carried out of the family home, the igloo, and be deposited alone on a block of ice that was breaking away from the rest of the ice floe, so she could drift away, separated—from—all . . . (*Two returns with a plate of sandwiches*) Back, back, take it back or I'll send you away!

TWO: Are you—

ONE: I am, I told you!

TWO: If you won't eat, I won't either. I'm not hungry tonight.

ONE: *I can't!*

TWO: What?

ONE: Play cards. I can't, I can't. Sorry, forgive me, I can't.

TWO: I think you . . .

ONE: What?

TWO: . . . want me to go . . .

ONE: Where to, where would you go?

TWO: I could—go to my room.

ONE: You say it's not air-conditioned, there's no TV, it's so small you feel suffocation when you're in it.

TWO: (*Sadly*) There's a TV set in the lobby of the hotel.

ONE: You've told me you can't stand the lobby of the hotel, it's full of dying old women that crowd around the TV as if they got their blood and their oxygen from it. The lobby of that hotel, just passing through it, its atmosphere rubs off on you and you come here carrying it with you. You come here like a sick dog after passing through that lobby; it's in your eyes, your voice, your, your—manner. When you knock and I open the door, you have a sick, frightened look as if you thought I'd slam the door shut in your face. You poor, dear little man! (*She suddenly catches hold of him with a sobbing intake of breath*) I don't have the strength any more to try to make you try to save yourself from your—paralyzing—depression! Why don't you stop looking like a middle-aged lost little boy? It makes it so hard for me to talk honestly to you! (*She catches a loud breath and pushes him away, turning her back to the table*) Every evening you have a frightened, guilty expression. I always say, "Oh, it's you," and you always say, "Yes, it's me." And then you put on that painful, false, sickly grin, blinking your eyes, your hands stuffed in your pockets. You teach school, but you've never got out of school, you're still in the—primary grades of—grammar school, or still in kindergarten. Oh, it's you, yes, it's me. My God, can't there be some other greeting between us? It would be better if you just stepped in and sat down to eat and then dealt out the cards or turned on television. But, no. We have to repeat the ritual, oh, it's you and yes, it's me; there's almost nothing else said, at least nothing else worth saying. I force myself to carry on a sort of monologue, with a few interjections from you, such as "Mmmm" or "Mmm-hmmm." And I tell you things I've told you so often before I'm ashamed to repeat them. But I have to repeat them or we'd just sit together in unbearable silence; yes, intolerable silence. Yes, and in summer, you say, "It's so nice and cool in here," and in winter you say, "It's so nice and warm in here," Oh, God, God. . . . (*She catches his shoulders, presses her head a moment to his back: then thrusts him away*)

TWO: It never was easy for me to . . .

ONE: To talk?

TWO: As long as I can remember it was difficult for me.

ONE: To talk?

TWO: To put what I think and feel into speech.

ONE: And even to look in the eyes of another person?

TWO: Yes. To look in the eyes of another person, that too.

ONE: You always look a little to the side with a guilty expression. What makes you feel guilty? Is it just being alive?

TWO: I . . .

ONE: —You?

TWO: . . . don't really know . . .

ONE: Take this piece of paper and this pencil and write me the first thing that comes into your mind. Quick. Don't stop to think. (*Two scratches something on the paper*) Good. Let me see what you wrote. "I love you and I'm afraid." What are you afraid of? Quick. Write it down. (*He scratches something on the paper again. She snatches the paper from him*) "Changes." Do you mean changes in yourself or in me or changes in circumstances affecting our lives? Quick, write it down, don't think. (*He writes again*) "Everything. All." Yes, well, I knew that about you from the beginning. Now I'll be it; I'll write down the first thing that comes in my mind. Pencil. Quick! (*She writes rapidly on the sheet of paper and thrusts it toward him across the card table*) Read it, read it out loud.

TWO: (*Reading aloud*) "If there wasn't a thing called time, the passing of time in the world we live in, we might be able to count on things staying the same, but time lives in the world with us and has a big broom and is sweeping us out of the way, whether we face it or not."

ONE: Well? Why don't you say something? . . . Nothing? Take the pencil and paper, write down anything, something, quick, don't stop to think (*He writes*) "I love you and I'm afraid." That's what you began with.

TWO: You said not to stop to think.

(*She reaches out to caress his face across the table. He catches hold of her hand and presses it to his mouth, then goes around the table to kiss her. She clutches his head against her for a moment, then thrusts him away*)

ONE: Sit back down where you were. There's no way back there, believe me. (*He drops his face into his hands*) Are you crying? (*He shakes his head*) Let me see. Look up. (*He drops his face into his hands*) Don't look so tortured. Did you eat in the kitchen? No? Then stop by the drugstore on your way back to the hotel mortuary and have a sandwich or something. It might be a good change for you, better than nothing. People need little changes now and then, and have to make them or accept them. I know some people are terrified of changes, hang on to repeated routines. I think it gives them a sense of being protected. But repetition doesn't make security, it just gives a feeling of it. It can't be trusted. You can walk one street every day and feel secure on that street, and then one day it collapses under your feet and the sky goes black.

TWO: We have to. . .

ONE: We have to what?

TWO: . . . try not to . . .

ONE: What?

TWO: . . . think about that. It doesn't . . .

ONE: What?

TWO: . . . help to . . .

ONE: What?

TWO: . . . think about that, it's better to . . .

ONE: What?

TWO: . . . to feel . . .

ONE: What?

TWO: . . . protected, even if . . .

ONE: What?

TWO: . . . the feeling can't be . . .

ONE: What?

TWO: . . . trusted.

ONE: You completed a sentence. It wasn't easy for you, but you got through it. Now please get me a glass of water for my drops. (*Two crosses from the card table into a dim area*)

TWO: (*To himself*) I can't imagine tomorrow. (*He returns with a glass of water*) Shall I put the drops in the water for you?

ONE: Yes. Thank you.

TWO: It says on the bottle five drops.

ONE: Tonight it has to be more.

TWO: Are you . . .

ONE: What?

TWO: . . . sure?

ONE: Give me the glass, the bottle, I'll do it myself. (*Two counts the drops aloud. One goes on. He seizes the bottle from her and places it on the table out of the lighted area*) All right, come back, sit down. (*He returns to the card table*) I'm going to tell you a story. (*She drinks the glass of water as she speaks*) It's about a small man. Well? Aren't you going to sit down? (*He takes a chair at the table*) A small man came to the house of Death and the uniformed guard at the gate asked him what he wanted. He said that he wanted Death. The guard said that's a very large order for a small man like you. The small man said yes, he knew it was a large order, but it was what he wanted. The guard asked for his documents. The only document he had was his birth certificate. The guard looked at the date on the birth certificate and said: "Too early, you've come too early, go back down the mountain and don't come up here again for twenty years." The small man started to cry. He said: "If you won't let me in for twenty years, I'll wait twenty years at the gate, I can't go back down the mountain. I have no place down there. I have no one to visit in the evening, I have no one to talk to, no one to play cards with, I have no one, no one." But the guard walked away, turned his back on the small man and walked away, and the small man, who was afraid to talk, began to shout. For a small man he shouted loudly, and Death heard him and came out himself to see what the disturbance was all about. The guard said the small man at the gates had come twenty years too early, and wouldn't go back down the mountain, and Death said: "Yes, I understand, but under some circumstances, especially when they shout their heads off at the gates, they can be let in early, so let him in, anything to stop the disturbance." Well? What do you think of the story?

    TWO: It's, uh. . . .

    ONE: It's uh what?

    TWO: Did you make up the story?

    ONE: No. You made it up. You've been making it up for a long time now. It's time to send it out for publication. Don't you think so?

    TWO: I, uh. . . .

    ONE: I uh what?

    TWO: Let's. . . .

ONE: Let's what?

TWO: Tonight you . . .

ONE: Tonight I what?

TWO: . . . you seem . . .

ONE: What?

TWO: . . . not as well as you . . .

ONE: Not as well as I what?

TWO: . . . not as well as, not as well as . . . (*He springs up with a soft, tortured outcry*)

ONE: Yes. I know. I know. You didn't eat anything, did you? No. You must stop at the drugstore on your way back and have something to eat at the soda fountain. They serve all kinds of things there and it's a popular place. You might even strike up an acquaintance with someone else eating there. When I go there for my prescriptions, I notice there's usually several people eating there at the soda fountain. I've heard them talk to each other. They seem to be acquainted with each other. It's easier to become acquainted with someone at a soda fountain than at a table in a restaurant because you're sitting beside them and a restaurant table is separate. And I think it's important for you to strike up some new acquaintances. Because it's possible that some evening I won't hear you when you knock at the door. I might be upstairs and not want to come down or not feel able to come down to the door when you knock, and in that— (*She closes her eyes and clenches her teeth in a spasm of pain*) — that—possible—eventuality—you should—have—other—acquaintances—to fall back on, in that case, if it comes.

TWO: I think you're still in pain. Aren't you?

ONE: If I am, it's my pain, not yours, and I have the right not to discuss it, don't I? I think a person in pain has the privilege of keeping it to himself. But try out the drugstore tonight and don't go in there with a long face, go in there with a bright attitude and sit next to someone that seems to have an extrovert air about them. Say something first, don't wait for them to say something to you because they might not do it. I know you will hate to talk, but you have to do things sometimes that are difficult for you, so go in there and sit at the soda fountain and have a milk shake and talk, speak, open your mouth even if you just open your mouth to say you heard an owl tonight, imitating your voice in a palm tree: Of course they won't believe you, but that could lead to an interesting conversation.

TWO: I think what you mean is . . .

ONE: What I mean is—things have to change in life.

TWO: The changes don't have to be sudden.

ONE: The changes are much easier to accept when you've already prepared yourself for them. That's why I mentioned the drugstore soda fountain.

TWO: It's bright and noisy and I would never be able to strike up an acquaintance at a bright, noisy soda fountain, I wouldn't know how and wouldn't want to attempt it.

ONE: Up till a year ago . . .

TWO: What?

ONE: What was I saying? Oh. Up till a year ago . . .

TWO: What?

ONE: Never mind. Whatever I was saying has flown out of my head.

TWO: (*After a pause*) Do you want me to slip away now?

ONE: Slip away is a way of saying dying. (*She sits up*) I've changed my plans for the night. I'm going upstairs, after all. I can still get up them if I take my time about it and hold onto the banisters. I can get up to the landing and rest there a while and then climb the rest of the way. And as for you, don't forget my advice to strike up some new acquaintances. It doesn't have to be at the soda fountain, it could be at a bar. Say something to somebody. That's my advice, but I can see it's wasted.

TWO: An acquaintance isn't a friend.

ONE: Who is a friend? Let it go. But eat something at the drugstore on your way back.

TWO: Shall I help you upstairs before I . . . ?

ONE: Lately I've been sleeping down here on the sofa. The stairs have gotten much steeper. But tonight I think I'll get up them. I'll climb to the landing first and then I'll rest there a while before I go on. There's a fairly comfortable chair on the landing that I can rest in till I feel able to go up the second flight. (*She goes up three or four steps to a platform and a chair*) Yes, I can rest here a while.

TWO: I'll stay till you've gone to your bedroom. Then I'll slip out.

ONE: No, don't wait. Slip out now. I like to talk to myself a little before I sleep.

TWO: You mustn't sleep on the landing; you can't sleep on the landing.

ONE: I'll do what I want to do!

TWO: I'm sorry, I—didn't mean to tell you what you. . . .

ONE: Go on, slip out now. Fasten the bolt on the door.

TWO: The bolt is inside the door.

ONE: Oh. Yes. You're right. That changes my plans a little, yes, I'll have to bolt it myself.

TWO: I don't think you ought to be left alone here at night.

ONE: That's your opinion, not mine. Good night, go on, slip away now, the evening has been an effort.

TWO: I'm—sorry, I—feel as if you'd lost all feeling for me. . .

ONE: That isn't true. I wouldn't have let you enter the house tonight if I didn't still love you. I did and still do. But we've gone into different countries; you've gone into a strange country and I've gone into another.

TWO: Could I stay on the sofa?

ONE: No, no, I'm sorry, no. You have to go, now.

TWO: You are . . .

ONE: I am what?

TWO: . . . my life, all of it. There's nothing else. I'll go to the clinic, I'll go back to the school, I'll. . . .

ONE: Don't make it so hard for me.

TWO: Please! Let me stay on the sofa!

ONE: No!

TWO: But. . .

ONE: No, I said *no!* Open the door, go out!

TWO: When I come back tomorrow, you'll . . . ?

ONE: What?

TWO: Let me in?

ONE: If you go now, yes, but if you . . .

TWO: I'm going now. (*He opens the door*) The air is—the sky is . . .

ONE: What are they?

TWO: . . . unusually light tonight. Like very clear shallow water, like, like . . .

ONE: The roosters will crow all night because they'll think it's near daybreak. Good night. Have a nice walk back. Perhaps the white cranes will still be on the lawn you passed coming over. Rest well. Don't ever doubt I care for you, but remember we're going into separate countries. (*He shuts the door silently from inside, walks back to the sofa*)

ONE: (*To herself*) Gone—better alone. It's hard because he has nobody but me and I have nobody but him, but in the Dragon Country, you leave your last friend behind you and you go on alone. —Oh. The door. Not bolted. I'd better go down and bolt it or the maid will get in tomorrow. Get up, get up, I said up! (*She rises with great difficulty and descends the stairs, clinging to the banisters. She doesn't see Two at the card table. She crosses to the door and bolts it: then to the windowframe and looks out. Two lifts a card as if to shield his face with it. She turns to the room and sees the man by the sofa*) Oh. You stayed, didn't go. —I can't imagine tomorrow. —Help me back up the stairs, please help me back up to my chair on the landing. (*He catches her as she seems about to fall and supports her up to the landing*) Let me rest here, please. I'll go on up to my bedroom in a while, even if I have to crawl up the rest of the stairs. . .

TWO: Let me help you up now.

ONE: No. Here. Stop. Impossible—further—right now. (*She sits in the chair on the landing*) Now. Go back down.

TWO: Let me . . .

ONE: *No, no, go back down, down, down!*

TWO: I—you . . .

ONE: Sorry. I have to be alone here. (*Two returns to the card table*) If I wake up and come downstairs tomorrow, it won't surprise me to find you still here. I think you've always wanted to stay in my house. Well, now's your chance, so make yourself at home. You know where everything is: the TV set, the liquor, the Frigidaire, the downstairs bedroom and bathroom. I leave you with all these delights. I'm going to sleep in a minute. I suppose it's still possible that tomorrow you'll pull yourself together and meet your classes. I wouldn't bet on it, though. Anyway, it's likely that you've been replaced at the Junior High School. You've probably been expelled from the Junior High School like some—incorrigible—student. They just haven't bothered to notify you about it, or you've been scared to pick up the phone if they called you at the hotel mortuary. Haven't you always wanted to move in here? You've paid so many compliments to the place, the evenings you've come here from the hotel mortuary you live in. You always tell me how lovely something is, the warm air in winter, the cool air in summer, the palm garden, even the sky, as if it belonged to the house. All right, now, you can stay here if you want to. You wouldn't get in my way, I wouldn't get in yours. After a couple of days we'd hardly notice each other. It would be like talking to ourselves, or hearing a bird or a cricket somewhere outside. Of course you have the alternative of creeping back to that mortuary called a hotel, but there's a time limit, a pretty short time limit, on your acceptance there in your present circumstances. They probably already know you're out of a job. Well, such things happen to people, all people, no exceptions. The short time limit runs out, it runs out on them and leaves them high and dry. (*There is a pause. Two collects the cards, puts them in the pack. Then One continues*) If I sleep well tonight, I'll be better tomorrow, and if you're still here, we'll drive out or take a cab to the Food Fair Market and stock up the Frigidaire for you, and then we'll go by your hotel and collect your things and check you out of that awful mortuary. After that? I can't think. Perhaps it's not necessary to think past that. That's far enough for thinking and planning the future. So make yourself at home here. Take a drink out on the screen porch, enjoy the sky and the sea that belong to the house. I'm going on upstairs now. (*But she sits back down*) Not quite yet. Going on up is like climbing a peak in the Alps.

TWO: Stay down a little while longer.

ONE: All right, just a little while longer. . .

TWO: (*Softly, after a pause*) Are you asleep now? Are you asleep now?

ONE: . . . I can't imagine tomorrow.

Curtain

Alun Owen
DOREEN

Alun Owen

Alun Owen was born in 1926 in Menai, North Wales, and was educated at Cardigan and Liverpool. He began his stage career at fifteen when he joined the Perth Repertory as a bit-part actor and assistant stage manager. During World War II, he was a "Bevin Boy" (one who worked in the mines as a public service, as an alternative to conscription during the war) in the pits in South Wales before a mining accident led to his discharge. An assortment of jobs followed. He worked as a waiter, a lorry driver's mate, a warehouse hand, a seaman in the Merchant Navy, for two trips; and then as an actor in repertory, pantomime, and on the West End stage and television. He had meanwhile published poems in the United States and Wales and had gradually become interested in dramatic writing.

After five radio scripts had been accepted by the British Broadcasting Corporation, his first stage play, *Progress to the Park,* was presented as a Sunday night production at the Royal Court Theatre in 1959, was then produced for a run at the Theatre Royal, Stratford East, and subsequently transferred to the Saville on the West End. His other plays include *The Rough and Ready Lot,* produced at the Lyric in Hammersmith, and *A Little Winter Love* which premiered at the Gaiety Theatre, Dublin.

In 1964, Mr. Owen's musical, *Maggie May* (with music and lyrics by Lionel Bart and starring Rachel Roberts) was an overnight success at the Adelphi Theatre, London, where it enjoyed a run of sixteen months.

A prolific author who transfers his allegiance from stage to television to films with equal facility, Mr. Owen received the 1960 award as Best Scriptwriter of the Year from the Guild of Television Producers and Directors and received the Television and Screenwriters' Guild award for the Best Original Television Play of 1961 in England—*The Rose Affair.* Additional honors subsequently came to him when he was nominated for a Hollywood Academy Award for his screenplay, *A Hard Day's Night* (The Beatles' first feature film) and acquired the 1967 Gold Star Award from Britain's Associated Television for his play, *George's Room,* which was published in this editor's collection of *Modern Short Comedies from Broadway and London*.

In 1969, the author scored a resounding success on American television with his three-part drama, *Male of the Species*. The production was introduced by Sir Laurence Olivier and starred Paul Scofield, Sean Connery, Michael Caine and Anna Calder-Marshall. The networks repeated the presentation in 1970, and at present a musical version of the work is being planned for Broadway. (The text of *Male of the Species* will appear in print for the first time in this editor's forthcoming anthology, *Best Short Plays of the World Theatre: 1968–1973*.)

During the seasons of 1969 and 1970, Mr. Owen was represented by three separate offerings on British stages: as a contributor (along with Harold Pinter, John Bowen, and others) to *Mixed Doubles* (Comedy Theatre, London), nine short plays about marriage; *No Trams to Lime Street* (Richmond Theatre), a musical based on his television play; and *There'll Be Some Changes Made* (Fortune Theatre, London).

Doreen—the girl from the typing pool who reduces a puffed up womanizer to a complete nervous wreck by playing cunningly on all his little prides and insecurities—began life on B.B.C. Television and drew considerable praise from the press. *Plays and Players* magazine noted that "*Doreen* is absolutely up Owen's street, the sort of thing he does incomparably well." The comedy, in its new stage form, appears in print for the first time anywhere in *The Best Short Plays 1971*.

Alun Owen lives with his wife and children "mostly" in a large Victorian house in Cardigan, West Wales, on the banks of the River Teify.

Characters:

ERIC

JOHN

DOREEN

EMMA

Scene:

A large, well-furnished flat in a suburb of London. Evening.

Eric is sitting on the settee, eating salted peanuts. He is about thirty and fair-complexioned. He is a nice worrier; at the moment, everything worries him, which makes him aggressive.

After a second, John comes in. He is slightly younger; better looking, better dressed, over-confident and on the make.

ERIC: Are they going to be long?

JOHN: You should worry, they're here, aren't they?

ERIC: Yeah, but . . .

JOHN: But what?

ERIC: (*Moodily*) Well . . .

JOHN: Relax, enjoy yourself.

ERIC: I just wondered, that's all.

JOHN: No, you didn't, you worried, that's all you ever do —worry. You never let it happen, you're always trying to control it instead of letting it happen.

ERIC: Oh, shut up. *You* sound as if *you're* trying now.

JOHN: Have a drink.

ERIC: Will he mind?

JOHN: It's got nothing to do with him—I bought all the drinks, he only lent me the place.

ERIC: Oh, it's your liquor then?

JOHN: Of course.

ERIC: I'll have a beer.

JOHN: Have a drink.

ERIC: I fancy an ale.

JOHN: Well, I don't want them two prancing in here and you with only a beer in your hand. Get a vodka or something.

ERIC: Got any rum?

JOHN: Bacardi.

ERIC: Tastes like gnats' pee.

JOHN: You've drunk it, of course.

ERIC: Bacardi, yes.

JOHN: No, gnats' pee.

ERIC: Oh, you get on my nerves.

JOHN: Oh, no I don't, you get on your own bloody nerves. Eh, they're all right aren't they?

ERIC: It's a bit near home.

JOHN: Take a chance.

ERIC: (*Uneasily*) Off the switchboard.

JOHN: It's done all the time.

ERIC: Maybe, but I don't like it.

JOHN: And, by God, you're making it obvious.

(*There is a pause*)

ERIC: Mind, they're all right.

JOHN: I'm glad you've come to terms with it.

ERIC: And that dark one, she can eat too; she went for that sirloin like a saber-toothed tiger.

JOHN: (*Grinning*) Doreen—and she's mine.

ERIC: Who said so?

JOHN: Why, do *you* fancy her?

ERIC: That's not the point.

JOHN: Look, don't start.

ERIC: Let them make up their own minds.

JOHN: I thought you liked blondes.

ERIC: I do.

JOHN: Well.

ERIC: Well what?

JOHN: Emma—the other one—she's a blonde.

ERIC: I'm not color blind, you know.

JOHN: Well, you never stopped chatting her up.

ERIC: Aye, but at the same time I had my eye on who's it?

JOHN:　Doreen?

ERIC:　Yeah, Doreen—common name that. (*Raises his voice*) "Eh, Doreen, go home, your knickers are torn."

JOHN:　Have you gone mad? They'll hear you!

ERIC:　Go on! They must know about it.

JOHN:　What do you mean?

ERIC:　They wouldn't be here unless they knew about it.

JOHN:　Oh, I don't know about that.

ERIC:　(*Doggedly*) Well, I do; we'd never have got them back here otherwise.

JOHN:　You're going to funk out on me, aren't you?

ERIC:　Are you expecting an answer to that?

JOHN:　Why else would I ask?

ERIC:　You like your own voice; you always did.

JOHN:　Look, I know you. (*Slightly louder*) I've *always* known you; are you going to abandon me?

ERIC:　You'll be saying, "leave me in the lurch" next.

JOHN:　I know you, son.

ERIC:　Don't go on about it.

JOHN:　I've got you sized and taped.

ERIC:　I'm fastidious.

JOHN:　What?

ERIC:　Wash the wax out.

JOHN:　Fastidious nothing! You start off all for it but when it comes to the in, you're off like a frightened first timer.

ERIC:　I am not!

JOHN:　Hare on a mountain, you are, son.

ERIC:　You'll do anything. It only has to flinch and you want it; you're over-sexed.

JOHN:　Oh, aye, changing the subject now that I'm tightening your braces.

ERIC:　Look, it was your idea; you picked 'em; you made the date.

JOHN:　Aye and I'll make the kill and all.

ERIC:　You're always landing me in it.

JOHN:　In what? Go on, define it.

ERIC: I like making my own arrangements.

JOHN: All right, I made the arrangements; you've come this far. Why can't you just drift?

ERIC: I don't like this flat.

JOHN: The scenery's that important, is it?

ERIC: To me, yes.

JOHN: I don't get you.

ERIC: (*Ironically*) Go on, surprise me.

JOHN: You always balk at the last fence.

ERIC: Well, I told you—I'm fastidious. Always have been.

JOHN: (*Fed up*) Yeah, you're known for it. (*Then, changing his tack*) Oh, come on, kid, it's a giggle, a bit of fun. Old Man Reilly lends me his flat for the weekend, they're two prime little movers. Let's have a few drinks and everything else will take care of itself.

ERIC: And you'll let 'em make up their own minds?

JOHN: I was set on that Doreen, but Emma's a good kid so I'm laughing fore and aft.

ERIC: Aye, I suppose so.

JOHN: Good man, what'll you have?

ERIC: Scotch and Yank.

JOHN: I'll join you. (*He crosses to the drinks table*) You know, there's a nip of success in the air tonight.

ERIC: You're like a kid with a party balloon. Don't slop the drinks!

(*John gives him his drink. They look at each other and go through their own private ritual*)

ERIC:

(*Together*) First today! (*They drink down in one*)

JOHN:

JOHN: Mind you, you're right, they're taking their time,

ERIC: Ladies' privilege.

JOHN: Eh?

ERIC: Women spend half their waking life in the Carsey.

JOHN: Aye, you're half-right.

ERIC: Well, let's have another.

JOHN: Are you working round to getting quietly smashed?

ERIC: No, just want to smooth out the wrinkles.

JOHN: Go on—you do fancy Doreen, don't you?

ERIC: Oh, she's got a definite undertow all right.

JOHN: Anyway, I'm easy.

ERIC: You fancy her as well, I know.

JOHN: No, I'm easy.

ERIC: Well, let's not have any of the "you wouldn't think Eric was eighteen months older than me" bit going on.

JOHN: I wouldn't.

ERIC: I've heard you.

JOHN: *Never!*

ERIC: "Oh, yeah, he's a great kid, old Eric, set in his ways, mind, of course. He's eighteen months older than me, you'd never get to change *old* Eric."

JOHN: I've *never* said that.

ERIC: Never? You said it to Hilda Formby.

JOHN: Oh, Hilda Formby's different; she doesn't count.

ERIC: She's a girl, isn't she?

JOHN: She's a shopping basket and you know it.

ERIC: I was doing all right there.

JOHN: She had you half way up the aisle blindfolded and you didn't know it. I was doing you a favor.

ERIC: We go to a party . . .

JOHN: Marriage on her mind.

ERIC: . . . I go for a jimmy . . .

JOHN: The branding iron was white hot, it was singeing your backside.

ERIC: . . . come back and she's lying on the sofa with you with her skirt half-way round her throat.

JOHN: You had a narrow shave, me laddo.

ERIC: Any road, we'll have none of the "saving me from meself bit" either.

(*There is a slam of a door*)

JOHN: What was that?

ERIC: It was a door, wasn't it?

JOHN: It was the front door.

ERIC: They've done a glide.

JOHN: (*Crosses to the door*) We'll see about that.

(*As he goes to the door, it opens and a dark girl enters the room; it is Doreen, she is young and attractive, cool, calm and collected*)

JOHN: What was that noise?

DOREEN: The front door.

JOHN: The front door?

DOREEN: The front door.

ERIC: *Our* front door?

DOREEN: Yeah, your front door.

ERIC: Oh.

ERIC: Who was it?

DOREEN: Emma.

ERIC: She's gone?

(*Doreen winks at him*)

DOREEN: You're quick when you try.

JOHN: You mean she's gone?

DOREEN: Over the hills and far away.

JOHN: What for?

DOREEN: She didn't fancy you.

JOHN: *Him,* you mean?

DOREEN: No, she didn't discriminate; both of you.

ERIC: Oh.

DOREEN: I saw it was in the cards.

JOHN: Did you?

DOREEN: And when she didn't have a sweet, I knew.

ERIC: I noticed she didn't have a sweet.

JOHN: What's that got to do with it?

ERIC: Yeah, she's the sort who'd be a natural for a gateau.

DOREEN: Ice cream and all.

JOHN: You might have let us know.

DOREEN: Oh, there would have been no point. When she gets the bit between her teeth, there's no stopping her.

JOHN: (*Annoyed*) We could have tried.

DOREEN: If it isn't putting anyone to any trouble, I'm dry.

ERIC: Scotch or gin?

DOREEN: Don't use 'em.

JOHN: You don't?

DOREEN: Don't need 'em.

JOHN: Oh, that's great.

DOREEN: Why, were you planning on getting me drunk?

JOHN: No—only . . .

DOREEN: What?

JOHN: Oh, give her a lemonade.

ERIC: There's only orange.

JOHN: (*Briefly*) Then give her an orange.

DOREEN: (*Amused*) Yeah, give her an orange and quick. The soft bitch is thirsty.

JOHN: (*Shocked*) I never said that.

DOREEN: No, you're a master of self-control, you are.

JOHN: Well, for God's sake, it's not very nice having someone walk out on you like that!

DOREEN: Particularly when you've paid for a slap-up meal and a bottle of wine.

ERIC: You only drank water.

DOREEN: It's good water in that café, best tap for miles.

JOHN: And she just pushed off?

DOREEN: Cantered.

ERIC: (*Amused*) Not a backward glance?

DOREEN: (*Smiling*) Like the clappers.

ERIC: As if Old Nick was on her tail?

DOREEN: In a manner of speaking.

JOHN: Shurrup the two of you, it's not funny!

ERIC: Don't you think so?

DOREEN: It had *me* in pleats.

JOHN: It's bad-mannered, that's what it is, bad-mannered!

DOREEN: Steak and chips, two gins before and a Drambuie after and she pushes off without so much as a how's-your-father. I was a bit shaken meself.

JOHN: It's not the food and drink I'm bothered about.

DOREEN: What's a quid to a big spender like you!

JOHN: (*Suspiciously*) Are you having a go?

ERIC: Don't blame *her,* she stayed, remember?

JOHN: Oh, aye, well, I won't forget this in a hurry, She's ruined my night.

DOREEN: Had a case on her, did you?

JOHN: Well, no. I don't like being made a mug of. Does anyone?

ERIC: Yeah, he's right, it was a bad stroke. Is she given to this sort of thing?

DOREEN: I don't know.

JOHN: Well, she's your mate.

DOREEN: You've got it wrong, brother, I just work next to her.

JOHN: But you were together in the canteen.

DOREEN: We were having our tea break together. I've only spoken to her about twice in my life.

JOHN: Then how did you know about the gateau and the ice cream?

DOREEN: She had that look.

ERIC: Yeah, she did, didn't she?

JOHN: Don't *you* start!

ERIC: Well, she did.

DOREEN: Yeah, she did.

JOHN: You two have got the team spirit, haven't you?

ERIC: (*Laughing*) Looks like it.

JOHN: Well, she was *your* date.

ERIC: Who says so?

DOREEN: Yeah, who says so?

JOHN: You never stopped talking to her.

DOREEN: Yeah, but he did a lot of *looking* at me.

JOHN: Well, he likes blondes; he always has.

DOREEN: Up to now.

ERIC: Yeah, only up to now.

DOREEN: (*To John*) Let him make his own mind up.

JOHN: He hasn't got much choice anymore, has he?

DOREEN: No, not really.

ERIC: *She's* the only one with a choice now.

JOHN: Who?

ERIC: Doreen.

JOHN: (*Pause*) Oh. (*He looks at Doreen who appraises him*)

DOREEN: Yeah, what have you got to offer?

JOHN: Oh, come off it.

DOREEN: Well, one of you've got to go.

ERIC: Yeah, I suppose so.

DOREEN: I'm not taking on the two of you.

JOHN: (*Hopefully*) No?

DOREEN: If you thought I would, you've got the wrong girl.

ERIC: Don't you ever drink?

DOREEN: Never felt the need.

ERIC: Christmas and weddings included?

DOREEN: Have you ever had a good look at a room full of half-drunk people?

JOHN: If they're half-sloshed, so would we be.

DOREEN: (*To Eric*) Does he do a lot of the talking for you?

ERIC: I speak up when he gets it wrong.

DOREEN: Thank God for small mercies. Any road, I can't stand people sweating gin all over you and women get very messy looking when they're drunk.

JOHN: You can say that again.

DOREEN: They look as if their mainspring's bust.

ERIC: They say a bit, too.

JOHN: (*Laughing*) And they've got lots of things to say.

DOREEN: You don't like women, then?

JOHN: Yeah, but like you, I don't like a drunken woman.

DOREEN: Funny, then why did you keep on trying to force the stuff down Emma and me?

JOHN: Just to get you in the mood.

DOREEN: What for?

JOHN: To enjoy yourselves.

DOREEN: Gerroff?

JOHN: Honest.

DOREEN: I hope you don't believe that.

ERIC: Give her the point.

JOHN: Why should I? Nothing's the matter with a couple of crafty drinks.

DOREEN: Just to loosen the stays?

JOHN: Yeah . . . no . . . it relaxes everyone, gives 'em the party spirit. No harm in that.

DOREEN: Some people don't need it.

JOHN: Yeah, you said you never felt the need, are you cold or something?

DOREEN: No, I'm pretty warm when I feel like it.

JOHN: (*Sexily*) And what makes you feel like it?

DOREEN: It's like an itch with you, isn't it?

JOHN: Aw, come on, if you go out with a couple of fellas, you've got to . . .

DOREEN: Got to what?

JOHN: Are you trying to show me up?

DOREEN: Is that what you think?

JOHN: You answer, I'll ask.

DOREEN: No, I'm not trying to show you up.

JOHN: Good.

DOREEN: You do a pretty good job without my help!

JOHN: What did I do? I just asked you to come out and have a meal; I'd have settled for the odd kiss. I'm not Bluebeard.

DOREEN: This isn't your flat, is it?

JOHN: No.

ERIC: Yes.

(*Doreen looks at them with her cool amused eyes*)

DOREEN: Well, one of you's a liar.

JOHN: Does it matter?

DOREEN: Not to me, but it worried the hell out of Emma.

ERIC: (*To John*) I told you not to lay it on so thick.

JOHN: What's it matter!

DOREEN: Well, for one thing it makes you lose faith, like.

ERIC: As bad as that?

DOREEN: Well, it gave her an acute attack of, "what'll me mother say"?

JOHN: And you're enjoying it, aren't you?

DOREEN: Somewhat.

JOHN: All right, it *isn't* my flat. A friend lent it to me for the weekend and I'm sorry if that Emma thinks I'm a liar, but that's the way it goes and the sooner she learns, the better for all concerned. And anyway what's the diff?

DOREEN: "Nobody likes being made a mug out of" was the way I heard it.

JOHN: That's different and you know it.

DOREEN: Do I?

JOHN: Yes, you do.

ERIC: You don't look as if you've made a case out from here.

JOHN: *Whose* side are *you* on, Eric?

ERIC: (*Shrugs*) I'm just letting it happen, I'm drifting.

JOHN: I'll remember that!

ERIC: You've been trying to teach me that lesson since the eleven plus; now, I've learned it and you're suddenly crabby. You're inconsistent, son.

DOREEN: Yeah, he is and it only looks good on girls.

JOHN: What's this, a gang-up?

ERIC: Take it, it happened, forget it.

JOHN: I know why you say that!

ERIC: You do?

JOHN: Either way, you're laughing.

ERIC: Let us in on what you're on about, will you?

JOHN: You think you've made a mark on this one and even if you hadn't you were going to funk out on me. God, I wouldn't want to be in a tight corner with you! You're a right double-facer!

ERIC: And it's different for you?

JOHN: Too right.

ERIC: There's only one way for you, son, *your way*. "I love myself and me only will I serve" was the motto in your cracker.

JOHN: (*Turning on Doreen*) And another thing, what's wrong with this flat?

DOREEN: Nothing, I never said there was.

JOHN: Good.

DOREEN: Lovely flat.

JOHN: Fine.

DOREEN: Just isn't yours, that's all.

JOHN: It was lent to me.

DOREEN: The fella who owns it must trust you.

JOHN: (*Grandly*) He owes me a favor.

DOREEN: I see.

JOHN: Well, at least it doesn't bother you whose flat it is.

DOREEN: No, doesn't bother me.

JOHN: Atta girl.

DOREEN: I've been here before.

JOHN: (*Surprised*) In this flat?

DOREEN: Sure, often.

ERIC: You know Reilly?

DOREEN: Well.

JOHN: Did you tell Emma this wasn't my flat?

DOREEN: I think it might have been mentioned.

ERIC: And you know Reilly?

JOHN: What do you want to do a thing like that for?

DOREEN: (*To Eric*) Have done for ages. (*To John*) Why shouldn't I.

ERIC: No reason, just a coincidence, that's all.

JOHN: No reason, just wish you hadn't.

ERIC: I can't see you with Reilly.

JOHN: Mind, I didn't fancy her. I'm more for brunettes.

DOREEN: (*To Eric*) Takes all sorts. (*To John*) You're entitled.

ERIC: I like brunettes as well.

JOHN: (*To Eric*) Will you get off the line!

DOREEN: I'm the one who's getting it from all sides and I'm not complaining.

JOHN: I thought you said you couldn't handle two at the same time.

DOREEN: Didn't say I couldn't, said I wasn't going to.

JOHN: Well, you're managing all right.

DOREEN: Aye, but I'm not going to make a way of life out of it. (*To Eric*) Have you known him long?

ERIC: Since primary school; of course, I'm older.

DOREEN: (*Approvingly*) I thought you must be.

JOHN: Not that much.

ERIC: (*Countering*) Eighteen months.

JOHN: What's that got to do with it?

ERIC: That year-and-a-half makes a lot of difference.

DOREEN: All the difference, I'd say.

JOHN: Eighteen months is nothing.

DOREEN: It's a different vintage.

ERIC: Oh, we were never in the same class but he was big so we played on the same teams, that's all.

JOHN: (*Indignant*) We lived two doors away from each other. Our mothers are cousins.

DOREEN: Oh . . . relatives?

ERIC: Distant.

DOREEN: (*To Eric*) I like the fella to be older.

JOHN: What for?

DOREEN: What?

JOHN: What do you want him to be older for?

DOREEN: Everything.

JOHN: Just like that, the lot, the whole kit and caboodle.

DOREEN: It's not a hard line, it's just a preference, that's all.

JOHN: I don't get you. When that Emma went, why didn't you sling *your* hook as well?

DOREEN: She was nothing to me. What she does is *her* business.

JOHN: Well, it's damned odd!

ERIC: (*To John*) Maybe she didn't want to go?

JOHN: Well, obviously, but why?

DOREEN: Curiosity.

ERIC: What do you want to know?

DOREEN: I'll find out.

JOHN: You don't help much, do you?

DOREEN: Do I have to?

JOHN: Yeah . . . a little.

DOREEN: (*Amused*) A steak and chips worth?

JOHN: Are you hung up on food?

DOREEN: Not particularly.

JOHN: Well, you go on about it enough.

DOREEN: Like you and humpty?

JOHN: Humpty?

DOREEN: Nooky, Nasty, Sex, whatever you want to call it.

JOHN: I haven't mentioned it once.

DOREEN: You don't have to.

ERIC: He was always like that, even on the Cubs' outing.

DOREEN: Was he? I was a Brownie.

JOHN: I'm sure you were, any road, you've got it all wrong. I haven't tried anything. I've behaved very well. A lot of fellas u'd have gone screaming mad at what's happened here tonight.

DOREEN: (*To Eric*) Would you?

ERIC: No, I can see the funny side of it.

DOREEN: I thought you had a sense of humor.

ERIC: It's a godsend.

DOREEN: I know. I'd be lost without mine.

JOHN: Honest, I don't believe you two—you've lost touch.

DOREEN: What with?

JOHN: Forget it. Eric, have a drink?

ERIC: I'm not bothered.

JOHN: Well, bother yourself.

DOREEN: Yeah, go on, keep him company.

JOHN: He can make his own mind up.

DOREEN: He did, he said no. I just thought you needed keeping company, you know. You'd feel better pouring out two than just your own.

JOHN: Look, he's been putting gallons of the sauce down while you were in the bathroom with the vanishing lady.

DOREEN: Was he? He carries it well.

ERIC: I always do. Only have as much as you can handle is my motto.

DOREEN: You're moderate.

ERIC: (*Smiling*) Yeah, I think you could say that—moderate, yeah, moderate.

DOREEN: (*Smiling back*) Yeah, moderate.

JOHN: (*Exasperated*) Oh, God in Heaven!

DOREEN: (*To Eric*) What's up with him?

ERIC: Search me.

JOHN: You ought to hear the two of you. "I'm moderate, yes, you are moderate. Oh, I'm moderate," all right.

ERIC: Well, I am.

DOREEN: He is.

ERIC: It's obvious.

JOHN: Look, it's Saturday night, you know—party night, music, dancing. You're only young once, you'll be a long time dead; you two sound like a couple of old aged pensioners on a wet Wednesday in Preston. Let's put a record on.

ERIC: We won't be able to talk.

(*John has started to put on a Bossa Nova record*)

JOHN: That's the idea; I can't take your level of boss chat.

DOREEN: Boss?

JOHN: They say that for the best, greatest, you know.

DOREEN: Oh.

JOHN: Knock it off! Can you dance?

DOREEN: Yeah.

JOHN: Unbend a little and prove it.

(*By now he has the record playing and John and Doreen start to dance; at first they dance apart then John, who is a good but flashy dancer, pulls Doreen close to him. While they dance, Eric and Doreen exchange glances. She raises her eyes to heaven in despair that her participation in the dance belies. Eric assumes a look of tolerant amusement that doesn't really come off. He thinks he is smiling sardonically, the smile playing around his lips; actually, he looks a bit gormless and Doreen sniggers*)

JOHN: (*Quietly*) What's up?

DOREEN: (*Semi-whispering*) I feel as if we're dancing for the "Master."

JOHN: (*Laughing*) Aye, he looks a bit like a dirty old pasha spread all over the chair-like marge.

(*They both laugh and this discomforts Eric, who lights a cigarette*)

JOHN: You're a neat little armful.

DOREEN: Well, I've had no complaints up to now.

JOHN: I bet you haven't and you just reach level with my heart.

DOREEN: I saw that one, too.

JOHN: What?

DOREEN: That picture.

JOHN: You don't make it any easier, do you?

DOREEN: If you wanted it easier you shouldn't have joined.

JOHN: (*Whispering*) We better get rid of old Eric!

DOREEN: What?

JOHN: Etgay-iddray foa Ricbay.

DOREEN: What makes you think you're "favorite"?

ERIC: Yeah, you're only the dancing master, son.

(*John breaks away in a pet and switches off the record*)

JOHN: Oh, this is soft; I mean, it stands to reason, *one of us'll have to go!*

DOREEN: (*Wide-eyed*) How about me?

JOHN: Not you! *Him or me.*

DOREEN: Oh.

JOHN: Well, you said you wanted it that way.

ERIC: God, you're crude.

JOHN: Maybe, but I'm practical!

DOREEN: And you don't exactly sweep a girl off her feet with your romantic approach.

JOHN: (*Indicating Eric*) Well, what about the buck here, Moderation Willy from Chatter Lane? You're not going to tell me he's the answer to a maiden's prayer, 'cause if he is they'll *all* stop going to church!

DOREEN: They've stopped, or haven't you noticed?

JOHN: (*Sharply*) Are you making a choice?

DOREEN: Don't rush me.

JOHN: I'm not rushing you. I just want you to make up your mind.

DOREEN: No good ever came out of a hurry.

ERIC: Oh, it's always the same with him; he sees something and right off he's got to have it—in a manner of speaking, like.

JOHN: Thanks very much.

ERIC: You'd always pinch the last chip off someone else's plate.

JOHN: She's a chip then, is she? Or is that just another manner of speaking?

ERIC: Don't be so hard-faced. It's always the same with you; we take two girls out and you do the picking and I'm left with Mother. Well, you're on the wrong steer this time, son.

JOHN: You're being a bit premature; she hasn't made her pick yet.

DOREEN: Oh, I think I have.

ERIC: (*Self-satisfied*) Yeah, I thought you had.

DOREEN: Well, you're the nicest, Eric, and you're more dependable and you're older . . .

ERIC: But?

DOREEN: Yeah, and it's a very big but.

ERIC: Are you turning me down?

DOREEN: I've got to.

ERIC: Why?

DOREEN: Look at it from my point of view, you say you like me . . .

JOHN: He didn't.

DOREEN: (*To Eric*) Am I a liar?

ERIC: I like you.

DOREEN: Good. But you always liked blondes up to now and I don't go for sudden converts.

JOHN: You're not a bad judge.

ERIC: I thought we were understanding each other.

DOREEN: We do and there's not much surprise in that—you're like a brother.

ERIC: Thanks for nothing.

DOREEN: Temper.

ERIC: It's the dancing that did it, isn't it?

DOREEN: It helped.

ERIC: I can't dance.

JOHN: Come 'round when you've taken the course.

ERIC: God, if a bit of dancing can wilt her, you can have her.

JOHN: Thanks very much.

(*There is a pause*)

ERIC: Right, I'm off.

JOHN: Good-night.

DOREEN: It was nice meeting you, Eric. You're nice.

ERIC: Fat lot of good that's done me.

DOREEN: Oh, I don't know.

JOHN: That's the way it goes. See you tomorrow.

ERIC: I wouldn't count on it.

DOREEN: (*Concerned*) You'll get a taxi all right?

ERIC: Yeah, I'm fine. (*He crosses to the door*) Oh hell, so long.

(*Eric goes out. John turns to speak to Doreen*)

DOREEN: Shurrup!

(*John is surprised, but holds his peace. There is the sound of the front door closing*)

JOHN: He's gone.

DOREEN: I'll just make sure.

JOHN: I'll go.

DOREEN: (*Snapping at him*) You needn't bother!

(*Again John is surprised by her tone, but he stands motionless as she hastens to the door, opens it and goes out, leaving him alone in the room. John sits. After a moment, she returns, all smiles*)

DOREEN: Have a drink.

JOHN: You don't mind?

DOREEN: Of course not.

JOHN: I thought . . .

DOREEN: It'll do you good, relax you.

(*He crosses to the drinks table and helps himself, then returns to his seat*)

JOHN: You had me worried there.

DOREEN: Where?

JOHN: Back there; I thought you were going to take the wrong turning and elect old Eric.

DOREEN: Is he your friend?

JOHN: We put it about together, yeah.

DOREEN: But when it comes to the crunch . . .

JOHN: You're always on your own.

DOREEN: You don't find it lonely?

JOHN: I can handle anything that comes up.

DOREEN: *Anything?*

JOHN: I've always managed up 'til now.

DOREEN: Yeah, but you've never met anyone like me before.

JOHN: Oh, I don't know.

DOREEN: I'm telling you.

JOHN: Well, apart from the obvious, what's so special about you?

DOREEN: This and that. (*Critically*) I don't think much of that suit of yours.

JOHN: (*Surprised*) What's the matter with it?

DOREEN: It wasn't made for you, was it?

JOHN: I'm a handy figure. I can buy off the peg.

DOREEN: Off the peg? Yeah, I thought so.

JOHN: That's right, what's wrong with that? (*Doreen ignores the question*)

DOREEN: Do you think those "sideboards" suit you?

JOHN: Well, I wouldn't wear them if I didn't.

DOREEN: Quite right, so you must have thought a lot about them before you grew 'em. Then you'd have to grow 'em and you'd wonder all the time they were growing if they'd suit you. And I suppose half the people you know don't like 'em. Didn't that put you off?

JOHN: Why should it? What is all this?

DOREEN: Don't you care what people think about you?

JOHN: Not much. It's what *I* think that counts really, isn't it?

DOREEN: What you asking me for; they're your "sidies", not mine.

JOHN: Don't you like them?

DOREEN: What's it matter what I think? It's what *you* think that counts.

JOHN: Yeah, but I reckoned they looked good on me.

DOREEN: Then that's you suited. Why did you grow 'em?

JOHN: (*Grinning*) Hair's sexy.

DOREEN: Yeah?

JOHN: Sure, enhances your masculinity, says so in the paper.

DOREEN: You worried about your masculinity, then?

JOHN: No, but I'm going to make the most of it and build it up. Girls like that.

DOREEN: I'm a girl and I don't.

JOHN: Well, you must be odd.

DOREEN: I told you I was different.

JOHN: You're that all right.

DOREEN: Do you want to kiss me?

JOHN: I was quietly working 'round to it.

DOREEN: And you're not in any hurry?

JOHN: I can wait. I know when I'm winning.

DOREEN: And you reckon you're winning now?

JOHN: All these questions! All right, well, Eric lost, didn't he?

DOREEN: Aye, but there are three of us playing.

JOHN: One down, one to go.

DOREEN: Oh, you're keeping score?

JOHN: I haven't got you figured yet, but it'll come.

DOREEN: I don't see how I fit in. You fancy yourself so much, two's a crowd.

JOHN: That line of chat doesn't bother me. I'm the only one I've got, so I've come to terms with it.

DOREEN: What *does* bother you?

JOHN: I'll trade you; give us a kiss and I'll reveal the lot.

DOREEN: Stand up then. (*He does and crosses over to her, preparing to take her in his arms*) Oh no, *I'm* doing the kissing. You keep your arms at the side.

JOHN: You're joking!

DOREEN: I'm real serious. One move and I call it off.

(*John is amused and stands stiffly. She takes his face in her hands and kisses him long and slow. The effect on him is considerable, but the moment he tries to take her in his arms she moves away angrily*)

JOHN: What's up?

DOREEN: I warned you, I was doing the kissing!

JOHN: Sorry.

DOREEN: Well, it's over now and you've spoilt it.

JOHN: Are you serious?

DOREEN: When it comes to kissing, I'm *always* serious. Now, you've got something to tell me.

JOHN: What?

DOREEN: We were trading a kiss for what bothered you.

JOHN: Oh, that.

DOREEN: Yeah, that.

JOHN: Well, give us a sec, you packed quite a wallop in that kiss.

DOREEN: I told you I was different.

JOHN: Pride yourself on it, don't you?

DOREEN: "I'm the only one I've got, so I've come to terms with it."

JOHN: You remember things and all.

DOREEN: Yeah, and now I'm waiting to hear what bothers you.

JOHN: (*Lightly*) Oh, nothing much—not getting my own way—that sort of thing.

DOREEN: Emma's pushing off bothered you, didn't it?

JOHN: Well, she's a liberty-taker. She had no right just walking off like that.

DOREEN: Makes you hot just to think about it, doesn't it?

JOHN: That's right.

DOREEN: She made a fool of you.

JOHN: Don't go on about it.

DOREEN: Oh, does it bother you, then?

JOHN: Everybody hates being made a fool of.

DOREEN: Some more than others.

JOHN: Maybe.

DOREEN: If a story like that got around . . .

JOHN: You wouldn't tell anyone?

DOREEN: *Every*one.

JOHN: No.

DOREEN: I promise you.

JOHN: That's all right, I'll blame Eric.

DOREEN: But I know it was *you*.

JOHN: Who said?

DOREEN: She did.

JOHN: She didn't.

DOREEN: Prove it.

JOHN: Oh, for God's sake, it's not important, it doesn't matter!

DOREEN: Then you won't mind?

JOHN: I've told you, I'll just say it was Eric. He put her off.

DOREEN: He won't have that; he'll blame you and I'll back him up.

JOHN: But what about Emma?

DOREEN: She walked out because she didn't like the look of you.

JOHN: Do you mean that?

DOREEN: May have been the suit, may have been the lice beds, I don't know; she couldn't belly you.

JOHN: You're just making it all up.

DOREEN: What for?

JOHN: 'Cause you're an oddy, you're funny. There's nothing the matter with me, I'm all right, I'm known. Why should a girl walk out because of me?

DOREEN: I don't know, but walk out she did.

JOHN: But you stayed.

DOREEN: I'm like that.

JOHN: Like what?

DOREEN: Well, I'd stay; I'm more interested in odd ones like myself.

JOHN: I'm not odd!

DOREEN: What are you getting all worked up about?

JOHN: I'm not!

DOREEN: You are, you know.

JOHN: I'm not! (*He has shouted and this has rather startled him. Pause. Doreen grins at him*) I think you'd better go.

DOREEN: I like it here; I'm stopping.

JOHN: Well, I'm having another drink.

DOREEN: Do you carry it as well as Eric?

JOHN: Better! (*He crosses over and gives himself a stiff drink*)

DOREEN: I know your bother now.

JOHN: Do you now?

DOREEN: One word.

JOHN: And what's that?

DOREEN: (*Pleasantly*) Vanity.

JOHN: Just 'cause I don't like being messed about?

DOREEN: No, you reckon yourself so much that if anyone doesn't fancy you as much as you do yourself, you bristle like our cat.

JOHN: I'm not like a cat!

DOREEN: You see, you take it for granted that you should fancy yourself; the only thing that bothers you is "cat." You don't see yourself as a cat, do you, son?

JOHN: Of course not. Fellas aren't cats.

DOREEN: No, not *real* fellas—I mean, that Eric, he's more a terrier but you're not even a ginger tom. Oh, you like to come on like one, but underneath you're just a flabby tabby.

JOHN: You're a great one for "scratching" yourself, if you ask me.

DOREEN: Try stroking me, I might purr.

JOHN: I don't like cats.

DOREEN: Go on, they're lovely.

JOHN: They get on my chest.

DOREEN: Do they *bother* you?

JOHN: Yeah, they bother me.

DOREEN: I'm a cat.

JOHN: Come again?

DOREEN: Oh, there are cat people, didn't you know? And dog people. Eric's a terrier, that Emma's a toy poodle and Mr. Reilly's a doctored Persian—you see the way it works out?

JOHN: Yeah, I suppose so, and what are you?

DOREEN: (*Moving closer to him*) I'm a stray . . . black and skinny . . . with claws.

(*John is fascinated, but resists*)

JOHN: It's soft, you're a girl, a bit of a girl!

DOREEN: Oh, don't you want to play?

JOHN: What for?

DOREEN: 'Cause that's the way I like it.

JOHN: Well, I don't. We haven't got the same ideas, you and I.

DOREEN: Well, we couldn't have really, could we?

JOHN: We could have if you'd stop messing about.

DOREEN: Am I doing that?

JOHN: I've got you now, girl, you're a tease; you like talking it but when it comes to the grappling irons—you're dead scared.

DOREEN: (*Laughing*) Try again. I just have different rules.

JOHN: They could get you into a lot of trouble.

DOREEN: Not much fear of that with you.

JOHN: Don't be so rude.

DOREEN: (*Grinning*) Sure, you told me cats bothered you.

JOHN: You're not a cat. You're a girl, a switchboard girl, that's all. You come on in shifts of two and it just wasn't my day when I started talking to you. Any road, if you were a cat I'd know how to deal with you, give you a tin of cat meat and a saucer full of milk and you'll lick my hand. All cats are like that.

DOREEN: That's what's bothering you, isn't it? You've given us our tin and some milk and we don't love you for it so your vanity's hurt.

JOHN: Look, you were welcome to that dinner, I don't begrudge it to you. But I'm entitled to something in return if it's only a kind word, so knock off needling me.

DOREEN: Yeah, it isn't fair, a bit of a switchboard girl having a meal with a junior manager. But that's the chance you take when you invite someone like me out.

JOHN: Well, it won't happen again; we won't be playing together anymore.

DOREEN: (*After a pause*) Yes, I used to know a boy at school like you. When we were skipping in the street he'd run through the rope and if you'd plaits he'd pull 'em. He kicked a top I had into the allotments, right into the long grass; but we fixed him!

JOHN: Who?

DOREEN: Me and a gang of girls. We followed him every-where and sat all around him in class; even when he went into the "boys" we stood outside shouting things at him. We made him cry in the playground, just by the tap it was—and he rubbed his eyes with his hands and dirt went all over his face in strings. We fixed him—fixed him good and proper.

(*There is a pause*)

JOHN: (*Quietly*) Poor kid.

DOREEN: What about *us*?

JOHN: It was different—yours was a plan. He was just being a kid—he didn't plan it.

DOREEN: I liked that top.

JOHN: Yeah, that was wrong of him.

DOREEN: If your mother had plaited your hair, you wouldn't like having it pulled.

JOHN: No, I don't suppose I would but . . .

DOREEN: (*Strongly*) But! Where do you get that *but* from! He got what he deserved. He was bigger than us; we weren't as strong so we made a plan.

JOHN: Well, why tell me, it wasn't me. What are you tell-ing *me* for?

DOREEN: It's just that you reminded me of him.

JOHN: That's no fault of mine.

DOREEN: Well, don't take it so personally, I just said you reminded me of that boy, that's all.

JOHN: You didn't have to go into the gory details, did you?

DOREEN: Are you squeamish as well?

JOHN: As well as what?

DOREEN: As getting bothered easily?

JOHN: (*After a moment*) How do you know this flat so well?

DOREEN: (*Primly*) I've been here on visits. Mr. Reilly is a keen photographer.

JOHN: And takes pictures of you?

DOREEN: It's been known to happen.

JOHN: Aye, aye.

DOREEN: (*Coolly*) Eric said you were *crude*.

JOHN: Are there any about?

DOREEN: He keeps them in a wooden chest in the dark room, locked.

JOHN: Like that, eh?

DOREEN: (*Simply*) They're private and wouldn't interest you.

JOHN: Oh, does he pay you?

DOREEN: Of course he doesn't! He told me about his hobby, so I said he could use me as a model. He usually makes me a meal after, he's a good cook, a bit fancy but it makes a change.

JOHN: (*Snidely*) Yeah, but he's carrying a few seasons, isn't he?

DOREEN: What?

JOHN: He's ahead of you by a few, isn't he?

DOREEN: What are you trying now?

JOHN: Aw, come on, you understand; he's older than you, he's too old for you.

DOREEN: Why?

JOHN: Well, you wouldn't say he'd be very able.

DOREEN: He's a good photographer.

JOHN: But a little lacking in other areas, bound to be.

DOREEN: You can only see the one thing, can't you?

JOHN: Why, is there anything else?

DOREEN: All sorts of things, but not for you! You want to be at it all over the place, sweating and stumbling out of the room, your eyes screwed up and you stiff as a board, all strain, that's you. Well, there are some of us who can find the odd moment off just as great!

JOHN: I was right, you *are* cold.

DOREEN: That kiss was cold?

JOHN: No, but it was funny, damned funny!

DOREEN: (*Grinning*) Yeah, it takes some getting used to. Did you like it?

JOHN: Sure, but it was all wrong.

DOREEN: Wrong? How could you like it if it was wrong?

JOHN: Oh, I enjoyed it, but it was funny. Yeah, and it was wrong.

DOREEN: (*Amused*) Why?

JOHN: Well, *you* were doing all the work. I felt as if you were using me.

DOREEN: And you don't like being used?

JOHN: Do you?

DOREEN: We're talking about *you*.

JOHN: Well—I felt like Joe Soap standing there.

DOREEN: (*Amused*) Like Soft Mick?

JOHN: You were fooling about with me.

DOREEN: But you enjoyed it.

JOHN: Sure, but I shouldn't have, it was queer.

DOREEN: Different?

JOHN: Aye.

DOREEN: And you can't cope if it's different, can you?

JOHN: Why should I? I know what I want, and what I want's right.

DOREEN: Why?

JOHN: Well, it stands to reason, it must be; everybody wants what I want.

DOREEN: *Everybody?*

JOHN: Well, all the fellas that I know, any road.

DOREEN: What about the girls?

JOHN: I've never had any complaints.

DOREEN: All right, you kiss me.

JOHN: Y'what?

DOREEN: You heard, you kiss me and I'll let you know how you rate.

JOHN: You think I won't, don't you?

DOREEN: If you're going to do it, get on with it, show!

JOHN: (*Annoyed*) All right!

(*He crosses to her and takes her roughly in his arms and gives her a kiss. He kisses her hard and moves his mouth about a lot. She is limp in his arms which he takes for acquiescence. After a moment, he breaks away and looks at her. Her eyes are open and have remained so during the whole kiss*)

JOHN: Well?

DOREEN: Well what?

JOHN: Well?

DOREEN: (*Coolly*) Oh, is that all?

JOHN: (*Quietly, turning away*) You bitch, you treble bitch!

DOREEN: Eh?

JOHN: You did it on purpose.

DOREEN: Did what?

JOHN: Nothing.

DOREEN: Well, nothing happened.

JOHN: I kissed you!

DOREEN: You did not.

JOHN: I damn well did and you know it!

DOREEN: Nothing of the sort. You dug your chin bristles into me, breathed heavy, then tried to dislocate my neck.

JOHN: I kissed you!

DOREEN: If that's what you call a kiss, my Aunt Nelly's in the Coldstream Guards. I thought you were trying to do me a mischief.

JOHN: I have kissed hundreds of girls.

DOREEN: Like that?

JOHN: Yeah, like that!

DOREEN: God help them and save them and keep 'em pure.

JOHN: They liked it!

DOREEN: They were having you on.

JOHN: (*Desperately*) They liked it, they said so!

DOREEN: You're so pleased with yourself you'd believe *anything*.

JOHN: I can tell when a girl's enjoying it and you didn't even try.

DOREEN: I just lay there and waited. It was up to you, but nothing happened.

JOHN: Nothing?

DOREEN: Well, you hurt me.

JOHN: I'd like to break you in two!

DOREEN: Oh, you'd manage that easy enough; you're big and strong enough, lots of muscle on you as well.

JOHN: Aye, I'm fit all right.

DOREEN: But you've picked the wrong lady. That wouldn't please me at all—not one little bit.

JOHN: Who wants to *please* you, I just want to show you!

DOREEN: Show me what?

JOHN: That you can't treat fellas like that!

DOREEN: Like what?

JOHN: You know your own tricks best.

DOREEN: So, there never was any question of pleasing *me* —just suit yourself and you're away, was that it?

JOHN: Look you, I'm fed up with all your questions, your knocks and clever remarks! You've done nothing but have a go at me since Eric went.

DOREEN: Oh, I was flicking you before he went.

JOHN: But you ditched him to stay with me.

DOREEN: And that didn't strike you as odd? Of course, it didn't! You're so full of yourself, you reckon yourself the first prize so much, that you'd think if I came your way you were entitled.

JOHN: What harm did I ever do you?

DOREEN: You're a type, that's enough.

JOHN: I'm a man.

DOREEN: You! (*Laughing*) You're a lady, a lady passing yourself off as a fella! I eat men like you with me cornflakes!

JOHN: You're mad.

DOREEN: Don't you wish it?

JOHN: Stark raving mad!

DOREEN: It's the first time you've ever heard the *truth* about yourself, so of course I must be mad, it figures.

JOHN: Oh, I'm fed up with you; you're a mistake and I don't have to wear it! I've tried everything, but you came here looking for trouble and you won't be satisfied until you get it. Talk about *me* fancying myself—God—God—you think you're some sort of dazzling wonder! Well, you're not. You're right—

you are a stray, black and skinny and you can keep your dirty claws off me!

DOREEN: (*Crooning*) Ah, is he panicking then?

JOHN: No, he isn't! He's just had you up to the gullet. Who needs you? You don't drink, I haven't seen you smoke . . . .

DOREEN: You never offered me one.

JOHN: Do you want one?

DOREEN: I don't smoke.

JOHN: You see! You're sly and everything you say is to put me down. (*Doreen laughs*) Well, I'm glad *something's* funny.

DOREEN: Yeah, it is, *you*. You're out of your depth and you're splashing around, swallowing water and popeyed.

JOHN: And you wouldn't help, would you?

DOREEN: Me? Not on your life. I need a swimmer. I like men who can control themselves *and* me—not little boys.

JOHN: Well, I like girls who are real girls, girls who know how to behave, who don't ask men little questions all the time, like you, girls who are soft and round, not spiky and full of thorns!

DOREEN: You like flop meat, that's what you like. Give 'em a few drinks and a meal, then get 'em 'round to the flat, only a *borrowed* flat, mind, 'cause you still live at home, cheaper. Couple of dances and a bit more booze and you're there. She just flops out and you batter her and you think that's passion! You're as passionate as a bulldozer, you're a spoiled kid who runs at his mother's apron full pelt and you think that's love. Get off, son, I'm for the carriage trade and you're on a tricycle!

JOHN: (*Cornered*) Why? What for? Why me?

DOREEN: You're not entitled to any answers.

JOHN: Well, what did I do to you?

DOREEN: I made up my mind, half way through that steak, you needed telling.

JOHN: You planned it?

DOREEN: One thing I'm good at is planning.

JOHN: You weren't to know it'd work though?

DOREEN: Once I'd frightened off that Emma, it was easy.

JOHN: You frightened her off?

DOREEN: She was half way there already. She's the sort who enjoys being frightened of men; says, "please don't," right up 'til "please don't stop." But I gave her a little push and she was real scared, she couldn't wait to scarper.

JOHN: You're rotten.

DOREEN: And what about you? You had it all worked out, didn't you? Only this time you were up against a fighter and not a piece of flop meat.

JOHN: Stop saying that!

DOREEN: Bothered again! For a fella on the make, you don't half bother easy.

JOHN: I'm not on the make and I'm not stopping here!

DOREEN: Ah, don't go, I'm enjoying myself.

JOHN: And I'm supposed to stop here and amuse you?

DOREEN: Well, you didn't get me back here for the good of me health, did you?

JOHN: There's no way of reaching you, is there?

DOREEN: Not for you.

JOHN: Well, I'm going!

DOREEN: You said.

JOHN: Are you coming?

DOREEN: I'm comfy, I'm fixed.

JOHN: Well, I don't suppose it matters. (*Emphatically*) After all, you've been here before!

DOREEN: (*After a pause; coldly*) Yeah, you look just like that boy I knew at school.

(*John glares at her but gets back more than he can give. He turns on his heels and rushes out, slamming the door after him. Then, after a moment, we hear the front door slam. Doreen smiles to herself, then crosses to the table and pours herself a drink, lights a cigarette. She takes a good drink, inhales and exhales, taking pleasure in the whole routine. She endows these simple actions with a great deal of sexuality. Then she crosses, drink in her hand, to the settee and stretches out on it. She is relaxed and happy. After another drag she kicks her shoes off*)

DOREEN: (*Calling*) Emma! Emma! You can come out, love. Emma!

(*Doreen looks at the door and after a moment Emma appears. She is blonde, pretty and plump. She looks into the room, checking on the occupants. She looks at the empty room, then at Doreen and both of them explode into harsh laughter*)

Curtain

James Leo Herlihy

BAD BAD JO-JO

James Leo Herlihy

Internationally noted for his novel, *Midnight Cowboy,* and the subsequent film version that won the Academy Award as the best movie of 1969, James Leo Herlihy was born in 1927 in Detroit, Michigan. At seventeen, he joined the U. S. Navy and when the war ended, he spent a couple of semesters at Black Mountain College in North Carolina, followed by two years of study at the Pasadena Playhouse, California. But, according to the author, his "real education was acquired in years of hitchhiking through the country," a period that also found him in a series of diversified jobs until he finally acted on West Coast stages and in television.

In 1956–57, he was an RCA Fellow at the Yale School of Drama and in 1958, his play, *Blue Denim* (written with William Noble) ran for 166 performances on the Broadway stage and later was made into a successful movie. Mr. Herlihy's next theatrical endeavor, *Crazy October,* was less fortunate. The play, directed by the author and which starred the late Tallulah Bankhead, ended its brief career during its pre-Broadway tryout tour.

Though a proven dramatist, throughout his life he has been continually at work at what he considers his true métier, the writing of fiction. His first volume of short stories, *The Sleep of Baby Filbertson,* was published in 1959 and won enthusiastic praise from the press. *The New Statesman* called it "brilliant, technically perfect, an absolute model of the genre." The following year, his first novel, *All Fall Down,* was received with equal enthusiasm. The reviewer for the *New York Herald Tribune* termed it "a remarkable first novel," while Orville Prescott of *The New York Times* editorialized that its "humor, charm and poignance are all peculiarly Mr. Herlihy's own. He has told his story with impressive skill and a light touch. A deft and superior novel." The work appeared in a dozen languages and was made into a film. But most importantly, it established James Leo Herlihy as one of the most original writing talents of his generation.

Five years later, his second novel, *Midnight Cowboy,* was issued and immediately became a national best-seller. The screen version—with Dustin Hoffman and Jon Voight in the principal roles—was one of the top-grossing films of 1969 and still is being shown in theatres throughout the world.

When *Bad Bad Jo-Jo* (which appears here in an anthology for the first time) opened at the Off-Broadway Stage 73, in March, 1969, as part of Mr. Herlihy's triple bill (the other two short plays: *Laughs, Etc.* and *Terrible Jim Fitch*) bearing the overall title of *Stop, You're Killing Me,* the press acclaimed him as "a talented and imaginative dramatist . . . with a gift for words and a capacity for dramatic power." Clive Barnes of *The New York Times* described the evening as "bizarrely brilliant", and the correspondent for the *Hollywood Reporter* considered it "the best example of native American playwriting currently on view in New York."

In 1971, *Bad Bad Jo-Jo* was presented on British television and *Variety* reported that it "built tension admirably . . . leading up to a nail-biting climax" as the author "adroitly manipulated his three characters, gradually turning them from figures of fun into macabre people."

James Leo Herlihy, whose latest novel, *The Season of the Witch,* was published in the spring of 1971, still is an ardent traveler, though no longer by foot and thumb. In recent years, he has lived in New York, Key West (Florida), Italy and Spain.

Characters:

KAYO HATHAWAY
FRANK JONES
DENNIS

Scene:

Kayo Hathaway's penthouse in Sutton Place. There is evidence everywhere of Kayo's imminent departure: packing crates, disorder, etc. Prominent on one wall is a large lobby poster for a movie, Bad Bad Jo-Jo. Its illustration shows a little old lady with tiny eyeglasses and sensible shoes leading an enormous ape-like young man by a chain. The young man wears an Uncle Sam hat that is too small for him.

Kayo Hathaway is lying on a chaise longue, having a nightmare. We see its effects upon him, slides showing scenes of mayhem and violence, the flashing of a strobe light, and we hear loud, acid-rock music, as he squirms and gasps, reacting to the dream-menace. At length, he recognizes one of the sounds as the telephone bell, and slowly, agonizingly, comes awake. Music ceases as lighting becomes normal, late-afternoon daylight. Kayo scrambles toward the telephone like a person accustomed to using it as an instrument of deliverance.

KAYO: Hello? Hello? Hello? (*He hangs up and looks about him, still frightened, and then dials a number*) Roberta? Kayo. Was that you? Did you phone me? Just now. Oh. Well then, it was someone else. I was having the most ghastly nightmare when the phone rang. Who could it have been? It must have been Seymour. I thought sure you'd be phoning me to hash over last night. Oh, I loathed it, Roberta. And when I think it was my own farewell party! I'm so depressed. Do you know what I discovered? . . . What's the matter, you're not in the bathtub, are you? Well then, you can damn well listen for a minute, surely, can't you? . . . I discovered last night that all of my so-called friends are sycophants. Of course, I'm not including *you!* You're not a friend, sweet Jesus no, you're an arm, you're a vital organ, a part of me. I breathe through you, you silly, tiresome pussy. But the others! Roberta, can you name me *one* who would have been there last night if I were someone other than Kayo Hathaway, creator of Bad Bad Jo-Jo? No, no, don't try. If it weren't for the fact that my Jo-Jo books are in every drugstore and my name in lights on half of the world's movie theaters, that room would've been empty. Hesketh was right, you know. He said Bad Bad Jo-Jo made Double-O-Seven seem as heavy-handed and old-fashioned as Sherlock Holmes, and I must say he's right. D'you know, Roberta, Jo-Jo still amuses me—far more than any of my friends do, certainly. The very idea just kills me: this dreadful, grinning little saint of a woman, and this ghastly monster of a son, running through the world like a dose of salts. You know, it is terribly funny, darling. "Bad, Bad!" she says, as Jo-Jo slaughters twenty-two Communists before breakfast . . . How did I get off on that? Oh, yes, Hesketh. Do you know what else Hesketh said to me last night? He said, "You know, Kayo, you might have been a *real* writer if you hadn't been born with such a genius for trivia." Oh, Hesketh is vicious. But it's not just Hesketh, it's all of them. I had quite a sobering moment on my way home, in the solitary splendor of my Carey Cadillac. Kayo, said I, you are completely a-lone. Completely. So, darling Roberta, you see that I shall be no more alone in Switzerland than I am in America. What do you mean, have I had second thoughts? About leaving? I should say not! I'm getting out! And if you were smart, you'd listen. Something dreadful is going to happen here, and I don't want to be around when it does. . . In America! That's where! I don't know, pet, but it's something foul. I can smell it. The stench of it is everywhere, it rises like fumes from the gratings in the streets, it lurks in doorways, it's the unwritten story on every front page. Nobody knows what it is, and yet everyone has a name for it. The liberals call it the John Birch Society, and the Birchers call it Communism. The white man says it's Black Power, the Negroes say it's the fuzz, the fuzz says it's the marijuana smokers. Meanwhile the poor dear potheads blame it all on the liquor lobbies. And Kayo Hathaway, well, he's just dizzy and terrified. My dear, I tell you, the hounds are snapping at our asses. Don't *you* feel it, Roberta? Well, I don't think it's exaggerated at all! Would you care to hear what I dreamed last night? I dreamed I was Marie Antoinette! And I trust you recall what happened to her fair white neck! (*The door-bell rings*) Oh, Christ, there's the door. Who can it be? What time is it? Am I expecting someone? *Don't* hang up! Don't you dare, till I can think who it is. (*He rummages through notes on his desk*) Roberta, did you make an appointment for me and forget to write it down? Oh, I know! It's someone from a fan magazine. It's not *Silver Screen,* and it's not *Photoplay,* but it's one of those. (*He picks up the house phone*) Harris? Who is it? *Two* young men! No, I will not see two, I made an appointment with one. Send *one* up. (*He hangs up the house phone and goes to the door, leaving it ajar—still talking all the while to Roberta*) Can you imagine? A personality interview with a writer, of all things, to be published in a movie magazine! Why, I don't even have any tits! Roberta, couldn't you just chat with me till the young man comes? I *hate* being left completely alone. (*Another phone rings*) Ha! There goes my other line. Apparently someone *wants* to talk to me. Goodbye. (*He hangs up*) You hideous, selfish twat! (*He answers the second phone*) Yes? Seymour? What's happening? Uh-huh, I see, well, here's my answer. You tell Miss Enormous Toosh that Mr. Hathaway is in an utter coma of pleasure, since she's consented to tour the barns in his poor little play. She's his favorite movie star in all the world. But then you whisper to her, Seymour, just whisper that between the two of you, Kayo Hathaway is totally unapproachable on the subject of money. If she wants more than ten per cent she'll have to get it from the producers.

> (*During the above, Frank Jones has entered. He is a large young man, with a powerful-looking body, but his man-ner is tentative, awkward, obsequious. This effect is so pronounced as to appear, at times, almost studied, and per-haps even vaguely disquieting. At the moment of his appearance, Kayo ushers him in with gestures*)

KAYO: Call me back and tell me what she says. I've got to go now, because I'm being rude to a perfectly delightful young man who has come to interview me for a fan magazine. And he has promised not to ask any questions about The Burning Issues Of The Day. Isn't that charming? All I've got to do, apparently, is tell whether or not I sleep in the raw. Are you titillated? Wait, wait! Don't hang up! Were you going to hang up on me? Oh, Seymour, don't ever hang up on me. I want to ask you something very important. But hold on for one moment, while I tell my guest to make himself a drink. (*To Frank*) Dear Guest, how do you do. (*They shake hands*)

FRANK: Wow! I just shook hands with Kayo Hathaway! Wow-wee, am I ever impressed!

KAYO: Ha-ha, you do admire me, don't you. I love your being so forthright about it. How ingenuous! (*Into phone*) Seymour! Are you clicking at me? Please, I will not be clicked at! (*To Frank*) Help yourself at the bar. There's ice in the bucket. Now, apart from offering you a drink and encouraging you to replenish it at your own discretion as the visit wears on, I will make no attempt whatever to put you at ease. If you're foolish enough to be nervous in the presence of my enormous celebrity—then that's your lookout. There's simply no relief for such obtuseness.

FRANK: I might've known you'd be, well, real down-to-earth and all.

KAYO: Down to what?

FRANK: Down-to-earth.

KAYO: Look around, if you like.

(*While Kayo talks on the phone, Frank looks around, inspecting the place with great interest. We might even see him reading a piece of mail, or listening on an extension phone in the hall. But he does not make himself a drink*)

KAYO: I want to know about the Swiss banks, have you checked on them yet? Oh, Seymour, god*damn*it, Seymour! I asked you weeks ago, I'm leaving in five days! Seymour, I'm extremely unhap— Oh, I beg your pardon, I thought you said you had *not* done it. Tell, tell! How much interest do they give? Ech, you call that interest? Well, if I can't do better . . . And listen, I've

decided I want ten thou each in Palma, Gras, Tangier and Tor-
remolinos. Then you'll put half of what's left of me in Swiss
banks and the other half in debentures. I do not want any growth
stuff, understand? I am absolutely through with growth! I want
security, and I want yield! I've earned what I've got and I
intend to keep it. Oh, Seymour, I had the most brilliant notion, it
came to me at three a.m., I almost phoned you then. Listen, I
want you to tell Columbia that my European profits are to be
placed directly into the Swiss bank—without *bothering* the
United States Internal Revenue people. Have I made myself
clear? If I'm going to be living abroad, not using these highways
or breathing this polluted air, why in hell should I go on paying
these exorbitant . . . Don't talk to me about illegal! This is
1969 and Richard Milltown Nixon is President: laws aren't something you obey, they're only there to be outwitted. Honestly, you
frighten me. Whose side are you on? Oh, Christ, I just had a god-
awful thought! Seymour, are these Swiss bank accounts insured?
Yes, but by whom? Oh, that's just fine and dandy, but what
happens to me if Switzerland falls? Use that noodle, earn that
fee! And phone me the minute you've talked with Nuestra
Señora Del Culo Grande. . . . Our Lady Of The Big Butt, to
you. (*As Kayo hangs up, he catches Frank reading something on
top of his desk*) I did tell you to look around, didn't I!

FRANK: Gosh, I hope I didn't take any, well, you know,
liberties! Because wow, I'm just—golly! So nervous anyway.

KAYO: Young man, there are three words in the American
language which I abhor. They are gosh, wow, and golly. You
have already exceeded your quota of each of them.

FRANK: I just knew you'd have a sense of humor.

KAYO: That's where you cheapen yourself, I have none
whatever. Now, proceed with your questions, Mr . . . What is
your name?

FRANK: Frank Jones.

KAYO: I'll call you Frank. Proceed with your questions,
Frank.

FRANK: (*Consulting notes*) What do you think of young
people today?

KAYO: You're kidding.

FRANK: I guess that sounded real dumb, huh?

KAYO: Is that your next question?

FRANK: Yeah, I guess it did. Gee, Mr. Hathaway . . .

KAYO: Remember what I said about *gosh, wow,* and *golly?* It also applies to *gee.*

FRANK: Right, right! Well, see, I thought I'd ask your opinions about various things, because I was afraid it'd be kind of impertinent to ask really personal questions.

KAYO: I adore personal questions. Why don't you ask me why I'm leaving the country?

FRANK: Why are you leaving the country?

KAYO: To beat the income tax. Put that in your article. I'm sick sick sick of supporting that endless, outrageously expensive tedium in Southeast Asia. And I'm not a peacenik either. Are you?

FRANK: Me? Oh no. No, not at all.

KAYO: I hope not. I'm only against the war because it's expensive! Some bearded little ass with a hideous complexion came to me last week, said he'd heard I was against the war and could he ask a few questions. The first was a classic. He deplored, he said, the fact that while Jean-Paul Sartre had gone to jail over the Algerian question, no distinguished American author had yet made such a bold stand against our own country's atrocities in Vietnam. Could I tell him why? Me! Well, I wasn't fooled for a moment, I knew full well that in his damp, soiled little world, Kayo Hathaway is regarded as the Whore of Babylon. Rich, successful, writes comedies, takes baths. I was being baited and I knew it. I said, "Tell me, young man, why haven't you taken your Burning Questions to Tennessee Williams or Edward Albee, hmmm?"

FRANK: Hah! Oh, that was great, great! What'd he say?

KAYO: He said that because my films had such a vast audience, I was the somethingest something in the world. King of Camp, I think it was. I thought that was actually rather sweet. His point seemed to be that while Edward and Tennessee win the laurels, Kayo wins the public imagination. And of course he's right. The public adores bloodshed and camp, because the public is a bloody camp, and that's what I give them. I give them themselves. I give them Jo-Jo and his mother, good-hearted murderers.

FRANK: Wow-wee! Excuse me, but wow! That's fabulous. You really think the public is bloodthirsty?

KAYO: Oh, surely *that's* been established by now, hasn't it? The impotent are *always* obsessed with murder. And the public is impotent. Let me explain. The public is made up of a large number of individual persons who do not like or respect or trust one another. Therefore it has no hope of solidarity, and solidarity is its only power. Ergo, the public is impotent. It quite literally "can't get it up any more"! Hence, it amuses itself with blood-shed—making me a very rich man. However, I said none of this to my hippy interrogator, a very distasteful young man. No style, no *panache*. (*Frank is writing in his notebook. Kayo repeats the word for his benefit*) Pa-nache! A study in dreariness. He seemed bound and determined to make one feel that one's every public act was freighted with social consequence. I said, "Young man, if I took you seriously I should never write another word. The only responsibility I accept is to amuse and titillate and astonish, and for one purpose only: to keep that lovely green river flowing across the box offices of the world—into my pocket. If in the process I should happen to give the poor, doomed public a moment's comic relief from both the anti-Communists and the anti-anti-Communists"—one's as tiresome as the other, you know —"I feel I shall have earned one tiny gold star in heaven."

FRANK: Right, right!

KAYO: In a sense, of course, I'm deeply indebted to both. If it weren't for Peking, there'd be no bad guys, and if it weren't for the CIA, there'd be no good guys. In which event there'd be no Kayo Hathaway.

FRANK: Gosh, don't even say that!

KAYO: But to return to my hippie. You wouldn't have be-lieved the impertinence. I'm certain he was a Communist, by the way. Communism always attracts the fuck-ups, the sour, angry little creatures who can't make their own way. I've always said that if religion is the opiate of the people, then Communism is the malingerer's dream of paradise. (*Repeats, for Frank's benefit*) Mal-ing-er-er. Who knows, if I were lazy, or poor, or utterly talentless, I might be a Communist myself! Except, of course, that my intelligence, meager though it may be, is quite adequate for understanding a very simple natural law—namely, that nothing in the world is free. You get what you give.

FRANK: Oh? Oh, that's very interesting! Oh, golly, that's something I'd like to hear a lot more about. (*He writes*) "You get what you give."

KAYO: Why are you writing that down?

FRANK: Well, frankly, it's just exactly the kind of thing I'd hate to forget. Tell me, sir, do you really believe it's true?

KAYO: Of course I do. But I can't believe you're really so impressed.

FRANK: Oh, but I am. You see, a person in your position obviously has some key, some philosophy that makes him so . . . successful. And of course that's what readers like to know about. Me, too. I like to know, too.

KAYO: You said your name was Frank, didn't you?

FRANK: Yes, sir. Frank Jones.

KAYO: Um. Frank.

FRANK: Yes, sir.

KAYO: Frank, tell me. Why are you acting such a fool?

FRANK: Whee! Did you ever hit the nail right on the old head that time! I am a fool.

KAYO: My, my, my my my my my my my my *MY!* You're agreeable.

FRANK: Agreeable. Listen, do you want to hear the honest-to-god truth? I'm not agreeable, not at all. Not usually. But with you I feel like, gee, this is me talking. It's like listening to my own thoughts. Everything you say is just, wow, right on the old button.

KAYO: Mm-hm. I see. (*Kayo looks. Frank perspires*) You're with a magazine called what?

FRANK: *Image.*

KAYO: Oh, yes. *Image.* Why does *Image* want an interview with me, Frank? I'm not even pretty.

FRANK: But gosh, you're so famous, and you must know all the stars.

KAYO: Frank. Frank, you haven't said one interesting word since you walked in that door, and yet you have me absolutely fascinated.

FRANK: Oh, but I'm so boring. We shouldn't be talking about me.

KAYO: What do you want from me? Apart from this silly interview?

FRANK: Want?

KAYO: Yes. Want.

FRANK: Well, you're right, of course. I could be interviewing just any famous show business person. But I've got this kind of fix on you. I had to see you, I had to hear you talk. I guess, mainly, I just wanted to be sure you were, well, *real!*

KAYO: No, dear boy, that won't do. You're not just a fan. You're restless. Restless people always want something. And in your case, it's something specific.

FRANK: Specific?

KAYO: Very. You want me to read a manuscript you've written. Is that it?

FRANK: Me, oh gosh, I can't write.

KAYO: Oh? But I thought you wrote for a living?

FRANK: Just hack stuff. But I'm no good or anything.

KAYO: Your eyes are quick. I suspect you're intelligent. And yet somehow it suits your, whatever it is, to play the fool.

FRANK: You give me way too much credit, Mr. Hathaway. Not that I think I'm real dumb. But intelligent? Nobody's ever accused me of that before! (*He laughs*) Do you know something? I'm beginning to get an inkling. Just a kind of an inkling of what it is you noticed about me.

KAYO: Do go on.

FRANK: But I'm afraid you'll, well, laugh at me like.

KAYO: I assure you I will not.

FRANK: It's about . . . souls.

KAYO: Souls?

FRANK: Is that word too dumb?

KAYO: Not at all, it's intriguing.

FRANK: Well, I don't have all kinds of words like you do, so it's awfully hard for me to tell you what I mean.

KAYO: But you must try.

FRANK: I think we're . . . kindred souls. Is that a fairly pushy thing to say? I suppose it is.

KAYO: I'll let you know when I hear more. In what way are we kindred?

FRANK: When I read your books, or see your movies or plays, I feel like I know exactly how you feel . . . about life and all.

KAYO: About life! Dear boy, I write nothing but gory, campy melodramas. Now please, I abhor flattery. Compliments are lovely, but they mustn't be empty.

FRANK: But I honestly do feel that my fate is connected with yours, in some real close way.

KAYO: How?

FRANK: How?

KAYO: Yes. How?

FRANK: Listen, I want to ask you a fantastic favor. Would you let me answer that question just a tiny bit later on?

KAYO: You feel that . . . your fate and mine are very closely related. Is that what you want to talk about a tiny bit later on?

FRANK: Yes, sir, because I've got to, you know, feel my way into it, into this talking about it. So far, it's only been a feeling. And if you'd just talk to me some more, about other things, I think it'd help a really awfully lot.

KAYO: You think it'd help a "really awfully lot," do you? And what would you like to talk about now?

FRANK: Well, I was just fantastically interested a while ago when you were talking about the public being bloodthirsty. Anything to do with murder is just fascinating to me.

KAYO: Would you like to give me three fingers of Scotch and the teensiest splash of soda? No ice.

FRANK: Sure. (*At the bar*) I can't believe it. I'm making a drink for Kayo Hathaway.

KAYO: You neither drink nor smoke, do you, Frank?

FRANK: I take a drink once in a while. But not today.

KAYO: Today's very special, isn't it?

FRANK: Gee, is it ever!

KAYO: I could have done without the *gee*.

FRANK: Right! Right! I hate people t' say gee. What makes me do that? (*Frank hands Kayo the drink*)

KAYO: Your hand is shaking.

FRANK: That's because I'm so mad at myself, saying all these dumb things, gee this and golly that.

KAYO: O-o-o-o-o-oh, Gawd!

FRANK: What is it?

KAYO: I just had a dreadful thought, I have virtually frightened myself half to death with it, in fact.

FRANK: What, what?

KAYO: I've allowed you to remain here because I imagined there might be something faintly interesting about you. But what, oh God, what shall I do if it develops that you're just as hopelessly dreary as you appear to be. The thought alone is enough to make me *gasp!*

FRANK: I'm sorry, I'm really sorry, honest.

KAYO: The thing I find most tedious of all is this constant apology. Couldn't we dispense with it?

FRANK: Right, sure, absolutely. It's just that I know what rotten company I am, and I'm just sorry that . . . whoops, there I go apologizing again. I'm sorry. Oh, gee, *again!*

KAYO: Perhaps if we change the subject. Back to your interview, hm?

FRANK: Fine, fine. Now, about this terrific statement of personal philosophy—I have it right here—"You get what you give." Beautiful. I was just wondering if you ever worry about that, though. I mean, about getting what you give?

KAYO: Worry?

FRANK: Yes, sir. I mean, doesn't the idea ever bother you?

KAYO: What the hell are you talking about, does the idea ever *bother* me; it's made me rich and famous, you fool!

FRANK: Oh.

KAYO: Oh, what? You really are peculiar. I'd give a whole bagful of nickles to know what goes on in that head of yours.

FRANK: (*Straining after a thought*) "You get what you give." See, I was thinking that if what you give to the world are these wonderfully campy murders, then maybe you'd be afraid that what the world would give back would be—well, the same thing!

KAYO: What in God's name does that mean?

FRANK: It's just—I wondered if you've ever been afraid of being—killed—in some wonderfully campy way?

KAYO: My! My, my! Whoopee! Goodness sake! And hib-bety-bibbety-bobbety-ZIP! You have come through with an original thought! I'll bet you have all sorts of ideas tucked away in there, don't you?

FRANK: Oh, gosh, sir, I don't have any ideas. I've just got all this crap, I mean, excuse me, junk in my head and I'm, well, I'm just a young, nutty guy trying to get his thoughts kind of sorted out. You know. So I say all this dumb stuff.

KAYO: Dear boy, I give the public entertainment. The public is king—a fat, disgusting king without power and without balls, as I've pointed out. But it does have money. And I am one of its grotesquely overpaid court jesters. Is it really and truly necessary to point out to you that I do not kill people? I am in show business.

FRANK: Oh, boy, have I ever made a fool of myself. I been trying to make you think I'm this great thinker or something. I suppose it's because I admire you so tremendously, and it's hard for me to be my, well, my*self,* around somebody of your fantastic stature. Does that make any sense to you?

KAYO: (*Bored*) I told you at the outset there'd be very little I could do to reduce that barrier.

FRANK: Well, I suppose the least I can do now is, you know, like *leave.* (*Kayo waves bye-bye*) After having fallen completely on my face. Wow-*wee,* I really do disgust myself. (*Starts to leave*) I just want you to know I wouldn't be nearly so dumb around, say, Tennessee Williams or Andy Warhol!

KAYO: (*Appalled*) Andy Warhol!

FRANK: Or anybody else. But you, you're the really, well, you know, like the Great Man. And—okay, okay. Excuse me. I'm going now. (*At the door*) Oh! Oh gosh! Oh wow! I forgot! I can't go down there now. He'll never forgive me.

KAYO: Who will never forgive you for what?

FRANK: It's this friend. He's in the lobby. He's waiting down there, and I just don't know how to face him after lousing everything up.

KAYO: Oh, come now, I'm sure you haven't acquitted yourself quite so shabbily as all that. And if you have, the marks of it are not tattooed on your face. You could lie, couldn't you? Pretend you were brilliant?

FRANK: You don't understand! I promised him!

KAYO: Promised him what?

FRANK: Well, it's . . . No, no, I can't ask you a favor now. This is my own problem, I'll just have to . . . get through it myself. Goodbye, sir.

KAYO: (*Curious*) Oh, come now, what is this all about? What favor did you want to ask of me? If it's so unthinkable, I can assure you I'm quite capable of refusing.

FRANK: Well, it's this: this friend is just a great guy, you know? His name is Dennis. He's a terrific kind of goofy, wonderful little guy. And he's just as hung up on you as I am. He hoped you'd say "Hi" to him.

KAYO: Hi?

FRANK: I guess you think that's pretty repulsive kid stuff, right?

KAYO: (*Grandly weary*) Where is he?

FRANK: You mean you're going to let him come up?

KAYO: Of course. Dear heaven, I thought you were going to ask for an arm, or an eyetooth.

FRANK: Oh, nothing like that. (*Kayo picks up the house phone, clicks the hook*) Wow! Dennis is going to get such a thrill. You can't imagine what this'll mean to him.

KAYO: I have a fair idea.

FRANK: Oh no, you don't.

KAYO: (*Into phone*) Harris? Harris, there's a young man down there. Let him come up.

FRANK: Oh, Mr. Hathaway, you're making two crazy, unimportant little guys awful happy this afternoon. Honest.

KAYO: Perhaps you'd like to know why I'm bothering.

FRANK: If you'd care to tell me, I'd love to hear.

KAYO: Sheer curiosity. I'm wondering if your friend can be half as disgusting as you are.

FRANK: (*Laughing appreciatively*) Oh, that's great!

KAYO: I *thought* you'd like that!

FRANK: Wow, I'll say! You just come out with whatever you're thinking. It's fabulous!

KAYO: Why don't you get down on your knees to me? That's what you really want to do, isn't it? (*Frank drops to his knees*) Ho-ho, I see! I'm a full-fledged god now, aren't I? I order you *not* to kiss my feet, I have a weak stomach. Get up.

(*A buzzer is heard*)

FRANK: May I get the door?

KAYO: Please do.

(*Frank opens the door*)

FRANK: Come on in, Dennis, and meet the greatest guy in the world, Kayo Hathaway. Mr. Hathaway, this is Dennis.

(*Dennis is small, skinny, adenoidal, probably a user of dexedrine or amphetamine. He moves like the sort of creature who lives in dark underground places. He is carrying a shopping bag*)

DENNIS: Oh, Mr. Hathaway, I'm dumbfounded, I'm absolutely nonplused and stupefied. I've got this whole speech prepared and I'm just too flabbergasted to . . . What can I say except "Gosh!"

KAYO: You might've tried *gee whiz*.

DENNIS: Frank, did you ask him?

FRANK: You mean if we could . . . ? Oh, golly, I didn't have the nerve.

DENNIS: Well, I'm going to blurt it right out. Mr. Hathaway, we want to show you our act. Not because we think it's any good or anything, but it'd be our little present to you, who've given the world so much. See, I do this imitation of Mama, and he does Bad Bad Jo-Jo, and our friends think we're very funny. So could we?

KAYO: Oh, *please* do.

(*Dennis puts on a lady's hat, a furpiece, tiny eyeglasses, and snaps a chain onto Frank's belt buckle. Frank, leashed now, with an undersized Uncle Sam hat on his head, takes an ape-like stance, and the two of them strike a pose under the* Bad Bad Jo-Jo *lobby poster, managing to look amazingly like it. Kayo, easily seduced by this enactment of his own creation, watches with pleasure. Dennis speaks now in a little-old-lady voice*)

MAMA: G'd afternoon, Mr. Hathaway. Has my Jo-Jo been botherin' you somethin' awful? He can be a real nuisance and don't I know it. But he's goodhearted, they's nothin' Jo-Jo wouldn't do for a friend. Or his mama. Or his country, or God. Them four: Mama, God, country and friend. Why, Jo-Jo knew the Pledge of Allegiance when he was three. He wandered away from his mama in a department store one day, and they took him to the lost-kiddies' department. The lady asked him, "What's your name, little boy, and where do you live?" And Jo-Jo said, "I pledge allegiance to the flag of the United States of America." Isn't that sweet? Didn't know who he was, but he knew the stars and stripes of his Uncle Sam. (*Vaudeville tears*) Oh, I was s'proud. Say the rest of it for Mr. Hathaway, Jo-Jo. "And to the republic for which it stands." Go ahead.

JO-JO: "One nation under God, with liberty and justice for all."

MAMA: Liberty and justice for all, except?

JO-JO: Except Commies and hippies and faggots and niggers and peace creeps.

MAMA: And? Sympathizers! You always forget the sympathizers, and they're the worst of all! Oh, how nice, thank you, Mr. Hathaway, a cup of tea'd be ever-so-nice. Or whiskey, if it's easier. Yes, I think a cup of whiskey'd be lovely.

KAYO: Now look, you boys have amused me enormously, you truly have, but now I think . . . (*He touches his watch*)

MAMA: Oh, don't you go frettin' yourself about time, honey, I got all the time in the world. Jo-Jo, bring y'mommy a nice warm cup o' Scotch, she feels a chill.

(*Jo-Jo goes to the bar, pours*)

KAYO: (*Tapping his watch*) Look, I'm terribly serious about this.

MAMA: What's that, son? Is it your watch that's botherin' you? What's wrong with it, does it itch?

KAYO: Now I'm afraid you're forcing me to be heavy-handed.

MAMA: Let me see that watch, honey. (*Jo-Jo hands Mama a glass of whiskey*) Oh, thank you, darlin'. (*She swallows it in a gulp. Then, to Kayo*) Hand it to Mama. (*Pause. Kayo is frightened now*) Jo-Jo. Fetch me that watch Mr. Hathaway's got on his wrist. (*Jo-Jo easily removes the watch from Kayo, who is more and more docile with fear*) Mr. Hathaway doesn't know what a temper it puts Mama into, having one of her boys go disobedient on her like that. I think he ought to have a smart little slap.

(*Jo-Jo slaps Kayo*)

KAYO: How dare you! You don't work for a magazine at all. You're nothing but a . . .

MAMA: Nothin' but a what, honey? Oh, goodness, now I know what's troublin' Mr. Hathaway. He thinks you're a robber, Jo-Jo. He thinks we've come to steal his watch.

KAYO: I wish you boys would take what you want and leave!

MAMA: Y'see? I was right. Here, Jo-Jo, take this watch and throw it out the window. Then he'll know we're here in good faith!

(*Jo-Jo obeys*)

KAYO: All right then. What *do* you want?

MAMA: Do you know what I think, Jo-Jo? I think Mr. Hathaway's a Commie. I felt somethin' funny the minute I come in here. What do you suppose he created characters like us for in the first place? Why, he's trying to make fools out of the plain, honest folk that tries to rid this old world of the Reds. I won't stand for it! Okay, mister, I'm giving you a fair and square deal. Are you a Commie? (*The phone rings*) Ha! The telephone! See? He's trying to change the subject! Pull that cord out, Jo-Jo.

(*Now there is a marked increase in tempo. As Jo-Jo pulls the telephone cord, Mama withdraws two tiny folded squares of plastic from her shopping bag, handing one to Jo-Jo. They unwrap the articles, and we see that they are raincoats*)

MAMA: Here, son, put this on. These are wonderful little things, Mr. Hathaway. Jo-Jo thought of them. "Mama," he said, "if we put these on at Mr. Hathaway's house, we won't get any on us." Wasn't that clever?

KAYO: Won't get any—what—on you?

JO-JO: Blood. (*Jo-Jo and Mama laugh fiendishly*)

KAYO: Listen to me, I'm a very rich and powerful man. You'll never get away with—whatever it is you plan to do. But if you stop, I can get you anything you want. Anything. I also have a—an appreciation of this sort of—wit. It's maniacal, of course, but it's also very clever, and stimulating, and—and if the joke stops at once, I'll see to it you're both well rewarded—for the—for amusing me—so profoundly!

MAMA: Oh, son, we couldn't stop now . . . (*Jo-Jo has backed Kayo onto a pouf, downstage. Mama hands Jo-Jo a large knife*) . . . we just couldn't. Why, if Jo-Jo and me was to quit, right in the middle of a commitment, we'd never be able to show our faces again.

(*The music of the nightmare is heard again now, and the lights are dimmed to black, as the two young men close in on Kayo Hathaway. The various stages of his murder, a deliberate, ritualistic event, are seen under the flashing lights of a stroboscope, while throughout the theater and on the walls of the set, a rapid succession of photographic blow-ups is projected: a policeman clubs a peace marcher; a GI stabs a Vietcong; an 007-type shoots someone in the face; soldiers burn an Oriental village; someone is mugged; blacks smash a store window; a close-up of Sirhan Sirhan;*

President Nixon waves and smiles; Tommy Smothers looks bewildered; Allen Ginsberg prays.

Dennis leans the body of Kayo against the Bad Bad Jo-Jo *poster, while Frank places in front of it an ornamental gold-leaf picture frame. The two young men bow to one another*)

Curtain

Ronald Ribman

THE BURIAL OF ESPOSITO

Ronald Ribman

"A writer with a personal vision, a depth of concern, an awareness of the stage and the craft to implement them," wrote critic Martin Gottfried, "such is the identity of art and Ronald Ribman is a part of our theatre's great tomorrow." The year was 1965, when the American Place Theatre staged the author's *Harry, Noon and Night*. (In its cast were two young performers who since have gone on to stardom: Dustin Hoffman and Joel Grey.)

In the span of six seasons at its permanent home in St. Clements Church in midtown Manhattan, the American Place Theatre has become a significant force in the development and encouragement of new plays and playwrights. Its record is enviable. Since its inaugural season, it has introduced an exceptional number of works of dramatic stature and provocative content, including Robert Lowell's *The Old Glory*, William Alfred's *Hogan's Goat*, Ed Bullins' *The Electronic Nigger and Others*, and three plays by Mr. Ribman.

A year after the premiere of *Harry, Noon and Night*, the organization presented the author's *The Journey of the Fifth Horse* (based, in part, on Ivan Turgenev's story, *Diary of a Superfluous Man*) and it won the 1965–66 "Obie" Award for the best Off-Broadway play of the season. In 1967, he was represented once again on the stage of the American Place Theatre, this time with an impressive historical drama, *The Ceremony of Innocence*.

Born in New York City in 1932, Ronald Ribman attended Brooklyn College, then went to the University of Pittsburgh, where he graduated in 1954. After serving two years in the army, he returned to Pittsburgh to pursue his Ph.D. in English literature. As with many of his contemporaries, his writing career had its genesis in poetry and, in time, his poems began to appear in such periodicals as the *Beloit Poetry Journal*, the *Colorado Quarterly* and *Harper's* magazine.

When, eventually, he turned to writing plays, he was one of the fortunate few chosen to receive a Rockefeller Foundation grant enabling him to write without interruption. As he freely admits, grants have been sustaining him for years: "Without grants it's very difficult to survive. What it does is keep my nose on the stage rather than moving it over into movies or television. The point is, I consider myself primarily a stage writer. I prefer the stage. When someone does your play, they're really doing *your* work, whereas when you're doing movies, the director becomes the center of the action, and it's *his* vision."

In spite of his pronounced partiality to the stage, Mr. Ribman turned his creative hand both to television and films in 1970. With Bill Gunn, he wrote the screenplay for *The Angel Levine,* which co-starred Harry Belafonte and Zero Mostel, and a television adaptation of his drama, *The Ceremony of Innocence,* with a cast headed by Richard Kiley, James Broderick, Larry Gates and Jessie Royce Landis. The presentation brought Mr. Ribman additional honors and firmly established him with a nationwide audience as a major new American playwright.

The Burial of Esposito, here published for the first time, opened at the Off-Broadway Sheridan Square Playhouse in December, 1969, as part of Mr. Ribman's triple bill, *Passing Through from Exotic Places.* (The other two plays: *The Son Who Hunted Tigers in Jakarta* and *Sunstroke.*) While its engagement was unduly brief, he once more was heralded as "a young playwright with a strong hold on theatricality" who is uncommonly "adept at devising strong central dramatic images." *Variety* singled out *The Burial of Esposito* as "a tightly-written tragedy about a lower middle-class Brooklyn barber whose pride indirectly leads to his son's death. It is a model of short play construction and economical characterization. The author enables the audience to understand a man's life in a matter of minutes. . . . Ribman's writing is taut and exciting."

Among the author's other dramatic works are *The Final War of Ollie Winter* (presented on television's CBS Playhouse) and *The Inheritors,* produced Off-Broadway in the fall of 1969.

Ronald Ribman lives on Manhattan's Upper West Side with his wife and young son. In 1970, he was awarded a Guggenheim Fellowship that will make possible a year's continuous work on a major project. For the theatre, of course.

Characters:

NICK ESPOSITO
HIS WIFE
HIS BROTHER-IN-LAW
HIS SON

Scene:

A room in a mortuary. The stage is dark. A voice is heard.

PRIEST'S VOICE: There is a final question we must ask. Who was Anthony Esposito? Beloved son to Nicholas and Angela Esposito. Yes. Older brother to Rudy Esposito. Yes. Cousin, nephew, grandchild, friend. Yes.

(The stage gradually lights up revealing Nick Esposito standing with a tape recorder near a flag draped coffin. He approaches the coffin, places the tape recorder down on top of it. He sits on a stool and listens to the recorder)

PRIEST'S VOICE: A boy born and raised in New York City, a devoted member of St. Ann's Church, a choirboy, a child of immigrants. Yes. These things Anthony Esposito was and more. And I say more because Anthony Esposito was also a soldier. And in service to his country, in a foreign war ten thousand miles from home, he died. Anthony Esposito was twenty years old when he died. Not very old you say, no, not very old. But soldiers are never very old when they are sent out to die. Had he lived, his parents tell me they had plans to send him to college, that Tony wanted to go to college and study medicine so that he could become a doctor. Tony Esposito was no stranger to me. He was baptized at St. Ann's; he went to church school at St. Ann's. I remember him still as a young boy in class, his hand always waving to be recognized because he always knew the answer and wanted to tell the world that he did. I am grieved as you are grieved that all we have left of this young man is our grief. As to the righteousness of the cause for which he died,

I have no easy words of comfort. I am aware that even as I speak, in front of me there lies the body of a young man I once baptized among us. I am reminded of the English poet who said of those who died in another war, that if the cause for which they died was not good, then those that sent them to it will have a heavy reckoning to make, that if these men do not die well, it will be a black matter for those that led them to it. Let us pray.

(*As the priest begins to pray, Nick shuts off the tape recorder and places it on the floor*)

NICK: You want to hear something? Your Uncle Carlo is outside. Eh? What do you think about that? He's sitting in the first row next to your mama and Rudy. He don't speak to me for ten years, and now he's in the first row next to your mama and Rudy. Rudy don't even know him. He says to me, "Who's that?" I tell him, "That's the bastard, your Uncle Carlo." (*Wandering around the room*) It's very hot today. The radio says they expect ninety degrees. It's nice and cool in here, though. There's a vent on the ceiling and they got cold air coming in. That's nice. They should have cold air coming in the other room where everybody is. It's very hot in there. Everybody's sweating a lot. You should see how everybody is mopping the face with handkerchiefs. You remember your friend, the Jewish boy? He's here with his wife. Nice boy. I always liked him. I'm surprised, though, they don't take him into the army. I don't know why they take you into the army and they don't take him. Father Balussi says some very nice things about you. Nice man. Very educated. I have to pay . . . (*Pulling out a slip of paper*) . . . $871. Who would think they charge so much money? I only have seven hundred dollars left in the bank. Maybe I have to close the shop and move to a different place. Business is not so good. You remember Mr. Singer, used to come in twice a month for a haircut? He move away. Mr. Parucchio, he move away. Everything changing. I don't know what I do now. Maybe I move, too. What do I have to stay around for? I don't like to live where they got so much colored. I don't want to cut their hair. Black, kinky, they ruin business for me! They think they can move in and ruin business for me! I cut their hair, nobody else want to come in . . . I don't know what to do with your clothes.

Your mama don't want the clothes in the house no more. I want to give them to Rudy, but he don't want them. (*Angrily, as if talking to Rudy*) Why don't you take the clothes? Eh? Put on the clothes! If they fit you, you take them. What's the idea wasting clothes? Eh? What's the sense in wasting clothes? (*To the coffin*) Nobody's rich like your Uncle Carlo. Big shot! Such a big shot. If he wasn't your mama's brother, I don't even speak to him now. I spit in his face. I don't know what to do with your fish. I want to put an ad in the paper, but your mama don't let me sell anything. "Throw it out. Give it away." Everything throw out, give away. How much money you spend on the fish tank? Twenty-five dollars? I should throw out? I should give away? Money come down from the sky? Money *don't* come down from the sky! I don't know what to do with anything. Nobody wants anything. The fish are going to die. I don't know how to feed them. (*Pausing for a moment*) Ruby is going away to college. You should see how much money they're gonna give him for a scholarship. He's a smart boy, like you. I ask him to take the fish. Maybe he keep the fish in the room with him where he go, but he don't want to take the fish. Stubborn, like you, always so stubborn . . . Why you always so stubborn with me? You think it's nice a son should talk to his father that way? You stay home from the war. It's better that you stay home. They want to fight? They crazy people. You let them fight. You stay home. You don't be so stubborn with me. They gonna kill you. I tell you they going to . . . they . . . you work in the shop. That's what I want you should do. You want to go to school later, you go to school later. First you work in the shop. You don't like to be a barber, I give you money to go to school later. Sure, I give you the money! What do you think? You think I don't give you the money? You're my first-born son. I give you what you want. You tell me what you want, I give it to you. I give you everything. Everything you want, I give.

(*His wife, Angela, enters*)

ANGELA: You come in the next room.

NICK: What for?

ANGELA: Carlo wants to talk to you.

NICK: I don't want to talk to him. (*Angela stands there*

just looking at him) Eh? Why do you stand there? Leave me alone.

ANGELA: I want you should talk to him.

NICK: What for? Eh? He don't talk to me for ten years. Now I don't talk to him.

ANGELA: He wants to pay for everything.

NICK: What are you talking about?

ANGELA: He wants to pay!

NICK: I don't want him to pay. I pay! You tell him *I* pay! Let him keep his lousy money to himself! (*Leading Angela out of the room*) I don't need his money. I pay! I pay!

(*Nick returns to the coffin*)

NICK: Big shot. I don't need him! I got enough money. I always got enough money. (*He sticks his hand in his pocket and jingles some change*) You don't want to work in the barbershop with me, okay, I give you the money for school. How much you need? You don't have to stay in the army. I don't make you do nothing you don't want. What do you think I save all the money for? For me? I don't work for that. I work for you. You and Rudy. I give everything to you and Rudy. You work a year in the barbershop and then we see. Next year you don't like, we going to see. You a little boy, you say all the time you want to work with me. All the time you run in and out. Eh? You remember that? You bring me the towels. I tell you to bring me the nice hot towels and you bring. (*Making cutting motions into the air with an imaginary scissors*) I'm going to teach you to cut the hair. Sure. No fooling. You're going to like that. We go into business together. (*To his imaginary customer*) My son, sure, who you think that is? (*Looking down as if addressing a small child*) Hey, Tony, you tell the man who you are. We're going into business together. Father and son. . . . You come around some day, he's going to give you a first class haircut. No different than me. First class. (*Carlo enters and, unnoticed, stands listening to Nick*) I tell you something. You listen to me. It's nice here. You stay. I don't want you should go to school and Rudy should go to school. It's not nice you both go away. Your mama don't like it if no son stays at home. One son should stay at home. . .

CARLO: Who you talking to, Nick?

NICK: What do you want?

CARLO: Who you talking to, Nick?

NICK: Nobody. I'm talking to myself. I want to talk to myself, I talk to myself.

CARLO: Sure, Nick. Nobody says you can't talk to yourself if you want to.

NICK: What do you come here for, Carlo? I don't see you for ten years, and now you come. What for?

CARLO: To pay my respects to Tony. You know I've always liked Tony.

NICK: Okay. You do that. Now you can go.

CARLO: How's things been working out for you, Nick?

NICK: Okay.

CARLO: You know, Nick, you don't look so good to me. Your face is pale. You oughta get out in the sun more often. Maybe take a vacation.

NICK: I don't need a vacation. You want to go on a vacation, you go.

CARLO: You know what kind of vacation you need, Nick? One of these vacations to the Caribbean. Lots of sun down there. You'd be surprised how much sun they got down there. You get on one of these big tour ships and they take you on what they call "island-hopping." You stay a couple of days in Jamaica, then you move to Barbados and you stay a couple of days there, then you move to Trinidad or St. John, the Bahamas. Always moving from one island to the next. Real nice. And not too expensive either. Didn't come to more . . . and this was for the wife and the two kids . . . not more than three thousand. Of course, Sophia bought some china and glassware in Barbados and that pushed up the expense, but outside of that we didn't spend much over three thousand. We were on what they call the "sun, fun, and rum" plan. You gotta get on one of these plans or else your expenses start skyrocketing.

NICK: I don't go on a vacation.

CARLO: Why not, Nick? How come in all the years you've been married to my sister, you've never gone on a vacation?

NICK: I save my money.

CARLO: Is that what you do with it, Nick? Is that why Angela never goes on a vacation? Why you never take her anywhere?

NICK: You want to go on vacation, you go. You don't tell me what to do with my money.

CARLO: You must have a lot of money saved up by now, Nick. You never take my sister on a vacation, you never buy her a dress, you walk around in twenty-five year old suits, you wouldn't give Tony a penny so he could go to school. You must have a lot of money saved up. You must be a very rich man.

NICK: I do what I want with my money.

CARLO: And what's that, Nick? What do you do with your money?

NICK: I mind my own business.

CARLO: What business, Nick? What business is that? (*Nick looks at him, but doesn't answer*) You don't have a business, Nick. You're what we call scraping by. You're what we call a marginal man. You know what that means, Nick? It means you live in a stinking, paint-peeling, roach-crawling shithouse in Coney Island. It means in thirty years you never take my sister anywhere, you never buy her anything, you never give your kids a chance to make anything out of themselves. If I were you, Nick, you know what I'd do? I'd commit suicide. I'd take out an insurance policy and commit suicide.

NICK: Disgraziato!

CARLO: Maybe I'm going to help you, Nick, Maybe because you don't have what it takes to be a man, I'm going to help you.

NICK: I don't want nothing from you!

CARLO: This funeral is going to cost a lot of money. You got enough money to pay for it?

NICK: I pay.

CARLO: What you pay? What? This funeral is going to cost one thousand dollars. You got a thousand dollars?

NICK: They don't charge me that much.

CARLO: What did they give you? A bill for eight hundred? Did you add in the cost of renting this hall for services? Did you add in the flowers, the use of the funeral cars? You going to give the priest something for the church? You going to screw the church out of its money?

NICK: I pay everything.

CARLO: I'm glad you told me that, Nick. It relieves me to know that you got the money to pay for everything, because I was just talking to Angela and she says you got less than seven hundred dollars in the bank. But now I'm relieved to know she's wrong and you got the money. It relieves me to know the ground they're gonna shovel over my nephew is paid for.

NICK: What do you want? You don't talk to me for ten years and now you come around and want to pay.

CARLO: That's right, Nick.

NICK: Why? Why do you want to pay?

CARLO: Tony was a good boy. I always liked him. You need help, okay, Angela is my sister. Her husband don't have enough money, why shouldn't I help out? I give you two thousand dollars. (*Using the coffin as a desk, Carlo starts to write out a check*)

NICK: Why do you give me the money?

CARLO: Because I got the money! You understand what I'm saying? I give you the money because I got the money! I got the money!

NICK: Big shot!

CARLO: That's right, Nick. Big shot. In this family, I'm the big shot. You remember that. You got seven hundred dollars in the bank; I got a hundred and fifty thousand. You live in a shithouse in Coney Island; I got a house worth eighty-five thousand in Westchester. I'm the big shot. I don't like to see my sister living the way you make her live; I don't like my nephew buried when nothing's paid for. So, I'm going to help you out, Nick. When you need a few bucks you're gonna come to me. Angela wants to buy a pair of shoes in the department store, you're going to let me know, and I'm going to give you a few bucks to pay for it. You wanna buy a suit, well, you tell me about it. You come to me and I'm going to give you a couple bucks. I'm going to help you out. From now on, you're gonna come to me!

NICK: I starve like a dog on the street before I take a *penny* from you!

(*Angela enters*)

CARLO: No, Nick, you're not going to starve, you're going to take money. (*He places Nick's hand down on the check*) I'm going to give you money and you're going to take. You're going to take money like Rudy takes money from me to go to school.

NICK: (*Pulling his hand away*) The *school* give Rudy money! He don't take nothing from you.

CARLO: I give Rudy money. You think the three hundred dollars they give him for a scholarship pays for everything? It don't pay for nothing. I give him the rest of the money. The money they give him don't pay for nothing.

NICK: He don't take no money from you. I make him give it back!

CARLO: .You're living in another world, Nick. You're stupid. You hear me, Nick? You're stupid. You always were stupid. If it wasn't for Angela, I'd let you cut your throat.

NICK: He don't keep your money.

CARLO: You go and tell him that. Go ahead! You go out and tell him he's not going to school. Maybe you send him into the army like Tony. Okay? You send him into the army.

(*Nick goes to the door. Angela blocks him*)

NICK: Get out of my way!

ANGELA: You don't take Rudy's money away from him!

NICK: *I* give him money. He don't take money from *him*. My son don't take money from him.

ANGELA: What money you give, eh? *What* money?

NICK: He don't take money from him!

ANGELA: What money you give Rudy?

CARLO: What money, Nick? Tell Angela what money you got to give.

NICK: Rudy go to school *next* year. He wait a year; I give him the money for school next year.

ANGELA: No. He take the money, now. He go to school, now!

CARLO: Next year maybe they don't give him the scholarship.

NICK: I don't care about the scholarship. I give him the money next year.

CARLO: Sure, Nick, sure. Like you give Tony the money.

NICK: You shut your mouth!

CARLO: Okay, I'm gonna shut my mouth. I'm gonna tell Rudy he don't go to school. I'm gonna tell him to stay home, work in the barbershop.

ANGELA: (*Grabs Carlo's arm as he starts out*) No. Everything is all right. He's not going to say anything. He's going to take the money

CARLO: He doesn't want the money.

ANGELA: (*To Nick*) Tell him you take the money. (*Nick just stares at her*) Tell him you take the money!

CARLO: I'll find something else to do with it.

ANGELA: Tell him you take the money. Tell him! (*Nick turns away*)

CARLO: I'll take care of the funeral. You don't worry. (*He kisses Angela and exits*)

ANGELA: (*Running after him*) Give us the money for school, Carlo. Carlo! Carlo!

NICK: *I* send Rudy to school. He go to school next year. He's a young boy. It don't make a difference to a young boy if he waits next year. (*He stares down at the coffin*) What difference does it make? (*Looks away*) Someday we all take a trip together. We going to drive across the country. You sit up front with me. I take you to visit my brother Dominic in Chicago. He's got a nice house there. I don't see Dominic in a long time. (*The flag begins to slide off the coffin, and then comes to a stop*) Hey, Dominic, what you think? You looking good. This is my oldest boy. Sure. Tony. Hey, Tony, say hello to your Uncle Dominic. We're gonna drive all over the country. Maybe we drive to Denver just to see the mountains. Maybe we just keep going all the way to the Pacific Ocean. Maybe. . .

(*The top half of the coffin opens. Tony, dressed in his military uniform sits up and looks at his father*)

TONY: (*Deeply breathing, as if trying to catch his breath*) Hello, papa. (*Nick, without surprise, turns around to face his son*) How are you, papa?

NICK: Good, I'm good, Tony. How are you?

TONY: (*Very animated, very full of life*) I'm fine, papa.

NICK: They told me you were dead.

TONY: It was just a trick, papa. I didn't want to stay in the army anymore, so I put myself in a coffin and they sent me home.

NICK: You don't have to be in the army no more?

TONY: I'm finished with the army now, papa. They sent me home.

NICK: That's good. That's good. I'm sorry I didn't give you the money for school when you ask.

TONY: How's mama?

NICK: She wants me to take money from Uncle Carlo to send Rudy to school.

TONY: How's Rudy?

NICK: He's a nice boy. Just like you. Both my boys are good boys.

TONY: I love you very much, papa.

(*Nick tightly embraces his son*)

NICK: I love you, Tony. I love you. I'm sorry I didn't give you the money for school.

TONY: It's all right, papa. I saved a lot of money in the army. I can pay for everything now. Rudy and I will go to school together, and when we graduate, we'll both be doctors and we'll make a lot of money, and you and mama can move to Long Island and live in a big house with me and Rudy. You won't ever have to worry about money again.

NICK: I love you, Tony. I want to do everything for you. I give you anything.

TONY: Don't cry, papa. We're all going to be very happy from now on. We're all going to live together in a big house and be very happy. You'll see. I'll tell you what. Why don't you bring mama in here and we'll give her a big surprise. I'll just lie down now and you close the coffin, and when she comes in you open the coffin and she'll be so happy to see that I'm alive and that we're all going to be happy living on Long Island.

NICK: We going to give her a very big joke.

TONY: Sure, papa, a big joke. (*Tony lies down and Nick closes the coffin and replaces the flag*)

NICK: Big shot, with his money. I spit on your Uncle Carlo's money! Did you hear how he was talking to me? We don't need his money. We're going to have all the money we need. Let him keep his bastard money! I have two sons. *Two sons.* (*Going over to the door*) Angela! Carlo! Angela! (*Motioning with his hand for them to come into the room*) We're going to give them a good joke, eh, Tony? Be ready.

(*They enter*)

ANGELA: What do you want?

NICK: (*Looking at one, then the other*) Eh? Eh?

ANGELA: I want you should apologize to my brother! I want you to tell him you take the money.

CARLO: (*Extending his hand to Nick*) You want to tell me something, Nick? You want to tell me you made a mistake?

NICK: Disgraziato! Disgraziato! (*He pulls the flag off the coffin and wraps it about himself*)

ANGELA: What are you doing? What's the matter with you?

(*They rush forward trying to pull the flag away from him, but Nick fiercely pushes them away*)

NICK: No! You leave it alone.

ANGELA: Crazy! He's crazy.

NICK: Not crazy. (*Knocks on the coffin*) Eh, Tony?

CARLO: What do you think you're doing, Nick?

NICK: I'm going to show you, big shot. You big shot. (*Knocking again on the coffin*) Tony? Tony?

ANGELA: He's crazy! (*Nick has now begun trying to open the coffin*) You leave the coffin alone! Leave the coffin alone! Tony is dead. What are you doing?

NICK: (*Pulling at the coffin lid, harder and harder*) He's not dead! Not dead!

CARLO: The coffin is bolted shut, Nick. It's bolted. You can't open it!

NICK: Not shut! Not dead! Tony! Tony!

ANGELA: Leave him alone! Leave him alone!
(*Frantically pounding on the coffin with his fists, Nick begins to sink down until his head rests on the lid. His rage increases each time his fist slams down, each time he calls out*)
NICK: Tony! Tony! Tony!
(*Lights out*)

THE END

Kenneth Pressman

STEAL THE OLD MAN'S BUNDLE

Kenneth Pressman

Kenneth Pressman was born on November 7, 1940, in Cynthiana, Kentucky. Formerly an English instructor at the University of Hawaii, he now is a resident of Manhattan and a member of the faculty of the New York City Community College of Brooklyn.

As teacher and dramatist, Mr. Pressman successfully has managed to blend both careers. Three of his plays originally were presented by the Playwrights Unit, a non-profit experimental organization (founded in 1961 by Edward Albee, Richard Barr and Clinton Wilder) that affords new and promising dramatists an opportunity to see their scripts performed on a professional basis before invited audiences. (The organization's most celebrated alumnus, Mart Crowley, whose *The Boys in the Band* originated at their Greenwich Village showcase, then moved uptown to Theatre Four where it ran for 1,000 performances.)

In 1965, Mr. Pressman's *Hunting the Jingo Bird* was presented by the Playwrights Unit at the Cherry Lane Theatre, New York. His second work to be staged under their auspices was *For Breakfast, Mr. Sachs.* Revised and retitled *Steal the Old Man's Bundle,* the play subsequently opened in May, 1970, at the Off-Broadway Fortune Theatre. Though the run was brief, Mr. Pressman's personal notices were laudatory, citing him as a new playwright of exceptional power and promise. Following its Off-Broadway showing, Mr. Pressman made further and extensive script revisions, and *Steal the Old Man's Bundle,* in its final form, appears in print for the first time anywhere in *The Best Short Plays 1971.*

In 1970, the Playwrights Unit staged a third work by Mr. Pressman, *The Fault,* and earlier, his short play, *Mrs. Snow,* was presented as part of the ANTA Matinee Series at the Theatre De Lys.

Recently, the author completed the libretto for an opera (with music by Michael Valenti) based on his play, *The Fault,* and, at present, he is working on a screenplay, *The Price of Admission.*

Scene:

The kitchen of a ground floor apartment on Manhattan's Upper West Side.

The room is drab and notably untidy with a peculiar assortment of grocery items, some in paper bags, some unwrapped and lying open, arranged around the refrigerator. The furniture is standard Salvation Army—an oilcloth-covered table with three chairs, and little else. There are two doors: one, at rear center, leads out into the hall of the building; the door at the right, to the rest of the apartment. On the wall nearby, a telephone.

Early morning. A transistor radio on the table is blaring out rock 'n' roll music. Charles is pouring orange juice, an activity he invests with a certain amount of formality. He appears even younger than his eighteen years, wears wire-framed spectacles, has a head of hair just short of mod length, and is dressed in pipestem trousers and baggy sweater.

A knock is heard at the door. Instead of answering immediately, Charles concludes his little kitchen chore, wiping his hands fastidiously on a kitchen cloth. A second knock at the door, louder, and more urgent. He finally crosses to door and opens it. Mr. Sachs, a middle-aged man, gray-headed, bespectacled, and in shirt sleeves, stands in the doorway.

CHARLES: Yes?

SACHS: (*A trace of a European accent*) Is . . . is your mother at home?

CHARLES: My . . . mother?

SACHS: Your mother, yes. Is she at home?

CHARLES: Excuse me. (*He goes to radio that has been*

playing loudly throughout, turns it off, and comes back to door)
You want my mother? Is that what you said?

SACHS: Yes, to speak with her. If I may.

CHARLES: Come in, won't you?

(Sachs enters, stands in extreme discomfort while Charles closes the door, then walks about, apparently examining the visitor)

SACHS: Perhaps she's not in, I shall come back.

CHARLES: You wanted to speak with her?

SACHS: It would be no trouble to come back later. Only I thought if she was at home . . . I wouldn't disturb . . . or if she is out. . .

CHARLES: Maybe *I* could help?

SACHS: Better, I think, if your mother . . .

CHARLES: Hold on, I'll see. *(He starts off, as if for the living room, but stops, turns back to Sachs)* Have a seat.

(Sachs sits. Charles goes to the wall telephone, dials a number, all the while keeping a baleful eye on the older man)

CHARLES: *(Into phone)* 'Lo, Babs? Yes, love. How are we this morning, Sexy? Yes, I am one of those early birds this A.M. . . . *(Looks at wrist watch)* Oh, seven-thirty, dear, time all good little girls were up and at 'em, don't be a spoilsport. Lord, yes, been up for eons. My eyes flash open at six, with or without the clock. Like I'm keeping watch over the world. I know, love, it's my hang-up, not yours. But something came up. I've got this gentleman here . . . *(Sachs squirms in his seat)* I do apologize, really am destroyed, but this gentleman here—he insisted, so . . . I told you, love, you *are* out of it, told you he's sitting here right now. Well, I can't say. Knocked on the door, it's all shrouded in mystery, pummeled down the door practically and demanded—quite insistent, really—wanting to speak to *you*. . .

(Sachs sits up in his chair, startled)

SACHS: *(His hand raised in a gesture of protest)* No! I asked was your mother . . .

CHARLES: *(Covers mouthpiece with his hand)* Was my mother at home and couldn't you speak to her . . .

SACHS: But . . .

CHARLES: Well, she is and you can—here. (*He extends the receiver toward Sachs who instinctively draws away*)

CHARLES: Damn it, go ahead! Do you have any idea how many units it is to call White Plains?

SACHS: Your . . . mother? White . . . White Plains!

CHARLES: Babs. My mother, yes . . . (*Again urging phone on him*) Will you please take the phone . . . (*Then, speaking into the phone himself*) A second, darling, he's mike-shy . . . Your guess is as good as mine. Doesn't seem to believe you're my mother. Moms. (*Laughs*) Mommykins. Charleykins' mommykins. (*Back to Sachs*) Take it, will you, I'm getting slushy.

SACHS: (*Stunned, he reaches out for phone*) Some . . . mistake . . .

CHARLES: (*Snatching back phone*) Wait. What's your name? Name!

SACHS: Uh . . . Sachs. You see, I am from up on the second, I live . . .

CHARLES: (*Into phone*) A Mr. Sachs to speak with you, Lambchop. Mater . . . (*He thrusts phone into Sachs' hand*) She's all yours. (*He flops down in chair and folds his arms across his chest*)

SACHS: (*To his dismay, finding the phone at his ear*) Uh . . . Mrs. . . . Mrs. . . . Some mistake here, I am afraid. Yes. (*Spelling*) S-a-c-h-s. From upstairs. He came to the door and I thought . . . (*Realizing how foolish he must sound*) About my, my . . . garbage . . . Garbage is . . . gone . . . (*He winces, as though thunder were coming over the line. He holds out receiver to Charles*) She wants you . . . your mother.

CHARLES: (*Taking the phone while Sachs shambles miserably away*) As I said, angel, I'm mystified. . . . No, it's not one of my pranks. Central European isn't even in my repertoire . . . A *real* Mr. Sachs. Apparently from upstairs. . . . You'll have to take my word, would Charleykins fib? . . . Well, don't eat out your liver, I expect one day we'll find out. You go back to bed now, have the girl bring you up a tray. Tell her Mr. Charles said you were to be spoiled today, all day. . . . No, I haven't heard a syllable. I expect she will. Have no fears, I'll keep myself occupied. You, too. 'Bye, love. (*He hangs up and without looking at Sachs, goes to stove where he begins to crack eggs into frying pan*)

SACHS: (*Watches him. Now over his embarrassment, he is furious at being made a fool. He waits for Charles to recognize his existence, but when the boy goes on cooking, Sachs strides forward in indignation*) What! Games you play with me? You young smart-face, you play games? Put me on the . . . the telephone. I asked was your mother home, you know damn right what is going on! Turn your face here, I want to see you when I ask—I am not a young man, with your baby tricks—when I ask you now *turn here to me!* Why you do this!

CHARLES: (*His back to Sachs, very calmly*) Have a chair. I make terrific eggs. Even better than the hens. You'll have a bite.

SACHS: Still with your smart mouth you give me . . .

CHARLES: (*Facing him, fork in hand*) You asked was my mother at home. You persisted. So I called her. She *was* at home. In White Plains. You just talked to her yourself. What's the mystery? Any chair, I don't care which you take. Traditionally, the cook sits nearest the kitchen, for efficiency in serving, but since . . . (*Gestures about the room*) It doesn't make a heckuva lot of difference. One nearest the stove, though, would do best for me. You take that one. Whoop, burning my eggs here. (*He turns back to stove. Sachs stands in amazement*)

SACHS: You . . . you want me to eat? To eat here with you?

CHARLES: Didn't you hear me invite you? Maybe I didn't get around to it. Sorry. Sometimes I leave gaps between the intention and the deed. Sit ye down. (*Facing Sachs again*) At the back of my neck, I feel this tension, like you're imperceptibly on your axis, leaning into me. Please, I'll have your eggs in a jiff.

SACHS: What eggs? I don't want no eggs. What is this? I come in to ask your mother because outside I . . . I come down the stairs with my can and I look . . . The first time I came down, I had two cans. I go up for the other. I come down again, I look. I think, "You are, old man, you are crazy. Down you brought two cans, you go up for the other, you come back down and . . . gone. You are a crazy old man, it cannot be." I walk around, around the pile, once, twice . . . nowhere. Gone. My garbage. Then your door—slam! it goes. I think, "maybe." I knock. It's you. A kid. What does he know? I'll ask his mother; she saw maybe what happened to my . . . my things. Then all this business, with the telephone, with your eggs. I go up to my place now. You should be ashamed; I am not young like you. To make fun. I go up. (*He starts out*)

CHARLES: Wait! This garbage. Could you describe it? (*Sachs stops*) You needn't be vivid, but something to go on in the way of distinguishing characteristics.

SACHS: Garbage. I have to explain to you garbage!

CHARLES: Well, somewhat. You can't just say "garbage." Was it heavy garbage, smelly garbage, what?

SACHS: Garbage garbage.

CHARLES: (*Goes to sink, pulls back the curtain and brings out the two cans of garbage, setting them before Sachs*) Tell me then—did it bear any resemblance to *this* garbage?

SACHS: So! And this is what you do to an old man, a stranger after all in your country, without the language. I can't speak so well your language; you do this to me who never did nothing to you. I should call the police! Play with me, sonnyboy, you see how fast I make them wipe that smile off your smart face when they get here! Lock you up, you punk. Drag you out of here so fast you won't be smiling no more, you lousy no-good . . .

CHARLES: (*Unruffled*) Take it easy, don't scream at me. I can't stand being screamed at.

SACHS: (*Raging on*) You punk, I'll scream at you! Think you're so good, you hoodlum, yes, I'll scream at you, you lousy, rotten filth, you . . .

(*Without rage, Charles strikes the man sharply across the face. Sachs stands, stunned, his lips quivering*)

CHARLES: (*His tone light, not at all threatening*) Gee, I wish you'd take your seat here. You're spoiling the party. I go to all the trouble, you spoil the party. For being so nasty, I am canceling the cake with the chlorine inside and the twenty-seven white doves. You get a prune Danish, baddums boy. (*Back to the stove*) These eggs are going by the boards. (*Heaps some onto plates*) Will you please take your chair. (*Sachs sinks wide-eyed into a chair*) Because chow is on. And hot. I don't know, Lottie says not to cook with butter, oleo's just as good. But you can't convince me. (*He has put the plates on the table by now and takes his seat*) Eat hearty! (*He digs in, but Sachs' plate remains untouched*) What's the matter? Eggs n.g.? If you find any shells in there, report me to the Board of Health. Stop me before I kill again! Something wrong, you're not eating? (*Sachs does not reply*) Hey! Like I forgot the most festive touch. (*He has been fishing around, under his capacious sweater, at last comes out with two pieces of cardboard*) Here! The difference between a low-class feed and a high-class *dejeuner*. (*He holds up the cardboard rectangles, which are place cards*) Charles. (*Points to himself*) *Moi*. And—A. R. Sachs.

SACHS: (*Dully, as he fingers the place card*) August Rheinhardt Sachs. You got my . . .

CHARLES: August Rheinhardt Sachs, what a mad moniker!

SACHS: I—I don't know you. Never laid my eyes on you. You got my initials . . .

CHARLES: Off the doorbell, no big feat. It's in the public domain—the doorbell. Frost is forming on your eggs, August Rheinhardt . . .

SACHS: Stole my garbage to get me in here, what is this?

CHARLES: I keep abreast of all my neighbors' garbage habits. *You* always make *two* trips. Once with the metal cans, then back up for the plastic one. Strange, you don't empty those two first, take 'em back up with you as you go for the plastic one. But we *all* have our quirks. . . . Listen, I don't want you to get upset now. What I want is for us to have a leisurely, lordly breakfast, get acquainted, exchange stories. Tell tales of our youth, which for me has a certain here-ness and now-ness about it. The whole bit. Neighbors. I want us to be good neighbors. Already I like you. Halfway home right there. Now when you get used to me, come to accept, and I hope, finally, ultimately, have the kind of affection for me I am most surely going to have for you any minute now, then it will be, as I've counted on, accomplished.

SACHS: (*Quietly and with great fear*) You are crazy. Oh, you are *crazy*. (*The response from Charles is a laugh so warm, so genuinely appealing that it gives the lie to Sachs' accusation*) You are. Don't you laugh. Only a crazy . . .

CHARLES: (*Controlling his giggles*) Mr. Sachs . . . A. R. . . . August Rheinhardt . . . *Gus* . . . Do I look, really look like a crazy man to you? I am eighteen years old, not even quite exactly to the day eighteen, a normal American teenager, Gus. You might even call me Super Normal since my life has been the life of all American teenagers writ large. For instance, *three* daddies had Charleykins, and three husbands, Charleykins' Mommykins. But lest you conclude this has been the unhinging of me—I see you frothing at the eyes—let me assure you each daddy has been better than the last and that I am three times as normal as the average mono-sired adolescent. (*Indicating his food*) Sort of tastes queer—rancid butter, I wonder . . . Daddy One, at any rate, was the athletic kind, skating at Rockefeller Plaza in the winter, swimming and fishing during the summer months, just the ticket for nurturing Charley here into the sleek, well-formed tiger you see before you. Daddy Two was the brain of the crew which explains my intellectual hunger but not my I.Q., somewhere in the 145–150 range. Fahrenheit. However they calculate these things. Must have been there from the beginning, this skyscraper of an intelligence quotient, though it couldn't have come from the genes of Daddy One, a far-famed dumbhead except on the subjects of flyfishing and breast strokes. So it probably was Babs, whom I've always suspected of brilliance if you could get her out of bed. With all those daddies you can imagine what bed meant to Babs. To be fair, she did get out of bed once to move from Greenwich to White Plains at the behest of Daddy Three, Sidney, the *sheik* of White Plains who, incidentally, rounded me out as the sensitive and finished person I am simply and entirely by virtue of his knowing the swingingest chicks on the Eastern Seaboard and eventually dumping the whole feathery, fluttery flock in my lap which I only discovered a couple of years ago. Discovered my lap, that is. So my heart belongs finally to Daddy Three who was the pimp and the Pan who led me out of darkness, who gave me or caused to be given unto me Lottie, about whom I could go on forever if I didn't smell the coffee burning (*Jumps up, goes to stove, comes back with coffee pot*) Hey. We've already begun. Our friendship. Twelve-and-a-half minutes into our relationship and we've already got past Daddies One, Two and Three and have arrived at the Feature Attraction. . . . Or have I done it again? Skipped. By gum, I have skipped. *You*. And your whole probably convoluted and Old World History of laughter and tears and Capitols of Europe and Disorder and Early Sorrow and the Third Reich no doubt coming up fast on the inside, followed I suppose, by Remorse of Conscience, Agenbite of Inwit and stealing away by night to Freedom and America and a second floor walkup in a dingy corner of the loneliest city in the world where you have at last found Peace of Mind and Security and possibly God and surely Inner Serenity and apparently have *not* found the way to the Super's apartment with this month's rent, he told me to tell you since "youse boids" is so thick. Have I omitted any salient details? If so, please fill them in. But with a fair amount of terseness, I want to get back to the Feature Attraction . . . You haven't touched your Sodium Pentothal. (*The telephone rings*) My sweepstakes number has come up, I'll bet my booties. (*He rises, goes to phone*) Hullo, Babs. I *thought* you'd be thinking . . . Okay, I invented him . . . 'Course I'm not lying. (*Attempts a European accent*) Zee? I inwented heem. Whole ting a yoke. Ja . . . Listen, you called to tell me I invented him, then when I admit I invented him, you claim I didn't invent him. What kind of a mother are you? Why don't you slide your sleep mask back down, pop another Nytol, and pretend it was all a bad dream? . . . No, I told you she hasn't called or written. Why should I be concerned over Lottie's safety, have you ever felt her muscles? She'll be in touch when the fit is upon her . . . look, love, I'm calling from a pay phone and there's a line outside the booth . . . Darn, caught me again . . . Okay, give me a buzz when you've figured out why I did not invent him . . . Ciao. (*He hangs up the re-*

ceiver, comes back to table) Your coffee has jelled; I can't turn my back on you for an instant.

SACHS: (*Utterly lost*) I am crazy. It is me and I am the crazy one.

CHARLES: Nobody's crazy. You oversimplify.

SACHS: Crazy. I must be. I am sitting here.

CHARLES: The world is full of you subway psychiatrists with your easy labels. Crazy this and sick that, it's the coward's way of coping. (*He casually picks up newspaper that is strewn about the table*) Look, take this body on page three in the river, which was formerly on page one in the river, what's to call sick? It exists. It is one of God's own creatures. Why should it be called sick for want of a head here, a limb there? I mean what do you want, the uterus is there intact!

(*Sachs bolts from his chair, his hands tightened into fists*)

SACHS: *What do you want, to kill me!*

CHARLES: (*The soul of passivity*) Sit down.

SACHS: (*Still on his feet, but considerably subdued*) Talk and you talk and you talk . . .

CHARLES: Sit down, Gus, I've asked you nicely.

SACHS: (*No more than a mumble now*) Want to kill me . . . (*He sits down*)

CHARLES: I'm going to pour you some more coffee, you need fresh. (*He fills a new cup for Sachs*) I don't want to kill you, Gus. I'm no killer. I'm an American teenager. Eighteen years old. Not even. I dig rock 'n roll and Bob Dylan and the Led Zeppelin. I love to dance, Gus, is that a killer? Come on and drink. Give you some milk? You take it with milk?

SACHS: (*Dully*) Yes. With milk I'll take it.

CHARLES: I haven't got milk. Just remembered. It's Half-and-Half.

SACHS: Half-and-Half, what's the difference.

CHARLES: (*Starts for refrigerator, stops, turns instead to paper bags arranged in a semi-circle around the refrigerator*) Here someplace. Saw it a while back . . . What happens to a guy when his old lady leaves him for a couple of days. Wrack and ruin. I told you about Lottie, didn't I? Yeah, I'm a child groom.

She's away visiting. Her mahmah and pahpah in Bahston. They're *from* Des Moines, but she would only visit them in Bahston, the snob. (*Holds up container of Half-and-Half*) Here we is. Run this up the flagpole. (*Pouring it into Sachs' cup*) Say when. When! You'd have let me flood the entire Upper West Side. You married, Gus? Huh?

SACHS: No.

CHARLES: No?

SACHS: I said no.

CHARLES: Boy, I am. And here you are unattached and unencumbered. Bet you get the eye from plenty of girls on Columbus Ave. You're a pretty spiffy gent. (*Clinking cups with Sachs*) To the unencumbered life!

(*They drink and an instant later, Sachs spits his coffee all over the table*)

CHARLES: What's your problem, buddy? You don't like the cuisine, say so. No need to be so juicy.

SACHS: Sour. The milk . . .

CHARLES: Half-and-Half? (*Looks into Sachs' cup*) Well, why didn't you look? Sure it is. When you see it all curdled on top that way, it's a dead giveaway. You got to learn to speak up, Gus. (*Mops off table*) My fault for leaving it out. All those groceries I bought for while Lottie's away, I just left them out. Lie there and molder probably before I put it away. Whole empty Frigidaire and I leave this stuff sitting. But I have my reasons, "crazy" as you'd think them. You want some more? On the shelf somewhere I might scrounge up some Pream . . .

SACHS: (*Quick to protest*) No. No, thank you.

CHARLES: No, thank you, *Charles.*

SACHS: (*A sickly smile on his face*) Charles. My brother is Charles. Karl it was over there. Here you say Charles.

CHARLES: (*Beaming*) Charles and Gus. The intimacy grows.

SACHS: (*Warily*) You know . . . about me? I come from Germany? Who told you this? That I come from there?

CHARLES: Back there when I was sketching you? I sketch

people sometimes, as a hobby. With words. Like you heard me tell Babs, I "inwented" you. Nobody told me, but I invented and I invented the truth.

SACHS: Can . . . Can I go now? I finished eating, thank you.

CHARLES: I'm not holding you, am I, at gunpoint? You're still afraid I want to hurt you, when what I really want is to befriend you. You can go.

(Cautiously, Sachs rises, goes to the door, but then stops and turns back to Charles)

SACHS: Befriend? Why do you want to do this? With a stranger? That never met you, don't care two cents for your life? In a big city like this, you better watch yourself you don't get knifed in the street, you don't get robbed and beat up with half the place standing around, all smiles! Who does such a crazy thing here—opens a house to *strangers?*

CHARLES: Didn't I say already we're neighbors? With only a thin ceiling between. Isn't that enough?

SACHS: *(Looking up)* Only a thin ceiling . . .

CHARLES: The *thinnest* of ceilings between. Don't you need a friend, Gus? Don't we *all* need a . . . friend? *(Sachs comes and sits down at table. Charles is delighted)* I'm going to get you that prune Danish! *(Forages in paper bags on floor, comes up with a pastry)* I know you're partial to it, I've studied your garbage, remember? *(Sachs begins to eat it, but without much enthusiasm)* You're right about it being a big city and strangers staying strangers and all. The very reason I'm taking the bull by the horns. Cliché, Charles, go sit in the corner! But it's going to work out, my friendship with you, despite the difference in our age, in our backgrounds, in our interests. Oh, I have plans for us; sitting here right now I'm bursting with ideas; long walks in the park, lazing by the boat basin, maybe hiking all the way over to the children's zoo. Maybe we'll even be allowed in—a child . . . *(Indicating himself)* . . . accompanied by an adult. *(Points to Sachs, who smiles)* But it won't be all game time either, this can be a constructive relationship. You, I notice—you won't be offended—have trouble expressing yourself. It's natural, this isn't your language—you don't have the words. I have them, though, and they'll be yours after a time. You'll be my tutor, too. Can teach me all about Europe in the days of the bloodletting. An American teenager should learn about it from one who's been there. And between these cultural exchanges, there'll be laughs. I have an idea you don't laugh too much.

SACHS: Not too much, no. Do I have reasons to laugh?

CHARLES: We'll laugh, I promise you. Make you a kid again, Gus, see if I don't. Teach you to dance. Do you dig dancing?

SACHS: Dancing?

CHARLES: Not your waltzing, but the new stuff with the beat. The rock sound. Don't look so baffled. Like what you see the kids doing. Here. (*He flips on radio, turns the dial till he gets some wild rock 'n' roll. Sachs, in comical amusement, covers his ears*) Doesn't this turn you on? (*He begins to sway to the music, becomes more intense, and starts dancing in earnest, letting his body go in an extravagant display of gyrations and arm flailings. He continues talking while he moves around Sachs' chair*) No rules, just groovy. Man!

SACHS: (*Over the radio's blare*) Dancing this is? I never saw such . . .

CHARLES: (*Still in motion*) Try it with me. Yeah, c'mon. No fink-outs. Everybody up.

(*Protesting frantically, Sachs is dragged to his feet. Holding onto him, manipulating him as if he were a puppet, Charles guides him through his paces as Sachs pleads, "I can't . . . This is crazy . . . What are you doing?"*)

CHARLES: Bend, Gus. Keep 'em limber. Let yourself go. 'Atsa way, you're coming along . . . To the beat . . . Pow . . . Pow . . . Pow . . . Pow . . . Now wail!

(*Charles, head back, emits a primitive cry and, under his prodding, Sachs imitates—a grotesque carbon copy. Then the older man sinks into his seat, laughing hysterically. Charles, too, is roaring as he plops down, exhausted, near Sachs and turns off the radio*)

SACHS: (*Through his laughter*) Whoo— Whooo . . . My sides . . . Oh, my sides . . .

CHARLES: (*Laughing even louder*) Told you we'd laugh! This is laughing; this is . . . laughing. You have a wonderful laugh, you old laugher, you.

SACHS: (*Gaining control of himself somewhat*) You, you too.

CHARLES: Have the most wonderful smile, you've been holding out on me.

SACHS: And you . . . you got, good teeth.

CHARLES: *Dank*. Oh boy, Gus. I'll say one thing: you don't speak English so hot but can you ever do the Funky Broadway!

(*This starts them laughing again, joyous sounds as if they were young children. When it finally subsides, they sit back very pleased with themselves and with one another. Charles is the first to break the silence*)

CHARLES: So I've invented myself a friend. I dreamed of it and here it is. It's my special talent. I invented Lottie, too, and she's real. It's my profession, actually. An author. What's *your* profession, Gus? A fireman? (*Sachs laughs*) Movie actor? Edward G. Robinson type, you're a natural.

SACHS: Me? I wait on the tables at Fines' down the street, you've seen it. Movie actor! Here I am just a dumb waiter.

CHARLES: Here?

SACHS: In this country here.

CHARLES: Before though. In the Fatherland?

SACHS: Ah. There I was *something*. A big shot. With a life. Here they got enough big shots, all the big shots got in ahead of me. From the First War they been here already. I can't shine their shoes, these goddam crooks. Sewed the place up, I didn't step off the boat yet. Shows you how much chance I got. A nickel-and-dime waiter in the delicatessen! An author you say you are? How can it be, a child?

CHARLES: Nevertheless, an author. Well, for the pulps. The cheap mags. *Women's Diary* bought my "I Was A Victim

of Birth Control," and currently I'm getting the kinks out of
"My Afflicted Child Couldn't Yell 'Rape'!" Products of my
imagination, every one, albeit drawn from life. Well, what *isn't*
drawn from life? Even the most outrageous grotesqueries are.
Lottie is. Hey, we got there after all! The Feature Attraction,
the light of my life, Lottie. I do want to tell you about her,
then you can give me the gruesome facts about your . . .

SACHS: I am not . . .

CHARLES: Forgot! You're not married. I sure am. Don't
get the wrong idea; wouldn't want to give the impression she
is unattractive—lacking desirability. In the first place it would
reflect on me and on the address book of the Sheik of White
Plains who gave her me. For the record, Lottie is, during certain lunar phases, at any rate, what you'd call not *too* beastly.
Unclothed—can we level about this? Unclothed, she is straight
out of Rubens, all lush pink and bedimpled, a valentine of a
female who will constantly surprise you by baking a loaf of
bread some morning, hot and aromatic, or some night weaving
the legend "Here It Is" with love knots into her pubis. Don't
tie me down to photographic realism, it takes a creative interpretation to do Lottie justice. This is Lottie sans everything.
Fully dressed, however, in mod cap and brown twill jumpsuit,
she is a living tribute to the United States Marine Corps. Even
more endearing in her mini-skirt and patent leather pumps—
King Kong in a Mary Quant. I don't intend to take away from
her femininity either. Crazy about jewelry, for instance, her favorite adornment being—outside of the wrecking balls someone
designed in papier-mâché and which dribble around her head
like unispheres—her most prized ornamental possession is the
one hundred percent vinyl bone she wears through her nostrils
for entertaining at home. There you have her, impressionistically
rendered, but it is God's truth that she tips the scales at one
hundred and fifty-three pounds and is as tall as a house.

SACHS: (*Chuckling*) You. You're a funny talker, ain't
you? You enjoy to make people laugh. Because you are a kid.
Wait, you will be my age, you will turn more serious and be
not so happy all the time. But for now, fine. Enjoy yourself.

CHARLES: Damn right, Gus. I intend to. (*Idly turns on radio, which again plays rock 'n' roll, but softly now*) Because let's face it: I am eighteen years old and pretty much where it's happening, baby. (*Irresistibly, he is drawn to his feet and performs a languid dance, using his movements to punctuate his speech*) I've got powers a guy more than twenty-five is already uptight about losing. Yesterday it was I found I'd grown an inch! Every day tends to be a growing day. There's nothing anybody'd rather be than these eighteen tender years of firm flesh and growing hair and low hips and skinny pants and youth. (*He snaps off radio and sits down*)

SACHS: I see. You done a lot of figuring on this. And me? In this rating system you got? Next month, I am fifty-three years old and nothing grows on me no more. Every year, I am smaller. In the bathroom glass, I see myself. Or in the store windows when I go by. Less and then less . . . closer to the ground. I grow the wrong way. Down! Every year . . . And for you it is all skinny pants and youth.

CHARLES: Not . . . all. Frankly, not as much as it should be. Maybe I misled you. Prevailing conditions, anyway up until a few days ago, sort of skim the cream, you might say, off the top of my, well—potential.

SACHS: Prevailing conditions?

CHARLES: I did . . . take a wife.

SACHS: Ah. This is a regret?

CHARLES: Finish your Danish. At noon it turns into a blintz.

SACHS: A regret of some kind? No, thank you.

CHARLES: My wife? Lottie? I suppose so, a regret of some kind.

SACHS: Too bad. I am sorry.

CHARLES: Spare me your sympathy. I said up until a few days ago.

SACHS: Yes. Until a few days ago when . . . ?

CHARLES: When I did something about it. Took certain steps without asking "Mother May I?" It's a game we have for prepubescents. A series of moves upon a chalk-lined pavement, presided over by this Mother figure, although it can be a boy, still playing the part of this Mother. And each move preceded by this question, "Mother May I?" Which is pretty dull as you can imagine. So you start—taking liberties, without permission, striding two giant steps or three without asking "Mother May I?" until—if you're lucky, if there is plenty of distraction and very little moon and you're not playing too near the street lamp —if you're very lucky, she or he, the Mother figure, is . . . usurped. Then *you* become the Mother figure, in effect your own Mother. Very Freudian, I'm sure, or primordially atavistic, depending on your particular bag.

SACHS: (*Unable to comprehend*) And this concerns your . . . ?

CHARLES: In an allegorical sense. Making it literal would only vulgarize. Since you press me, I killed her. So I'm vulgar.

SACHS: Again with your jokes. Such things are not to joke.

CHARLES: Nevertheless, I unloaded Lottie. Gus, will you do me a favor? Will you not think ill of me? Really, because I want you, of all people, to understand how impossible it was. You can't take a guy eighteen, who, my God, is still growing and saddle him with a girl of Lottie's ilk. Or of Lottie's size. Thrown to the wolves by my own family. "You married her, Charles. Support her." Support her? When I can't *bear* her! Could not bear her.

SACHS: But—but you did not do this? What you said.

CHARLES: I am an author, Gus. A creator. I need hours in my day for creating the works that may one day put this sagging ventriloquist's dummy of a world up straight again. Where am I supposed to get those hours, Gus? Her ideal Sunday is to pass a pigskin in Central Park, then back here for nude wrestling in there on the parquet floor! I am a man with bruises, Gus. I suggest a concert, she suggests I shut my face I don't want a fat lip. I cajole, she threatens me with a dildo she had smuggled over from Paris in a rolled up copy of *Le Figaro*. Take me seriously, Gus, I beg you. These are truths too fictitious to be unreal.

SACHS: You make no sense. All the time you talk, you make no sense to me. You don't speak three words I understand the whole time.

CHARLES: Shall I *make* you understand, Gus? Shall I? (*He picks newspaper off floor, starts flying through it*)

SACHS: What now, you read me the funny papers? I go upstairs you start in with your monkey business. (*Starts to rise*) I go up now. You want nothing but to joke, I understand. You're a kid, why not? What . . . what you said, I won't tell nobody. (*He goes to door*)

CHARLES: (*Finding his place in the newspaper*) Wait! I have to read you this. To clarify. *I said wait!* (*Sachs returns to his seat. Charles reads from the paper*) The story on page three: "The nude and dismembered body, stuffed into a blood-drenched laundry bag which one bystander termed 'a womb of death'"—only the *Daily News* could find the bystander who would say that!—"still unidentified three days after Fifty-seventh Street dock workers found it moored on pilings near Pier Ninety-six appears to be the corpse of a young woman, although police this morning admit to being in the dark as to other facts surrounding the mystery . . ."

SACHS: (*At table, hands clutched together*) Oh, my boy, my boy . . .

CHARLES: (*Repeats*) ". . . in the dark as to other facts surrounding the mystery . . . blah blah blah . . . the decapitated trunk of the body apparently had been brutally slashed, according to the coroner's verdict, no less than twenty-eight times . . . blah blah blah . . . Coroner's Assistant, Edward Fleem . . ." Edward Fleem! I knew him well, Horatio! "Edward Fleem termed it 'one of the most mutilated corpses' I've ever had the pleasure to meet." . . . Darn it, I wanted to find the place about her dentures, but I keep reading over and over about her frigging uterus being intact!

SACHS: (*Unable to bear it, he reaches across the table and grasps Charles by the shoulders, shaking him violently*) No! You must not . . . It cannot be . . . IT IS NOT YOUR WIFE!

CHARLES: (*Calmly removing himself from Sachs' grip*)
I never *said* it was my wife, did I, Gus? I put Lottie in the *East*
River. This is the body in the Hudson. Lottie is in the East. See,
Gus—Gus, it's all right. Don't cry. No one else would dream
of contaminating the East River where the rich people live;
over here we get all the crap. Anyhow, Lottie would have ap-
proved. I dropped her in over the rail at Beekman Place.

SACHS: Oh, God, God, my God! You did not do this!

CHARLES: Did not what, Gus?

SACHS: Not . . . in the East River! What you said!

CHARLES: Why not, for crying out loud? Why shouldn't
I? You put yours in the Hudson. Pass me your Danish, Gus,
I'm ravenous.

SACHS: (*Only now regaining his power of speech*)
My . . . ? My . . . ? MY?

CHARLES: Your wife? Yeah, I said your wife. Well, it is
your wife, isn't it, Gus?

SACHS: No! It is not! Don't you say that, you . . .
(*Bounding to his feet, sending his chair flying out from under
him*) MONSTER, DON'T YOU SAY IT IS MY WIFE!

CHARLES: Easy, now, easy.

SACHS: (*On his feet raging, but it is almost like a plea*)
It cannot, *cannot* be my wife! Take it back, I tell you—take it
back!

CHARLES: No can do, Gus. Says right here: the uterus is
intact. She's yours.

SACHS: *Cannot be!* My wife, my wife is . . . is gone. In
Florida. My wife is in Florida!

(*Pause*)

CHARLES: (*Finishing the last bit of pastry, he wipes his
hands of the crumbs*) Said you didn't have a wife, you told me.
Now I don't know what to believe. Unless she was heading
south in a laundry bag and using her femur as a paddle.

SACHS: I said? Said I didn't . . . ?

CHARLES: Didn't have a wife, told me a couple of times
so there wouldn't be any mistake.

SACHS: Because of you! Because you make me afraid
when you ask, because I see right away you are crazy. I'm going

to tell to a madman I have a wife, he shall sneak up some night and kill. . . .

CHARLES: (*Bursts out laughing*) Gus, you are a riot. August Rheinhardt Sachs, you are a one-man panic. (*Imitating*) "I shall sneak up some night and kill!"

SACHS: It is true, you would! So I lie, I tell you I have no wife—to save her. (*Advances on Charles, knocking his plate to the floor, and laying his hands violently upon the boy's throat*) To save her!

(*They tussle briefly, but Charles is the stronger and throws Sachs to the floor where he lies among the grocery bags and newspaper*)

CHARLES: (*On his knees beside the gasping man*) Listen to me, *you listen to me!* This is me talking to you, Charles is speaking to you, goddamn it, you listen! (*A moment; when he speaks again, he has regained his composure*) Why do you think I got you down here, stole your garbage, lured you in here? Because your deed has fathered my deed. Because your wife is in the Hudson, mine is in the East. For these reasons you are here and we are together.

SACHS: (*Face averted*) My boy, oh, my boy . . .

CHARLES: As I learned from my first father to swim, as I learned from my second father to search, as I learned from my third father to fornicate, so I learned from you, my fourth father, Gus, though we had never met, to kill. And you would still deny!

SACHS: I . . . I cannot say it. Never. That I . . . I killed her. Never. My poor boy.

(*Silence. Charles rises stiffly, goes to table, and sits. He picks up newspaper and begins to read in a shaky voice*)

CHARLES: "One—one of the most baffling aspects of the puzzle—of the puzzle concerns itself with the thoroughness with which the killer obliterated all possible avenues of identification. The Coroner's Assistant reported not only the mutilation of the victim's fingertips, making futile a fingerprint check, but, even more gruesome, the careful removal of fillings and denture plates from the mouth of the severed head . . ."

SACHS: Inhuman, you are an *animal!*

CHARLES: What *is* your profession, Gus?

SACHS: (*No more than a croak*) An animal!

CHARLES: Your profession, Gus? What's your profession? (*Still in his seat, he reaches down and grasps Sachs roughly by the collar*) Son of a bitch, I'm asking you!

SACHS: What I told you before. At Fines'. Only a waiter, that's all. You will kill me. Go on, animal, and do it!

CHARLES: Only a waiter. But *before!* In the Fatherland you were more. A big shot, you said.

SACHS: No. I wait tables. Always, before, now. Always.

CHARLES: (*A broad grin*) Look at me, Gus. I am smiling. Look at what a gorgeous smile I have. But you didn't say that. You said, "You got good teeth." Professional opinion. A dentist!

SACHS: No, never. Believe me, I was never . . .

CHARLES: (*Letting him go so that he falls back into the rubble on the floor*) Dentist! I have a job for you. I want to put you to work, dentist! Get you back in harness. I need a professional opinion.

SACHS: Leave me alone! I must—must go now. To work. Nine o'clock they expect me. Let me go!

CHARLES: *After* you advise me. I have followed your lead in this, you'll advise me now. I have been your disciple . . .

SACHS: They will miss me at work, will send for me. *I must go!* (*He has risen to his knees*)

CHARLES: . . . down to the most minute detail, down to the subtle filings of the fingertips.

SACHS: I want out of here!

CHARLES: (*Rises*) I have followed your lead—but for one step: "the careful removal of fillings and denture plates from the mouth of the severed head."

(*Sachs leaps to his feet and breaks, moaning, for the door of the apartment. Simultaneously, Charles rushes over to the refrigerator and flings open its door*)

SACHS: (*His hands fumbling wildly with the doorknob*) LET ME OUT!

CHARLES: (*At open refrigerator*) Here, Gus, catch!

(*Sachs turns, shrieks, instinctively extends his hands and catches "the severed head"—a leafy green cabbage. He stands there, crying freely, embracing the vegetable, hugging it to him as if it were a child, as if he were tenderly holding a baby)*

SACHS: Yes. Yes, yes, yes. Yes!

(Charles goes to him, puts an arm about his shoulder. Tenderly)

CHARLES: Sorry, Gus. Oh, Gus, I am. I tried not to, hoped you wouldn't make me . . . go so far. There were other ways, kinder ways, and I did try, truly, Gus, to spare you. *(He leads Sachs to the table, the man still clutching the cabbage to his breast, and together they sit down)* Cry, Gus. Better for you if you can cry.

SACHS: Yes. Yes . . . To cry.

CHARLES: I didn't want to hurt you. But you understand, don't you, it was necessary. For you to claim it as your own.

SACHS: *(Through his tears)* It is mine.

CHARLES: *(Reaches over, tears off a bit of cabbage leaf, nibbles on it)* Lottie makes soup of this, her renowned cabbage soup—the murkiest of all liquids, black as a pool, and with a stench that rises. And to make matters worse, on top of creating the soup, itself a crime, she *slurps* it. Naturally, I refuse all offers but cannot escape the spectacle of her at the trough. I watch her, and as I watch, I eat saltines. In immaculate silence. She is alive, Gus. I must admit it, if you haven't already guessed. I'm no killer, a normal American teenager like myself. With you its different—you have a history of slaughter. The camps, the ovens I still can't conceive of with all my imagination, were the backyard of your home. For me, for us, it is fiction. So she lives. In Bahston with mahmah and pahpah. . . . She lives and because she lives, you and I will be the best of friends. When she returns day after tomorrow, sooner even if she has sucked the meat out of the last claw of the last lobster in Bostontown before then, when she returns, I'll introduce her to my new friend, a Mr. Sachs from upstairs, who is a stranger in this country and whom I have befriended. We will be seeing a great deal of Mr. Sachs, Lottie; he is in need of friends and he has endeared himself to me with his clean-cut habits and his neighborliness. We have grown to be fast friends. He . . . he is helping me with my writing, has a vast store of knowledge, you'd be surprised, has Mr. Sachs. And I'm going to help him with his English, bring him out of the cave of his inarticulateness, and when he has found a tongue, he will have a voice again, be the man to whom the voice belongs and be free . . .

SACHS: Alive . . . the whole time . . . and mine . . .

CHARLES: Soon forgotten. Hardly worth the paper she's printed on. By Tuesday week, the *News* will have found a passel of fresh dismemberments and yours will have passed into oblivion, unsung, scarcely a memory. Just a private smile between us—two old pals. I like that! Between the two of us. Now tell me, Gus, since I have a share in it, you will explain. *Why? How?* Did she pry up the lid of your soul and . . . ?

SACHS: (*Flaring for the first time with dignity*) You know as much as you will *ever* know! And it is *nothing*. Why? How? You get no answers from me! Even the way she looked, you will never find out! Read what they got to say in the papers, they will tell you what she weighed, the color of her hair. And it is nothing! What you heard through the ceiling—sounds, not words to explain! If blood came down from there, rained down, you still would not know, will *never*! It is mine!

CHARLES: *Ours,* Gus! Ours! Just as *Lottie* is ours. And if, after a time, you should want to kill again . . . kill just once again if you find her the insupportable creature she is, after all, to me, then, believe me, Gus, for once in my eloquent life I'll not utter a single word!

Curtain

Joseph A. Walker

TRIBAL HARANGUE TWO

(A Domestic Comedy)

Joseph A. Walker

Until very recent times, the black playwright had scant opportunity to raise his voice in the American theatre. With just a small number of exceptions (including Lorraine Hansberry, James Baldwin, Langston Hughes, Loften Mitchell, Abram Hill), comparatively few gained professional stature or even had the experience of seeing their works staged. Then there suddenly emerged on the wave of our rapidly changing times a sizeable group of compelling black dramatists such as: LeRoi Jones, Ed Bullins, Adrienne Kennedy, Bill Gunn, Ronald Milner, Ben Caldwell, Douglas Turner Ward, Charles Gordone (the first Negro dramatist to ever win a Pulitzer Prize, for his 1969 play, *No Place To Be Somebody*) and Lonne Elder III (whose *Ceremonies In Dark Old Men* was a strong contender for the 1968–69 New York Drama Critics' Circle Award). They inspired a literary awakening and most brought new vigor and innovative forms and styles to the theatre.

One of the newest of black playwrights to move up into this influential vanguard is Joseph A. Walker whose *Tribal Harangue Two* is published for the first time in this anthology. The play is from Mr. Walker's *The Harangues* which opened at the St. Marks Playhouse, New York, in January, 1970, and which Clive Barnes of *The New York Times* termed "a remarkable series of white-black vignettes in an evening that makes a plea for less racial racism and more racial understanding."

The Harangues was presented by the Negro Ensemble Company, founded in 1968, and as Mr. Barnes reported: "How quickly the company has established itself as a vital part of our cultural life. In little more than two years it has become one of the significant theatrical forces in the country—a force that is honest, stimulating, provocative and as valid for the white man as for the black."

Although only lately "discovered" as a forceful playwright of individuality and mettlesome dramatic spirit, Mr. Walker, admittedly, is no newcomer to the theatre. As an actor, he has appeared in many stage productions and has been seen on television and in films. He also has directed plays, written lyrics, choreographed, designed sets and, upon occasion, taken a turn at the backstage lighting control board.

In 1968, he collaborated on the book and lyrics for the musical, *The Believers,* that ran for 295 performances at the Off-Broadway Garrick Theatre. And in 1970, the Negro Ensemble Company once again opened their season with a work by Mr. Walker, a musical entitled *Ododo,* which he also staged and choreographed.

The author received his B.A. in philosophy from Howard University and his M.A. in drama from Catholic University. In addition to his diverse activities in the theatre, Mr. Walker taught for three years in various high schools in the Washington, D. C. area, for four years in New York City schools, and has conducted a drama course at Yale University.

Characters:

ZOE WALTON

CAL

JAKE

WALTON

DOCTOR

TWO BLACK MEN

Scene:

A fairly expensive efficiency apartment somewhere near Dupont Circle, Washington, D. C.

The kitchen, dining area, and living room are one. The furnishings include a small walnut table, two chairs, a convertible sofa, a rug and a large lounge chair, in front of which is a coffee table. There is a door behind the chair which leads out of the apartment. There are two doors in the right wall: one leads into the bathroom, the other to a closet. Next to this door there is a huge window.

The time is the present; it is six o'clock on a Wednesday evening.

A young white girl in her early twenties is busily setting the table, apparently for three. She is an attractive girl of any description. It is easy to tell that she has lived, at least up to this point, a jolly carefree existence. It is obvious that she is extremely worried and anxious about something of grave importance. From time to time she goes to the window and looks out nervously. She finishes the table and goes to the stove, inspects her cooking. Suddenly, she feels faint. She makes her way to the lounge chair and plops into it, mopping her face with her handkerchief.

The doorbell rings and a happy, but fearful look crosses her face. She runs to the door. An imposing Negro man enters. His hair is very long. He has a beard and an earring in his left ear. He is neatly, not flashily dressed. His personality is a mixture of amazing calm and boundless *energy. She embraces him, trying to kiss him, but he refuses her.*

ZOE: Cal, why don't I get a kiss?

CAL: 'Cause you don't rate a kiss, ya dig?

ZOE: I haven't seen you in one solid month. A whole month!

CAL: That's your fault. No kisses until after, ya dig it? Until it is over and done.

ZOE: Yes, Cal.

CAL: (*Throws bag in the corner, crosses to table*) What's for dinner? I'm starving.

ZOE: Chili.

CAL: Smells good. Nice layout you got here. What does daddy have to shell out for this?

ZOE: How was your trip?

CAL: Ridiculous.

ZOE: What?

CAL: Ridiculous. I will never again take a Trailways Bus 'cause they are not where it is.

ZOE: Why, what happened? (*She attends to the food*)

CAL: I tell this okie at the ticket counter I want a one-way ticket to Washington, D.C., the country town in which I was born. And he tells me the twelve-thirty bus is a Five Star Special Luxury Express or some old shit and that for the privilege of riding on this hotel on wheels I have to pay one dollar and seventy cents extra.

ZOE: It's a new service they started a few years ago.

CAL: Yeah, well anyway. I tell this cat, "Man, I could see a flick for a dollar and seventy cents." But this does not phase him. I shell out my coins and make it on down to track five, and there in front of this bus—a bus, mind you—is this dingy red carpet and these polished silver railings and this big high-busted blonde, also dressed in red. All this shit, like this bus is an airplane in disguise, ya dig?

ZOE: Cal . . .

CAL: This okie bus driver finally gets this airplane bus

out on the highway and along comes this stewardess bitch whose name, by the way, was Jeannie Spicer, and she's smiling and grinning and shit and showing her cleavage, both cleavages, ya dig? And lo and behold, she's taking down people's last names.

zoe: Cal!

cal: Taking down the last names of over seventy people. Like who in the hell is going to remember the last names of seventy-some-odd people on first meeting? This, you see, is personalized service.

zoe: Cal. I'm scared!

cal: And then they serve the food: one-half turkey sandwich, one-half cream cheese sandwich, a cookie. One cookie, ya dig? A dollar and seventy cents. Can you imagine? One goddamn cookie.

zoe: You really want to go through with it?

cal: You know what I did? I just kept ordering sandwiches. I ate so much I thought I was going to pop. I was determined to get my dollar and seventy cents' worth. And then to top it all off, Blondie asked me if I was enjoying the trip, and I got mad. All I could see was my dollar and seventy cents. And I yelled at the top of my voice, "I protest, I protest!" I'm sure they thought I was crazy. The bus driver stopped the bus and came back. But I pretended to be asleep.

zoe: Can't we talk about it?

cal: The only reason I took Trailways is because my father used to work for them. Ain't that dumb? My father killed himself, slinging bags and lifting boxes and I, his stupid son, took Trailways because Trailways killed my father. Ain't that dumb?

zoe: Please, let's talk about it! (*Cal abruptly gets up, crosses to his bag and starts out*) Where're you going?

cal: If you still have your little reservations about it, then I'm going back to New York, you dig it?

zoe: Cal, please!

cal: Look, *you* called *me*, right? I mean I didn't call you, right? Didn't I tell you not to call me until you had made up your mind? I mean once and for all.

ZOE: Yes, Cal.

CAL: Dig it. My blue prints did not shape this world. But I am forced to live in it, and I have made certain determinations. Now I expect my woman to follow my determinations, no matter what they are, ya dig? It just be's that way.

ZOE: Cal, I'm carrying your baby! A woman wants the father of her baby around her.

CAL: You are not just a woman. You are a white woman. And that means you have to pay certain dues. The price for a black man gets higher and higher every day, and you have to decide whether or not you want to pay the price. It be's that way.

ZOE: How can you ask me to do it, Cal?

CAL: I will not argue with you, you dig? I will not discuss or talk about it any goddamn more. I do not wish to hear about it any more. Are you with me or not? That's all I want to know. (*Pause. He hesitates another minute and then picks up his bag once more*)

ZOE: Cal, please.

CAL: Are you in my corner or not? That's all I want to know.

ZOE: You know I am. It's just that it's not . . . it's just that it's not . . . easy. You don't seem to understand. It's not easy.

CAL: I don't want to understand. I am not interested in understanding, you dig? Dig it, baby. Nothing has been easy for me in this life. I have been gasping for air and spittin' and clawin' and tryin' to cover up my balls to keep 'em from being kicked in my ass ever since I first dropped from my mother's womb, so don't you tell me what's easy.

ZOE: Cal, I am only human. He's my father, Cal.

CAL: That's an accident of fate. He's just a big mass of vicious white protoplasm as far as I'm concerned. You said so yourself. Now, do I go back to New York or do we go through with it?

ZOE: Anything you say, Cal.

CAL: (*Puts his bag down*) Jake should be here pretty soon and then we can get it all together.

ZOE: You sure he'll go through with it?

CAL: Sure he will. I told you before, Jake's like I am. We have always been alike. With just one difference. My development has always been a little ahead of his. I reach a conclusion this month; he reaches it the month after. That's always the way it's been. He'll do it all right. (*Stares into space*) Dig it, he has to!

ZOE: What took you so long to get here?

CAL: This city. This old Washington D.C. My old hometown. I knew Jake was an hour behind me so I took the opportunity to do a little walkin' and talkin' with my old hometown. You know, I hate to say it, but this city is total, complete and unbelievable jive. Makes me mad. That's why I don't come back here any more than I have to. You know, I was down here about six months ago, me and some other guys, and do you know even though black people dominate this town in numbers, we still couldn't get these niggers to take over this mother? I mean, they're so happy with their clerkships and post office jobs and their teacherships and doctor and lawyerships and Howard University and their split level homes in Woodridge and the Capitol and the Washington Monument which never did look like anything but a giant penis. And The White House. That name White House alone should make them furious. I mean they'll loot and riot and shit. But these black bastards are so happy you couldn't get them to rip this mother away from the pigs, even if you took away their wigs. That's okay, D.C. I am gonna have my *own* little individual private revolution right here tonight in about one hour from now!

ZOE: Where's it all gone? The smile, the quietness in your eyes? I sometimes wonder who it is I love. What's happened to you?

CAL: The weight, baby, the weight. I am tired of bearing the weight. You ever hear of the story of Atlas and Hercules? This cat Atlas was holding up the world and old Hercules came walking by and Atlas said, "Here, I got to take me a pee, bad. Would you take this world thing and hold it on your shoulders while I run into the bush?" And old Herc, being the considerate cat that he was, thought about it a while and then he said, "Okay, Atlas," and he put that world on his shoulders and it almost broke his back. And the sweat was running down and his veins were sticking out and shit. It was no gettin' used to it. The weight was unbearable. And Atlas came runnin' out of the bush zippin' up his fly, and Atlas took one look at Hercules and he could see the strain on his face and he remembered what the world felt like on his own back, and Hercules said to him, "Come on, man, take this damn thing back." And Atlas squinted his eyes and grinned and answered, "No, no baby. You got that motherfucker now, you keep that motherfucker 'cause I am tired of the weight." And that's how *I* feel. I am tired of the weight. I can't bear it no longer, baby!

ZOE: I am not sure what is right and what is wrong any more. I do know that my love for you goes past all other considerations. My family, my friends, even myself. And every time I feel our child moving inside of me, it brings tears to my eyes. The beautiful thing about our baby is not merely that it's the result of a man and a woman, but that it was sown here . . . (*Hugs stomach*) . . . by love. Love is the father and mother of this child. (*Pause*) Cal, I *have* to have you with me! There've been many nights when I have stood on the Calvert Street Bridge and watched the cars crawl underneath no bigger than ladybugs and wanted to throw myself over the railing. I wanted you back so bad but I couldn't bring myself to do what you wanted me to do. I could kill myself, I'm nothing. That would have been easy. But I couldn't kill our love. Every time I would grab the railing, it seemed as if our love sensed it and kicked its tiny feet in protest. I love you, Cal! Remember how we used to walk up and down Second Avenue across One Hundred and Twenty-fifth Street? Remember, Cal? Holding hands, laughing and bumping into each other. And Central Park, do you remember—making love in the valley of rocks that time and the children who caught us—how we continued in spite of their stares? Remember? Why was that, Cal? How was it that we could continue in spite of their stares? In spite of everything?

CAL: *You're* talking.

ZOE: It was because we had built an invisible fortress

around us and nothing could get in. No one could see it, but it was there. That was only six months ago, Cal. Just six months. You've become so different—so alien in six short months!

CAL: That's what you say. I'm thirty years old, and I say it's been *thirty years!* How do *you* know how long it's been? What I have been through to get to where I am at? When I first met you, I was playing games, white girl—black boy games. White girls are just as good to screw as other girls and it was fun seeing how frantic they were for my blackness. I was a child playing games and then I met you. Who ever thought I would fall in love with a white girl? I tell you one thing, baby, I didn't. Dig it, I had one thing on my mind when I met you and that was getting you in a horizontal position—nothing else, but I fell for you. Can you imagine? I fell in love with mine enemy. Do you remember what happened six months ago? You casually remarked that your daddy was rich and you told me what kind of rich son-of-a-bitch he was, and all of a sudden I found myself going around angry all the time. I do want you, and I want my baby just as bad as you do, but I knew that Texas motherfucker. I have never met him, but I knew him. I knew he wouldn't let me marry his snow white daughter without taking away her inheritance and I said to myself, "Ain't that a bitch. Ain't that a bitch, that I—as smart, as well educated, as unique and talented as I am—I am gonna be denied that money simply because I'm black." . . . That's when the weight pressed down so hard until it turned inside out! I awakened one morning and found that all the calmness, all the self-control, all the attempts to love my white brother had flown the coop. I am desperate. Do you hear me, *desperate!* I *want* that money. I have things to do with your father's money.

ZOE: But Cal, what about love?

CAL: Love is mine enemy too, and I am not gonna make peace with love until I get what I want! The foundation upon which this world is based is hate. We all know that. Dig it? It be's that way!

ZOE: Cal, you know there's no love lost between me and my stepfather. While my mother lay in a hospital, gasping her last breaths in an oxygen tent, my chivalrous stepfather was frantically trying to seduce me. He gave up only after I became hysterical. So hysterical, in fact, that I had to be carted off to a sanatorium where I rested for two whole weeks, Cal. The day I left the sanatorium, I learned that my mother had died the very night I was admitted. Cal, I had just turned fifteen!

CAL: Then what the hell are we arguing about!

ZOE: I'd be the first to agree he's the lowest point on the scale, but he's a human being, Cal; what we're talking about is a human being!

CAL: That's debatable! (*She tries to embrace him*)

ZOE: Cal.

CAL: Is he in town?

ZOE: Yes.

CAL: Did you call him?

ZOE: Yes.

CAL: Then he'll be here?

ZOE: I'm supposed to let him know when you get in.

CAL: Then do it!

ZOE: I can't reach you anymore.

CAL: I'm hungry. Reach me that way.

ZOE: Don't you want to wait for Jake?

CAL: No. (*He sits at table, picks up magazine. Zoe crosses to stove and prepares dinner*) You still reading these jive-ass magazines? If you're gonna marry a black man you better find out who he is. You better start reading *The Liberator, The Negro Digest* and *Jet.* (*Crosses to chair, picks up book and examines it*) And what's this shit you're reading? *The Feminine Mystique?* Feminine mystique, my ass. You a female, and you don't know about the feminine mystique? You better start reading *Invisible Man, Another Country, Manchild, Malcolm.* Feminine Mystique! Ain't that a bitch.

> (*The doorbell rings. Cal crosses to door and opens it. It is Jake, an attractive Negro in his late twenties. Intense, but calm, he is not nearly as jittery as Cal. He has long sideburns and a heavy moustache*)

CAL: Hey, brother. Come on in. Zoe, you remember Jake.

ZOE: Yes. How are you, Jake?

JAKE: Fine, Zoe. You're lookin' awful sexy.

ZOE: Don't be funny, Jake.

JAKE: Oh, but I'm not. Dig it. Pregnant women always look sexy to me.

ZOE: Have you eaten?

JAKE: Yeah, I guess so.

CAL: What do you mean, you guess so?

JAKE: I mean I ate on the bus and man, was that jive. They call it the Five Star Special for which they charged a dollar and seventy cents extra.

CAL: (*Laughing*) Man, you too.

(*They both slap each other's palms and dance about the room laughing. Zoe crosses to sofa and lies down*)

JAKE: I ain't never seen so much jive in my life, baby. I mean it was completely off the wall. (*Cal laughs*) Man, what we have to put up with in this phony damn country. I'm going to Canada or South America or something. I can't fight this crap no more. Like nobody really gives a damn about the little man. They just use him for everything he's worth.

CAL: That's right, brother. If you had been rich, you could've caught the plane and avoided that jive.

JAKE: Man, do you know I was so pissed with that four-eyed bus driver and that southern redhead that kept runnin' up and down the aisles until I took out my pencil and did some figuring. And do you know these mothers are making one hundred and nineteen dollars per bus load, and with an express every hour that makes $2,856 every twenty-four hours—which means $1,042,440 a year. This is what they're making off that extra one dollar and seventy cents. And that's just that one bus going to D.C. That's not counting the twenty-four hour service from D.C. to New York, and all the services in all the hundreds of towns in this great nation of ours. Man, those white folks are cleaning up off us little men. And you know who's getting kicked in the ass the most! The black man.

CAL: That's telling it like it is. Don't you agree, Zoe?

ZOE: I guess so.

CAL: You guess so? (*Glowers at her*) Sit down, Jake, baby. Relax. You don't mind if I eat, do you?

JAKE: On second thought, I would like some of that chili. It smells too good to refuse.

(*Zoe gets up and dishes out a bowl for Jake*)

CAL: Didn't I tell you he's exactly like me? Didn't I tell you that, Zoe?

ZOE: Yes.

CAL: Will ya dig this, Jake—*Feminine Mystique.* This is what my fiancée considers profitable reading. While my black brothers are out there being chased by the National Guard.

ZOE: I am tired of the racial problem. I'm just sick and tired of it, that's all.

(*Cal smacks her furiously*)

CAL: Don't you ever let me hear you say that again! You're not half as tired of it as I am. Do you dig where that is?

ZOE: Yes, Cal. (*She places bowl in front of Jake, crosses to sofa and lies down once more*)

JAKE: Man, you're really getting vicious.

CAL: That's right, brother. And you should be too.

JAKE: You need to take a little personal inventory.

ZOE: We've just been through it, Jake.

CAL: We're wasting time. Why don't we get our heads together.

JAKE: Yeah, baby. Why don't you run me down some of the details?

CAL: I already told you.

JAKE: Tell me again.

CAL: Dig. It's actually very simple. Did you bring the stuff?

JAKE: I said I would, didn't I? (*Jake opens suitcase. Brings out paper bag from which he produces a plastic bag containing a large hypodermic needle*)

CAL: Groovy, baby. Right on time.

JAKE: Getting this stuff almost cost me my job.

CAL: When we finish this you won't even think about your job! Zoe, call him.

ZOE: Now?

CAL: Right now, bitch. Right now!

JAKE: Why do you put up with him, Zoe?

(*Zoe ignores this question, rises, goes to the phone and dials*)

ZOE: Hello! This is Miss Walton. May I speak to my father, please? . . . Hello! Yes. Okay, I guess. Cal's here. Yes, I do. It's very . . . very important to me. About twenty minutes? (*Looks at Cal who nods assent*) Yeah, that's good. Twenty minutes is good. See you then . . . 'bye. (*She hangs up phone*)

CAL: Have you been doing any writing lately, Jake?

JAKE: Not much.

CAL: You'll be able to get all your plays done when we're finished. We'll be the most perfect combination in the world, baby. You writing and me directing real, nitty-gritty black spectaculars.

JAKE: Okay, Cal, lay it on me now. What's this all about? I mean you're joking of course—I mean all that stuff about killing Zoe's father. I mean that's a bit much.

CAL: You damn right it's a bit much! It's a bit much what they've been doing to us, too. This country is a bit much. Every goddam thing is a bit much.

JAKE: Okay, Cal, cool it now. I'm listening. You paid my fare down here so I'm listening, baby.

CAL: (*Laughs, relaxes*) You dig that, Zoe? I knew my main man would go along with the program. I knew it.

JAKE: Hold on a minute! I didn't say I was going along with nothing.

CAL: Jake, Jake—remember the things we used to do together? Like the time we came across that closed down parking lot and reopened it? Remember? People didn't have no place to park so we opened this abandoned lot. Charged a buck a car. Made five hundred dollars.

JAKE: Hey, yeah, that was wild!

CAL: They still don't know who did it. That money paid half of my tuition that semester. Why'd we do it, Jake?

JAKE: 'Cause we needed the money.

CAL: A lot of people need money, but we took it into our hands to do something about it. Why?

JAKE: I guess we were desperate. They were threatening to kick us out of school if we didn't cough up some bread.

CAL: Desperate! That's the word. We did it because we were desperate. We needed money. Whitey had it so we took it from him.

JAKE: What's your point?

CAL: I'm desperate now. I grow more and more desperate every day. I want to instruct black brothers about the revolution, and I want to do it now. I need money to do it. I've found a white man who has all the money in the world, and I plan to take it from him. I plan to ravish whitey, to rape him—same way he's been doing me all these centuries.

JAKE: But Zoe's father!

CAL: Dig it!

JAKE: You can't be serious.

CAL: Dig it. He's got more oil wells than I've got spigots in my apartment, and half of 'em belong to Zoe, willed to her by her rich southern mother. Only Zoe can't get it if daddyo doesn't sanction her marriage. How is it your thought, baby, that he'll give us his blessing? Alas! Dig it! But if he dies before he gets a chance to have the will changed, Zoe will get mamma's half and daddy's half also. Ya dig that!

JAKE: Like I said before—wow!

CAL: Wow is right, baby. Now's he's coming over here in a little while, and we're going to discuss his racial attitudes. If he talks the wrong way, we're going to do him in, and you will get one third of the take. One third of nine flourishing oil wells! And then we're going to produce that play you gave me to read last month.

JAKE: You must be joking!

CAL: You think so?

ZOE: He's *not* joking.

CAL: Dig it!

JAKE: If he's that rich, he's probably well known. We can't hassle that.

CAL: It's all figured out.

JAKE: I thought *I* was insane! (*Pause*) No, no, I don't know why I came down here. I can't go along with that.

CAL: Think about it, Jake. Three oil wells—all your own —three!

JAKE: I've thought about it. For one month I've thought about it, and I'm telling you you've flipped, baby. That must be what I came down here to tell you.

CAL: Come off it, Jake.

JAKE: I should have known. As soon as you told me about it, I should have known you had gone off the deep end.

CAL: Think about it, Jake! When was the last time you paid your rent?

JAKE: Not me. I don't want no part of it. I'm going back to the city. (*He picks up suitcase and exits*)

ZOE: What're you going to do?

CAL: He came down, didn't he? Don't worry about it. (*Picks up magazine*) Says here: "The FBI, which we all know is run by a racist, seeks to infiltrate, divide and destroy the Black Panther Party." (*Flips through magazine*) Says here: "Spiro T. Agnew is really a genius in disguise." (*Flips pages*) Says here: "At the current rate of population growth, we have about thirty-five more years left on this earth before we all starve to death." (*Flips pages*) Says here: "The FBI in conjunction with the CIA may have set up the Black Panther Party as a release valve for black dissatisfaction."

(*The doorbell rings. Zoe answers it. It is Jake. He comes in quietly and sits at table*)

JAKE: The play you read last month, you really dig it, huh? You'll do it first? You promise?

CAL: I promise. Now here's what we have to do. I'm going to give him a chance, ya' dig? I'm going to let him use that big Texas mouth of his to dig his own grave.

ZOE: Cal!

CAL: That's what I'm going to do, baby, so you may as well start strengthening your stomach to the idea. And when he's gouged out enough earth with that big mouth of his, I'm gonna shove him in his own hole. The signal is *Moby Dick was really a black whale.*

JAKE: What?

CAL: The signal. When you hear me say, *Moby Dick was really a black whale,* I want you to grab that knife and . . . Zoe, come here. (*She obeys*) Zoe is Mister Walton. Now we'll make sure he sits here. Jake you'll sit directly opposite him, and I'll sit next to the coffee table. Ya dig it?

JAKE: Exactly like you told me before?

CAL: Right. When you hear the signal, you are to grab that butcher knife and hold it to his throat and dare him to make a move. At the same time I will open this innocent looking box . . . (*Demonstrates*) . . . remove from it this wad of cotton and this bottle of chloroform. Once he's out, we get the hypodermic needle which will be in this drawer. We fill it with one hundred and fifty cubic centimeters of air and zippo, sock it to him. Dig it! The air causes a vacuum to constrict the heart, and zippo, he's gone to hell where he ought to be anyway, and we've done our good deed for today.

JAKE: Just one thing. You say you want me to use the knife?

CAL: Yeah, why?

JAKE: Well. I was thinking . . . that since I work in a hospital . . . I mean, maybe *I* ought to be the one to use the hypo? I mean, I've seen it done quite a bit.

CAL: While you've been watching other people doing it, I've been reading and practicing on myself for a solid month. I've developed an excellent technique!

ZOE: Then you *knew* I would give in?

CAL: I was kinda counting on it.

JAKE: I've never known you to be so serious.

CAL: Dig it, let me tell you the rest of the plan—now check these happenings. Right after bastard slips on into hell, Zoe runs screaming into the hall like a typical Miss Ann, gathers the curiosity seekers with her hysteria and shit and tearfully guides the dummies back here to witness sweet daddyo. In the damn meantime we call an ambulance. Now, dig it, when the doctor cat arrives on the scene, we tell him how I asked for daughter's hand in marriage and how daddy became so deeply and joyfully moved, how he got so choked up 'til he dropped stone cold dead on the spot. The doctor makes his examination and reports the cause of death as a heart attack due to severe shock.

JAKE: Wow! Wow!

CAL: And you get three damn oil wells which pump, ironically enough—black gold! (*Doorbell rings*) This must be him! (*Doorbell rings again*) Well, don't just stand there, Miss Ann, answer the door. (*Zoe goes to the door*) Dig it. Be cool and remember the signal.

JAKE: *Moby Dick was really a black whale.*

CAL: Dig it.

(*Zoe answers the door. A tall red-faced, happy-go-lucky white man enters. He appears to be the typical Texan, complete with string necktie, boots and ten-gallon hat. He even has a slight pot-belly. He wears a dark blue suit with a large belt into which he constantly sticks his thumbs. His manner is effusive*)

WALTON: Howdy, daughter. Long time no see. My, my, but don't you look healthy!

ZOE: Come in, Dad.

WALTON: My pleasure.

ZOE: This is . . .

WALTON: Don't tell me, child. This is Cal. (*Extends his hand which Cal ignores*) Intensity. That's what you got, boy. I could tell from your intensity that you-all just *had* to be Cal.

CAL: Sit down, Mr. Walton. (*Walton sits*) I want you to meet my best friend, Jake Johnson.

(*Walton shakes Jake's hand*)

WALTON: (*Takes out a cigar*) Y'all don't mind if I smoke, do you? (*Lights up without waiting for an answer*) Daughter, what on earth has happened to you? You look so radiant, like a lightning flash across a dark prairie sky. You know boys, this little gal is the spitting image of her mother, may the mightiest foreman of them all rest her soul. I mean, I think I have about the most beautiful daughter in the Western Hemisphere, don't you boys agree? (*Abruptly*) Now, what's on your mind, Cal.

CAL: I hope you don't mind Jake. He knows all my secrets. I would like for him to sit through our little talk. Is that all right with you, Mr. Walton?

WALTON: Call me Jim. All my partners do.

CAL: Yeah, baby, Jim. Now I got exactly . . . (*Looking at watch*) . . . twenty-two minutes.

WALTON: You're running the show, Cal. Whatever you say. Now what's y'all's problem?

CAL: Well, Jimmy, your daughter and I would like to get married.

WALTON: Uh-huh.

CAL: How does that strike you?

WALTON: Very h'ard, son, very hard.

CAL: And what am I to understand by that statement?

WALTON: That the whole idea hits me as a pretty hard pill to swallow, son.

CAL: Does that mean you're against it?

WALTON: Well, now, that's too simple. I don't believe in simplicity. Every shade of black contains a million shades of gray, I always say.

CAL: And what does that mean?

WALTON: You see, you keep looking for a simple answer.

CAL: A *direct* answer.

WALTON: But by direct you mean simple.

CAL: Dig it, my man, anyway you want to take it. Just give me an answer.

WALTON: I can't give you a *yes or no* answer.

CAL: I see.

WALTON: No, son, I don't think you do see. I mean not really.

CAL: The floor is yours, baby.

WALTON: Well, look at it this way. I'm not prejudiced.

CAL: Of course not.

WALTON: I'm practical. I see y'all don't believe that. Zoe, have you been lying on me again? What has my lovely daughter told you anyway?

CAL: Only that you tried to screw her when she was fifteen, that's all.

ZOE: Cal!

WALTON: Now, Zoe, that's unfair. You see, son, Zoe happens to be . . .

CAL: Your stepdaughter. I know.

WALTON: And a very lovely stepdaughter.

CAL: Which is why you felt no guilt about trying to screw her when she was fifteen!

WALTON: Now, boy . . .

CAL: Don't call me boy!

WALTON: I beg your pardon. I was about to say, let's not be vulgar. I do despise vulgarity.

CAL: You don't call me boy, and I won't be vulgar, okay?

WALTON: Hedging, that's what we're doing, hedging.

CAL: Then why don't you come to the point?

WALTON: Yes, the point. Let's get to know each other, Cal. Is that all right with you?

CAL: By all means.

WALTON: You see, son, I believe a little understanding coupled with a little money can solve all problems. I say, have you ever watched tumbleweed? I don't suspect you have. Well, let me tell you about tumbleweed. I have flown over my ranch many times as you can imagine. And I have watched the tumbleweed from up there in the sky, and I tell you it is a sight to behold. Any breeze, any breath of air is sufficient to toss that little old tumbleweed this way and that way. I mean, son, it has absolutely no direction whatsoever. Well, what I'm trying to say is I am the exact opposite of tumbleweed. I *plot* my course. I have *always* plotted my course. Everything about me is plotted. Every aspect of my life has been thought out and plotted.

CAL: Which means?

WALTON: Which means I don't like ten-gallon hats, don't like boots, and I don't really like suspenders, and I absolutely despise shoe string ties. As a matter of fact, I don't like things Western. To put it bluntly, I hate the west. I don't even like Western movies. I confess, I'm a bourgeois man. I like everything bourgeois. Which means I like money, prestige, position

. . . all things acceptable. I love acceptability, son. It's the cornerstone of my life. And I'm proud to admit it.

CAL: Now it seems to me that *you're* hedging, baby.

WALTON: You know where I'm from? I'm from East Harlem, New York. I'm a second generation Italian. My father owned a shoe repair shop in East Harlem at One Hundred and Seventeenth Street. The limit of his vision was lasagne. I left good old New York City because I hate lasagne. Thumbed my way to Texas, discovered the game Texans play and decided that I could make a fortune playing that particular game. I knew I could play it with supreme agility. One thing I can say about me is I'm a very agile man, son. I played the game so well until I am now worth eight million dollars, after taxes. So now I'm respectable. It's a wonder they don't bottle my urine I'm so respectable. But bear in mind, son, the essence of Texas respectability is Texas acceptability. I mean, I had to learn a new way of talking and a new way of walking. I learned very well.

CAL: I might add that you talk like a *Texan*—very long. Now, get to the point.

WALTON: The point is, I don't *dislike* colored folks. I think they're vital—just brimming with life. I can't imagine this country without colored folks. My stint in the army taught me that all men are pretty much alike—more or less. But the point is, colored folks just ain't acceptable, son. No matter how you cut it, they just ain't. Now if you were to marry my daughter— stepdaughter—you would reduce my entire empire to social unacceptability. And that's a horror I cannot in good conscience, son, allow.

CAL: Your mind is made up?

WALTON: Absolutely. I have here a certified check for five thousand dollars. All you got to do is fill in your name.

CAL: You stick that check up your . . .

WALTON: Well, now son, you shouldn't say things like that.

CAL: You undignified bastard!

WALTON: Don't be a fool, son.

CAL: Don't you think me a fool, whitey! You're offering me peanuts, man. Well, I don't want your leavings, whitey. I have use for that money, and I want it all. Dig it. Everything that my young bride is entitled to. I'm gonna open me up a school with that money. I got the building all picked out. Right up on One Hundred and Twenty-fifth and Eighth Avenue. You know what I'm gonna call it? I'm gonna call it Harlem's Academy of Black Revolutionary Drama. During the day I'm gonna teach my brothers and sisters how to take a gun apart, how to set fuses, how to make a time bomb, Molotov cocktails. And at night I'm going to put on plays depicting the white man in his usual attitude—with shit on his face.

WALTON: Intensity is what you got, boy.

CAL: Our first production will be Jake's play. You know what it's called? *My White Shadow.* It shows how the white man is a pale imitation, a mere shadow of the black man. Truth is the black man's. Black is truth, and white is lies. The shadow is always the lie, for it is always insubstantial. Black is concrete—hard and real.

WALTON: Are you aware that your boyfriend here is insane, Zoe?

CAL: Yes, I'm insane! Insanely anxious to see ten-gallon hats, and Five Star Luxury Specials, and all such shadows of reality, demolished. So that good old black truth can shine, do you dig me, shine through this Texas bullshit. 'Cause all America, baby, is Texas. Dig it!

WALTON: Well, son, here's five thousand dollars to help you get started and I wish you all the luck in the world. 'Cause you gonna need it.

CAL: And this is where we stand?

WALTON: This is where we stand.

CAL: Do you know, Jim, boy, do you know that white ain't never been right? That Moby Dick was really a black whale? (*Jake does not move*) *Moby Dick was really a black whale!* Jake! (*Jake still does not move*) What's the matter with you, man? (*Jake does not move*) That's it, that's it. Keep on sitting there, nigger! I'll do it by myself.

(*Cal reaches for the knife while Jake slowly pulls an automatic from his inside coat pocket*)

ZOE: Jake!

JAKE: It just be. . .'s that way.

(*Cal, who does not even see what Jake is doing, angrily continues advancing upon Walton. He raises the knife to a threatening attitude. Zoe, who realizes what is happening, rushes to stop Jake. Jake holds her off with one hand and shoots Cal twice in the back. Cal spins around in amazement, sizes up the situation in the hair of a second, makes a desperate and furious lunge for Jake who shoots him again in the chest. Cal falls. Jake steps over him. Zoe drops on top of Cal, screaming hysterically*)

WALTON: You sure do a thorough job, Jake!

JAKE: (*Returning gun to pocket*) That's what you're paying me for, ain't it?

WALTON: Oh, yes. (*He takes out pen, writes Jake's name on the same check Cal refused*) That's Jake Johnson.

JAKE: Jacob B. Johnson. (*He takes check*)

WALTON: Send the rest of 'em in here.

(*Jake nods, takes a last look at Cal and exits. Three Negro men enter. Two of them are large and robust. The last one to enter is small, meticulous and foxy—impeccably dressed*)

WALTON: Take her to the sofa, boys. Good. Now hold her down. (*To the Doctor*) I've been informed that there should be some chloroform in that box there.

(*Zoe understands what is about to occur and begins struggling frantically*)

DOCTOR: Excellent.

(*Walton takes an envelope from his coat pocket and hands it to the Doctor. Doctor counts money quickly, takes off his coat and begins preparations for the abortion*)

WALTON: You just get busy. Pull that black bastard out of her, that's what you do! When will colored folks learn they just ain't got the means?

Curtain

Rochelle Owens
THE KARL MARX PLAY

Rochelle Owens

Rochelle Owens stepped into the international theatrical lime-light with her first play, *Futz,* which excited considerable critical and audience interest. Described by Edith Oliver of *The New Yorker* as "a witty, harsh, farcical, and touching dramatic poem." it was presented at Café La Mama in 1967, subsequently toured England and Europe and was performed at the Edinburgh Festival. In 1968, the drama returned to Off-Broadway, this time at the Theatre De Lys where it ran for 233 performances and garnered an "Obie" award for distinguished playwriting. *Futz* and his companions, however, would not stay ballasted to Greenwich Village, and soon they were to be seen in theatres of Sweden, Germany, Canada and other countries, as well as on the screen in a movie version released in 1969.

Innovative and, admittedly, often controversial, Miss Owens' plays have engendered much journalistic space, both approbatory and disparaging, but whether one is pro or con, it must be conceded that she has an exceptionally gifted hand for stirring the cauldron of theatrical excitement. Harold Clurman, one of her many distinguished votaries, has written, "Her work is not realism; it is real. It is the product of a complex imagination in which deep layers of the author's subconscious emerge in wild gusts of stage imagery . . . I know of no contemporary playwright like Rochelle Owens."

In response to a request for biographical information, Miss Owens supplied the following: "I was born in Brooklyn, New York, on April 2, 1936. Having completed my public school education, I moved to Manhattan where I studied at the New School for Social Research and with Herbert Berghof at the HB Studio. At that time, neither an academic degree nor a career as an actress appealed to me, so I worked at numerous jobs, read a great deal, and wrote poetry. In 1959, my poetry began to appear in several of the most prominent 'little magazines,' and since then I have published three books of poems and have contributed to many literary journals and anthologies.

"In 1962, I married George Economou, poet and college professor, then editor of *Trobar* poetry magazine. Shortly before meeting my husband, I wrote my first play, *Futz.* Since then, I have written five full-length and nine short plays, including: *The Queen of Greece, Istanboul, He Wants Shih!, Beclch, Homo,* and *Kontraption.*

"Although I wrote *The String Game* after *Futz,* it was the first of my plays to be staged, in 1965, at the Judson Poets' Theatre. Subsequently, my plays have been produced Off-Broadway, Off-Off Broadway, in regional and college theatres, on television, and abroad.

"I am a member of the Playwright's Unit of the Actors Studio, the New Dramatists Committee, and in 1967, I was awarded an American Broadcasting Company grant to work at the Yale School of Drama. In the fall of 1969, a Rochelle Owens Collection was started at the Boston University Library, to which I have contributed many of my manuscripts and personal papers.

"While New York City always has been my home, I have traveled extensively in this country, Mexico, and in Europe, sometimes in connection with a production, sometimes as a guest speaker, and, of course, as a vacationer."

A collection of the author's plays, *Futz and What Came After,* was published in 1968.

The Karl Marx Play, a dramatic tapestry rich in texture and language and imaginative in design, is Rochelle Owens' latest work for the theatre and appears in print for the first time anywhere in *The Best Short Plays 1971.*

Author's Note

This play, this tragedy/comedy with music and many directorial possibilities, is a "fantasy" but is structured on the truth of Karl Marx's life: this is a theatrical investigation of a very "special" family. This play is apolitical; some of its concerns are about what was happening within the Karl Marx household before the manifesto was written. This play is about a driven man, a blighted genius who was also a poor father.

Characters:

LEADBELLY
ENGELS
KARL MARX
JENNY, *his wife*
ERIKA
TRINKA
SHIRLEE } , *his daughters*
KRISTA
BABY JOHANN, *his son*
LENCHEN, *the cook*

Scene:

A glittering chandeliered ballroom. A life-size Hellenistic plaster of paris statue of a nude male is in view. The sleek black portion of a piano is toward the side.

Leadbelly, Karl Marx and Engels are in the ballroom. Attached to Karl Marx's rear-end is an old, dirty enamel basin. Marx has had his lower intestines plundered away some time before. He holds a mass of entrails over his arm like a jacket. His face is angry and judgmental. Leadbelly is black, agile and quick. Engels is "Mittel European" and always full of plans. He frequently touches his fingertips together. Leadbelly glides to the piano and

pulls something out from underneath. It is half of the
bloody and cut-up rear-end of Karl Marx.

LEADBELLY: It's it's it's Marx's ass! Lord o' mighty, it's
Karl Marx's ass!

ENGELS: *Gott in himmel! Mein Gott!*

LEADBELLY: (*Holding the flesh out*) That ain't no world
spirit, baby! That a half-ass of a man! (*Pointing to Marx and
laughing*) You got guts! Give us the guts! Your right side
portion near the heart.

ENGELS: Ze fat entrail. Ah hah! Make it the sweetest!

LEADBELLY: The liver is the sweetest! Sounds like you
want his liver. Give us your liver, Karl Marx. It's so juicy!

ENGELS: Yah! So heavy und juicy. Hey, Leadbelly, is dis
here sentence structure right? I demand the glands of Karl Marx!

LEADBELLY: (*Enunciating*) His balls so white!

ENGELS: (*Repeating as a lesson*) His balls so white!

LEADBELLY: White as snow!

ENGELS: (*Scornfully*) It ain't not as white as snow! Karl
is a Jew!

MARX: I am a European! A German! Engels, Engels, my
friend. Why do you betray me?

ENGELS: It's slipping! His liver is slipping!

LEADBELLY: (*Mock surprise*) The liver is slipping between his fingers? His fingers so white? (*Laughs*) White with
a splash of red? Bloody white fingers?

ENGELS: Marx, vere are your testicles? Ze balls! Ze balls of
the leader of the Socialist Party! Hey, Leadbelly, is zis right? I
will pose the question to you, Karl Marx! Are you, Karl Marx,
the leader?

MARX: I *am* the leader! I have my theory! My vision!
Engels, my friend. *Our* vision!

LEADBELLY: Vision? What do you mean by vision?

MARX: New Jerusalem! I see New Jerusalem. Created by
Socialism!

LEADBELLY: You just a horse's ass! Where's your proof?

MARX: You idiotic clown! You black clown! (*Leadbelly lunges at Marx and rubs Marx's face in his entrails*) You will never do a complicated mathematical equation! Never will you comprehend intellectual systems of European thought!

LEADBELLY: I'm gonna beat that half-ass off 'til there ain't *nothing* left.

ENGELS: Enough! A revolution will create a disturbance without you two quarreling. Enough! Enough! Karl! Karl! You must not insult Leadbelly. And you, Leadbelly, must not goad Karl Marx. He is the leader of a science!

LEADBELLY: Why can't he take my teasing! It's just strong nitty-gritty down-on-mother-earth teasing.

(*Jenny appears with three of the four Daughters*)

JENNY: My God! Such noise. What on earth is happening? Karl, you've been hurt! How? Why?

ERIKA: Papa!

TRINKA: Papa!

SHIRLEE: Papa!

JENNY: Engels, my husband is *always* in pain. Why? My Karl, my Karl has so much suffering. Why?

ENGELS: Karl himself will explain.

LEADBELLY: Hey, Jenny Marx. Your man, Karl—gotta roast his meat on the fire for the good of us all!

JENNY: For the good of us all? And why? Why for the good of us all?

LEADBELLY: Humanity! All of us. The human race!

JENNY: So, my poor Karl, explain! Explain it to me. And what about money for the weddings of our daughters? In *our* case, Karl, a proletarian life-style is not the best thing for the girls.

MARX: (*Fuming*) Labor! Sucking Capital! Capital! The exploiting class! The milking class—the ruling class! (*To audience*) Is everybody happy? Engels, my friend. The girls are ready to get married. Well, Engels, you good Christian! You loyal friend!

ENGELS: Christian? I am your loyal friend, Karl. But . . . Christian?

MARX: I mean that you are worthy of my necessity and trust. You, Engels, are worthy of my trust!

(Jenny and the Daughters go to Karl and tidy him up; washing his face and hands with a cloth and brushing his clothes off)

ERIKA: Our father, Karl Marx!

TRINKA: The husband of our mother, Jenny!

SHIRLEE: Our mother, a Prussian aristocrat!

DAUGHTERS: *(Together)* Must have proper sons-in-law!

JENNY: Karl Marx, we must have rich sons-in-law!

TRINKA: We want rich husbands!

LEADBELLY: I, Leadbelly, say the girls should definitely have rich husbands. They so pretty!

JENNY: Karl, a proletarian reality is not good for our daughters. Karl, explain life to Engels, and how we want life to be for our children. Our girls!

MARX: Sometimes, Engels, there is a conflict between laws and the facts of real life. *(Frantic)* Engels, lend me the money for new dresses for the girls and Jenny!

JENNY: *(Looking disgustedly at herself)* What a lousy dress this is!

DAUGHTERS: *(Together)* Look how we look . . . so shabby! Uncle Fred, give Papa Karl some money!

LEADBELLY: Yeah, give him some *gelt* for the fancy silky stuff that a woman puts on for her man. Wow! Wow!

ENGELS: *(To Marx; friendly tone)* You Jew. Always bargaining and cajoling, trying to grasp! Grasp! You Jew!

MARX: *(Hotly)* My father was a Christian! An admirer of King Frederick!

ERIKA: Grandpapa and Grandmama were converted before we were born!

TRINKA: We are not Jews!

SHIRLEE: We are Revolutionists!

JENNY: My girls are not Jews! Perhaps, Karl . . .

LEADBELLY: Karl Marx is a universal man!

MARX: I am a German! And a European!

LEADBELLY: Some days you are a universal man, other days you are a German. But woo, woo, woo never a Jew!

ENGELS: Tu! Tu! Tu! Marx is never a Jew. But those that he hates are always *Babylonische* Jews!

JENNY: Enough! Enough! Enough! No more talk of Babylonians and Jews. We are more concerned about good married futures for the girls.

MARX: (*Proudly*) Karl Marx sired good-looking daughters. And Karl Marx sired the workers revolution!

ENGELS: And a mania has been sired in you—for bleeding Engels—your lifelong friend—dry!

MARX: Ah, Engels, you are right. For years I've been using your money. The money you made in your family's manufacturing business—but Engels! Engels, the inevitability of the proletarian revolution, beyond a doubt and amazingly, will force our theory to become actualized! Engels, the bourgeoisie, the fat enemy will get their reactionary asses *schtupped* up with horseshit and whipped cream! A new era will dawn!

JENNY: Karl Marx, your language! Our daughters!

ENGELS: Yes, Karl, your daughters! You have five children, Karl. (*Counts to five in German*) Five *kinder*, a wife and a lousy case of boils! Our theory! Our theory! Where is our proof? Where is our proof for our theory? *Proof!*

MARX: (*Abstracted, as if he has not heard*) Proof. Proof. About what, Engels? (*Poetic*) Jenny, Jenny, tell me, tell me about your breasts, describe to me the delicate spiderweb of sweet veins under your apricot sunny nipples . . .

JENNY: (*Feigning dislike*) Crazy Karl Marx! What about decent dowries for the girls?

TRINKA: Mama's breasts!

SHIRLEE: Our Papa Karl has never forgotten our mama's breasts!

ERIKA: When mama was a young girl!

LEADBELLY: Ole rubber-mouth devil Karl! Wow! Wow! Like a suction cup on his sweet woman's tit-tee!

MARX: Jenny, your slate-gray eyes rolled back with the taste of your first sip of champagne . . .

LEADBELLY: Of love! Wow! Sexy lady! Wow! Hey, Karl Marx, your eyes are slobbering!

JENNY: Enough! Enough! I am a much grown-up

woman. A girl no longer. I have four daughters. Very marriage-able daughters!

TRINKA: (*Teary*) Papa—he's always. . . . Oh, mama!

ERIKA: Papa's always peeking at mama!

SHIRLEE: Through keyholes! When papa thinks mama is not looking!

ENGELS: Peeking! Peeking! Not writing the manifesto! Peeking at your own wife! What kind of a crackpot . . .

LEADBELLY: Mmmmhhhuh! He is a crackpot.

JENNY: Karl, do you peek at me? Why, Karl, why? That's not a good thing to hear! Why do you peek at me, Karl?

MARX: I peek at you because I peek. I like to see you—so I peek.

ENGELS: *Mein Gott!* Who cares about Karl peeking at Jenny! When will you write the book? Karl, the book about our *cause!*

MARX: Yes! Yes! The revolution will force our theory . . .

ENGELS: Crackpot and my friend! What about writing—sitting down and writing the book?

MARX: I hate to write and I don't sit down—my affliction. Affliction! Engels, I would appreciate it if you would give me some of your money for my daughters' nuptials. Weddings! Ah joy, when children grow up and marry! Engels, my girls and my wife want nice things. Jenny and I . . . (*Pause; poetic*)

Jenny, Jenny, tell me
About the hollow above
Your golden-lovely rosy
Cheeks. Mmmmsweet Jenny.

LEADBELLY: (*Grabbing Marx in a choking hold*) I don't like hot talk poetry red pepper talk! You think about the man-i-fes-to! Man-i-fes-to!

ENGELS: Right! Leadbelly is right. Karl, you get your mind off your wife's flesh. *Und* write the manifesto.

(*Lenchen, the cook, appears with Krista and Baby Jo-hann, who has a Viennese accent*)

LENCHEN: Beatings! Oh, no more beatings on poor Karl!

Mrs. Marx, I have no money left for the house. The little boy is hungry.

KRISTA: Me, too, Lenchen. I am hungry! And my sweet sisters are hungry, too. Mama, also. And papa is, too. Even after a beating. We are hungry!

MARX: See, Engels. How hungry we all are! Please, Engels, money, some little bit of money! (*Leadbelly gives him a rabbit punch*) Do not beat me anymore! Stop beating me! (*Leadbelly crudely juts his rear-end out*)

ENGELS: (*Friendly*) You greasy Jew. Here—take, take, take! (*He shoves coins into Marx's hands*)

Interlude Music

The Party

Everyone is joyously moving about. All but Marx, who leans against a wall. He eats pickled beets from a jar which he holds. Whenever he chews a mouthful, he looks happy, otherwise he scowls. Lenchen and Baby Johann stand near him.

LENCHEN: *Fressen, fressen, gut* Herr Marx.

BABY JOHANN: Papa, papa, smooth mein little brow. Papa, mein eyes are clear gray like beautiful mama's!

LENCHEN: Yah! The Baby Johann's eyes are sweet just like his mama's.

BABY JOHANN: Lenchen, I peeked in the keyhole and I saw papa kiss mama on the belly. Her titties turned red like the beets papa eats!

MARX: Ah! My son peeks, too. Ah, red is good! These beets are good! Engels is good! Baby Johann is good! Little rolls with butter is good! Viennese torte is good! And a revolution is good! Ah, these beets are fit for a king!

(*Leadbelly, The Daughters and Engels go to Marx*)

LEADBELLY: (*Mockingly*) I'm so hungry I could eat my foot. There's no food here—nothing! You, Karl Marx! When

you going to be a wizard? When's the wizard going to write
Das Kapital? (*To Jenny*) Hey, Jenny, smile, Jenny. So I can see
your gums. Hey, woman, your gums are red like a baboon's ass.
An Asiatic ape! What do you think about that, woman! (*Jenny
looks angry*) What righteous anger, woman! You are full of the
storm! Jenny, Karl Marx suffers so much—like he is in hell, right
here. His sickness. His boils.

JENNY: Karl don't look so bad now. He's enjoying his
beets. My God! Sometimes he's in so much pain. My God! My
heart is hurting me because of Karl's pain! I'm full of . . . I'm
full of . . .

LEADBELLY: Anguish! (*He grabs Jenny and they dance
lewdly together. Lights dim. Marx's voice is heard*)

MARX'S VOICE: A sense of ful-fill-ment? Des-truc-tion?
Economics! The food sticks to the ribs. Man is fed—man is fed—
manisfedmanisfedmanisfed!

(*The mood changes to cold gloom. Lights come up; they
all look grim*)

ENGELS: (*To audience*) I have put my hands into my
pockets a thousand times for Karl Marx. Giving all the time,
little sums of money and big sums of money to Marx, who is my
lifelong friend!

MARX: Engels, there is not enough for the necessities of
life. Engels, so many unpaid bills! From shopkeepers—the
butcher, the baker, and everybody. I have pawned my suits . . .

LEADBELLY: I can't eat meat because the butcher's bill ain't
paid!

BABY JOHANN: My little body will not grow because there
is no meat! (*To audience member*) Please give a little sum of
money to Karl Marx's baby son.

LENCHEN: No! Baby Johann, no! Your mother will be
ashamed.

KRISTA: Mama's side of the family has *never* begged!

MARX: And your papa's side of the family has not begged
either!

ENGELS: (*Slyly*) Jews have been known to crawl for a
piece of fish and one onion. In mad Poland!

MARX: Engels, that reminds me! The pamphlet I wrote in Munich. It was called, "A World Without The Bargainers— The Jews."

LEADBELLY: I read it! I read that one. And you were criticized for writing it! The intellectuals of Hamburg thought it was naive.

MARX: Leadbelly, are you a Prussian?

LEADBELLY: Yes. I am a Prussian.

MARX: Who are the most intelligent of the Europeans?

LEADBELLY: The Prussians!

MARX: And we are Prussians! And we are concocting the revolution!

LEADBELLY: Con-coc-ting the revolution!

ENGELS: Concocting! Concocting! Marx says concocting the revolution! And Marx has not even written the manifesto! He has not written the first line of the book which is to prove our theory!

MARX: Engels, my friend. I had a grandmother who would make a soup out of beets from her garden. Engels, the girls and my wife Jenny and you and Leadbelly and the cook and the baby—we would glow with health if we ate my grandmother's beet soup.

ENGELS: I am talking about events of historical importance and you are concerned with soup made from your grandmother's beets!

JENNY: Even the King of Vienna likes beet soup!

BABY JOHANN: *Und,* I, the baby, like beet soup, too!

KRISTA: From the old King to little burping Baby Johann. We *all* love beet soup!

ENGELS: *Das Kapital! Das Kapital!* The manifesto! When will Karl Marx write the manifesto?

MARX: Stop tormenting me, Engels.

ENGELS: *I* stop tormenting *you!* I stop tormenting you! You unforgivable shilly-shallying wretch!

(*He has a fit of hiccups. The Daughters try to soothe him*)

MARX: Engels, I have bad luck. Sickness comes more frequently to my house—to me. Inflammation of the liver, jaundice, piles, boils, headaches, rheumatism—the boils. Engels, I know what misery is. But Engels, amid all the misery of these days, the thought of you and your friendship has kept me going, and the hope that you, Friedrich Engels, and I, Karl Marx, may *still* find it possible to do something worth doing in the world.

JENNY: Engels, Marx loves you more than his own family!

MARX: Jenny is a sentimentalist.

BABY JOHANN: Papa Karl is an intellectual, a thinker, a philosopher!

LEADBELLY: I, Leadbelly, am a man of revenge, you wahdjunkaga! Wahdjunkaga! Give us another piece of your gut! And when you can endure the pain no longer, I want you to say, "Ouch, this is too much!"

ERIKA: Our papa's!

TRINKA: Ancestors endured!

SHIRLEE: Torture and martyrdom!

KRISTA: And our papa can!

JOHANN: Endure it too! Yi! Yi! Yi!

LENCHEN: Herr Marx, where did your ancestors come from?

JENNY: Karl's people came from the Mosel valley.

LEADBELLY: That's a fine place, known for its wonderful wine. And its meat. They quartered a pig alive—till it was just chunks that squealed!

JENNY: Leadbelly, who is they?

LEADBELLY: The people in the Mosel valley. Where Karl Marx's good people come from.

ERIKA: My little brother must not hear these fearful things.

TRINKA: Lenchen, put your hands over the little boy's ears.

SHIRLEE: Leadbelly, I won't teach you trigonometry if you tell those horrible stories!

KRISTA: About what happened in the Mosel valley!

JENNY: Ah, my daughters are so emotional. So gentlehearted.

MARX: They are the sweet and pretty girls of Jenny, their

good mother and Karl, their proud papa. Ah, my sweet virgin daughters!

ERIKA: Papa is so amusing! Talking about our purity.

LENCHEN: It's all funny to me! And silly! Talking about purity. Girls *should* be pure.

DAUGHTERS: (*Together*) And we *are* the pure and sweet virgin daughters of Jenny, our good mama, and Karl Marx, our wonderful papa!

LENCHEN: *Mein Gott!* Listen to those girls talking! I said before, girls should be pure!

LEADBELLY: Hey, philosopher, Karl Marx! That mean the girls' ori-fices ain't never been poked?

BABY JOHANN: Are my sisters virgins? Are my mama and papa virgins?

JENNY: What bad manners everybody has! Johann, a child should not listen to and speak about things of that nature! Your papa is an intellectual, a thinker—a philosopher!

ENGELS: And poverty-stricken! But when he writes the book on economics, when Karl Marx is a published author of a book, the book on economy, the book is called . . .

ALL: (*Together*) *Das Kapital!*

LEADBELLY: The book that will tell it like it is!

JENNY: God be willing! Karl Marx, my husband, will write his economics book.

MARX: With such a family and such friends behind me, how can I not write my book! Ah, Europe waits for the book that I, the Red Prussian, will write! The book that will put iron flesh and sinew on the workers of the world! The people will believe in me, as a scientist, an economist! Karl Marx will have no equal! Engels, you are right! The book, *Das Kapital,* must be written! But first, my beloved friends, Engels and Leadbelly, my beautiful and noble wife, Jenny, my children and Lenchen—I must tell you what . . . what . . . (*He falls in a writhing, wild, demonic fit*) . . . boils . . . boils in my blood! I scream unto you, the world is full of loathsome riffraff! Scum! Ought not a righteous dethroner of God! I damn you, grandfather Yahveh! Yahveh! I am a righteous dethroner of God! Ah, Jenny! I stuff your fingers into my mouth! Ah, Baron von Westphalen, I adore,

adore your aristocratic flesh—my wife, Jenny! Praise be the creator of my lifelong friend Prince Friedrich Engels! Engels! Engels! You are my brother! My King! I am your Queen! Europe—Yahveh—Europe—Yahveh! Europe, I search for flakes of salt on you with my tongue! Europe, let me cling to your belly! Europe, let me kick my hind legs, let me be an Oriental pasha on thee! Europe! Europe! Be a big hill of meat for me! Let me be a hundred African Negroes eating chunks of thee! Metheeme-theemetheeme! Europe, I am scared out of my wits by the Slavs and Chinese! They are not nations of progress! They have no historical future! Oh, beloved! Beloved! Beware the eternal, unredeemed Jew, the everlasting bargainers! They are hot for buying and selling, they would kill my beautiful revolution! Working men of all countries unite! The proletarians have nothing to lose but their chains! (*Pause; calms down; speaks in a stern voice*) The proletarians have nothing to lose but their chains! Jenny, children, Engels, Leadbelly, Lenchen. Say what I say! The proletarians have nothing to lose but their chains!

ALL: *The proletarians have nothing to lose but their chains!*

MARX: Beware the Russians! The Chinese! The Jews! The Jews! Always beware the Jews! My family, my friends, in every case of international friction, take the side of Germany! For Germany is true Europe! It is counterrevolutionary to do otherwise!

ENGELS: Karl, we will never be popular with the democratic mob, the Red mob or even the Communist mob!

MARX: The mob! Those asses! The stupid workers who believe everything!

BABY JOHANN: Papa, workers have feelings also!

LENCHEN: (*Laughs*) The boy is a little Christian. He knows the catechism.

BABY JOHANN: I know also papa and Engels' theory! "The forces of production generate after a time the seed of . . . of . . ."

LEADBELLY: De-struc-tion! Which the system bears within itself!

KRISTA: So have risen!

SHIRLEE: And fallen!

ERIKA: All human institutions!

TRINKA: Up to the present time!

BABY JOHANN: The background of all great historical convulsions!

MARX: Everyone! All of you know my theory. What a theory! What a dazzling mountain of logic! Engels, our theory! Our theory!

ENGELS: Our theory will liberate humanity! It will make the human being free!

LENCHEN: Ah, our religion teaches us that.

BABY JOHANN: Religion is the opium of the masses!

JENNY: Ah, Papa Karl, our Johann is so smart!

MARX: (*Sings*)
My little son
Baby Johann
The golden apple
Of his papa's eye.
May money drop in your hands!
May you always laugh
And never cry.
My son, my son, my son
May you travel foreign lands!
And may you wear
Fine clothes,
Have the best false teeth
And silken hose!
My son, my son, my son!
My tender little lad,
You're the best son-of-a-revolution
That Karl Marx ever had!

(*He turns to the Daughters*) And my daughters! My daughters. My daughters are good-looking and so clever! My dear sweet girls. Papa Karl's little royal princesses! Lenchen, bake a white iced cake for the children!

LENCHEN: There is no money!

MARX: No money! No money for white cakes?

LENCHEN: No money for white cakes. No money, not even for potatoes!

JENNY: It's true! We have no money. No money for only . . . plain living!

MARX: No money for white cakes or even potatoes. (*Pause; smiles*) Or white dresses made of French lace for my royal princesses.

TRINKA: We *love* French lace.

MARX: My daughters will wear *wedding dresses* of French lace!

DAUGHTERS: (*Together*) When, papa, when?

MARX: (*Sings*)
Comes the revolution
My daughters will be brides!
And we'll eat meat pies and berries,
Apples and halvah!
Despair no longer
Will bite me!

DAUGHTERS: (*Sing*)
Comes the revolution
We'll don wedding dresses
And wear pretty flowers!

MARX: (*Sings*)
I'll eat cucumbers and apples
And slap-slap my thigh
When my enemies die!
Comes the revolution!
Despair no longer
Will bite me!
Comes the revolution!

(*Pause; sighs*) If my mother died I'd have my share of the fortune.

KRISTA: Papa, grandmother's money was spent a long time ago.

SHIRLEE: We spent it for medicine for papa's boils.

ERIKA:　And it was the same week that Baby Johann was born.

TRINKA:　We have no money!

JENNY:　The girls remember, Karl. We have no money. There is the Hellenesche sculpture. We can sell it.

LEADBELLY:　(*Mockingly*) Never! We cannot sell the Hellenesche sculpture! Such a beautiful work of art!

MARX:　I bought it after I wrote my paper on Greek philosophy. When I was a student. The statue's beauty devastated me! (*He goes to the statue and begins to suck at the chest/breast*)

KRISTA:　Our papa is like a hungry little one.

BABY JOHANN:　Mama, mama, Papa Karl is sentimental!

LEADBELLY:　Karl Marx, the plaster of paris's going to make your boils blow up!

ENGELS:　Karl, Karl, that is reactionary!

MARX:　(*Hugging the statue; slow, painful*) Ever decreasing wages, burden of toil ever increasing. Growing misery! Continual lengthening of the working day. Machinery sweeps away every moral and material restriction, in its blind unrestrainable passion, its werewolf hunger.

LENCHEN:　Werewolf! My God! If we had one we could throw it in the soup pot.

MARX:　Progressive deterioriation of factory buildings! (*Engels and Leadbelly pull him away from the statue*) Progressive deterioration in the quality of food. The adulteration of food! The adulteration of bread! The adulteration of bread! The adulteration of medicine! With what swiftness and grip capitalism has seized the vital power!

LEADBELLY:　The vital power of the people seized by the very roots!

DAUGHTERS:　(*Together*) These are the forms of misery in the past!

LEADBELLY:　And yah! Today!

MARX:　Jenny, Jenny, my boils! My wounds! Everything is torturing me!

JENNY: Karl suffers so! My husband, Karl Marx, suffers like poor Job!

ENGELS: Two *Babylonische* Jewish crackpots!

MARX: Engels, I am an internationalist and a . . .

LEADBELLY: Euro-pean! (*Laughs*) Hey, Karl, you are out of a Euro-pean nightmare! (*He kicks Marx*) Feel the kick of the king of Africa!

KRISTA: Don't kick my papa, you animal, Leadbelly!

ERIKA: No lessons, Leadbelly, in trigonometry for you!

TRINKA: No lessons in European science for you!

SHIRLEE: No higher knowledge for you! You savage!

JENNY: Girls, stop shouting! Leadbelly, stop kicking Karl Marx! Papa Karl has said economy, only, is a cause for arguments!

MARX: Economics is not only a cause. But the *only* cause for all human rancor. All human exploitation!

JENNY: Karl, wipe your mouth, there is some plaster of paris from the statue on it. It's bad for your boils.

MARX: Jenny, my loving wife. You worry about me too much. (*Sings*)

Jenny is my Jenny
Ya-ta-ta
What a wife
She is to me!

LEADBELLY: Karl Marx's Jenny von Westphalen!

MARX: (*Sings*)

Jenny is my Jenny
Ya-ta-ta
She always tickles me
She always tickles me!

LEADBELLY: When God created the day! He created the life!

MARX: (*Sings*)

And gave Karl Marx
Such a wonderful wife!
She always pleases me!
She always pleases me!

Ya-ta-ta
Ya-ta-ta
My children listen to me!
My children listen to me!
LEADBELLY: Listen to your philosopher father!
ALL: *Karl Marx! Karl Marx! Karl Marx!*
MARX: (*Sings*)
My children, I am he!
My children, I am he!
LEADBELLY: Hey, philosopher! You lie! Lying to us about your great book! Manifestoes! Yah! Manifestoes! I ought to chop off your toes! You should be quartered into pieces like a roasting pig until you just a stump!

LENCHEN: Ach, all of us have terrible troubles! Today, in the morning, I strained a ligament in my foot.

BABY JOHANN: I'm so hungry I could eat my foot! If only the revolution would come!

JENNY: Lenchen, put baking soda on your foot. It's good for the ligaments. Lenchen, you are right! We all have troubles. Years ago, my uncle, my father the Baron's brother, drowned out a field of potatoes belonging to a poor peasant. That peasant had the worst trouble! That poor man.

MARX: I am a poor man—unknown by the world.

ENGELS: Write the economics book and you'll become rich!

DAUGHTERS: (*Together*) And famous, Papa Karl!

MARX: I don't have it in me.

LEADBELLY: What don't you have in you?

MARX: I hate economics!

ENGELS: Write the book, Karl! You *must* write the book that will prove our theory. Write the book that will free us!

LEADBELLY: Anytime I look at your face, Karl Marx, I get mad! You're really nothing! You don't even have a lard ass! Not even no lard ass. Lemme see your gums! Blah! Yah! They red like the ass of a baboon! You white goo! Spewed out of a white bug! You—die—like a bug! Squish!

BABY JOHANN: (*Laughing*) Squish! Squish!

JENNY: (*Laughing*) Listen to Baby Johann. Squish!

LEADBELLY: (*Stern and angry*) Listen to me, all of you! Something is wrong with all of you! You need discipline, you do not yet understand my righteous anger!

ENGELS: Shu-tup! Shu-tup! I compel you to shut up!

LEADBELLY: (*Kicks Engels*) I compel my foot to kick your ass! (*Engels falls down in pain*) Marx and Engels! Do not say a word while I speak! You will listen to what I say—carefully. After completion—the completion of my statements—you well repeat exactly what I—have said.

BABY JOHANN: (*Crying*) This is not good! Not good to hear! Papa, Uncle Fred! (*Lenchen and Jenny cover Baby Johann's mouth and eyes. Everyone is terrified*)

LEADBELLY: (*Eerie, menacingly*) Marx, Engels, even before your gorge, like an obscene pocket, holds something foul, hold air, breath, life! (*Whistles*) Man-i-festo! Man-i-festo! Mine! Man-i-fest-o! A confession of faith! Man-i-fest-o! A confession of faith! From the heavenly twins! Marx and Engels!

ENGELS: (*Whining*) It is Marx's obligation! It is Marx's obligation to write the manifesto! Karl, you are a Jew. *Nicht* me!

LEADBELLY: (*Ignoring Engels' outburst*) Marx and Engels, you will repeat what I have said as I have instructed you to. Repeat! Now! One, two, three, go! Even before your gorge, like an obscene pocket, holds something foul . . .

MARX & ENGELS: (*Together*) Even before your gorge . . .

LEADBELLY: No! Say, our! Our gorge! Our gorge! Start again!

MARX & ENGELS: (*Together; humble, afraid*) Even before our gorge, like an obscene pocket, holds something foul . . .

LEADBELLY: Holds air, breath! Life! (*Whistles*) Manifesto! A confession of faith! From the heavenly twins! Marx and Engels!

MARX: (*Falling on his knees*) Holds air, breath! Life! I hold air, breath, life! (*Whistles*) Man-i-festo! Man-ifesto! Mine! Mine! A confession of faith! A confession of faith from me!

(*Anguished*) I am a wretched man! I have not any inspiration for writing the book. I haven't the urge! I have too much financial worry! A man cannot write with so much worry over money. My family! I have boils! I have chest cramps—it might be angina pectoris—and always, always I have boils and the stifling lack of money. (*Laughs*) No marks for Marx! The revolution must come soon to solve my problems! Leadbelly, my heart will be filled up with joy—after the revolution comes! (*High laughter*) Maybe, maybe I will have my mouth full with a delicious white iced cake that Lenchen will bake—in celebration of the revolution.

LEADBELLY: I will stuff your mouth up with your own brains! (*He flings Marx's entrails in his face. Everyone is frightened*)

MARX: (*Pathetically*) Ah, ah, ah, my anguish ascends!

LEADBELLY: I feel invigorated! I feel invigorated by this physical activity! Do you, Karl Marx? First-born stink bug! Do *you* feel invigorated?

Daughters, Jenny, Lenchen, Engels and Baby Johann: (*Sing*)

> You are like a dead man, papa!
> No longer able to predict
> The course of politics and history!
> And now the faith of those,
> Your family,
> Who had most firmly believed
> Is shaken!
> We doubt you! Papa!
> We doubt you! Papa!
> We doubt you!

MARX: It's true! My family! Everyone! Engels, *especially* you, Engels. It's true! I have shirked responsibility! I want to do something worth doing in the world!

ENGELS: You must write the book on economics!

MARX: Ah, Jenny! Help me! My sweet, sweet Prussian gentle lily, for the third time I dish your breasts into my mouth!

LEADBELLY: You not getting any suck-titty from Jenny or nobody! You will write the book—or die!

ENGELS: (*Placatingly*) Leadbelly, he got the point. Look at him. Marx got the point! He wants to write the book!

MARX: (*Surging, intense*) Izzy sells out the workers' party! I'm the prophet! The dreamer! The mystic! The plumber! The plumber of fat, sweet, sweet revolution! I love my family! I want them to laugh! I have all the perception and intelligence to write the book on economics! I will sit . . . I will sit on my boils in the British Museum and write on economics. I am the coming judgment! Economics! My veins are religious with economics! Who is Karl Marx? *I* am Karl Marx! I hate the passage of time without revolution! I want to cheat the day and the night! Yahveh! Yahveh! I am a fish sticking out of the hand of God! I would like a new gold watch for Christmas! Yahveh! Yahveh! I have pain! I have pain. I am abused by historical forces. Revolution which is past and revolution which is to come! Yahveh! Let me play Karl Marx! Let me play a workman! I have got big calluses! Boils! Calluses! Boils! Calluses! Yahveh! I do a jig for thee! I have a big izzy in my pants, let me hang it out for thee! Give me back my foreskin, Yahveh! I have heard of the Socialist party! I've never heard of the Socialist party! Look in my eyes! Do you see politics in my eyes? Or economics? Rage? Rage and pain? Yahveh! Yahveh! You gave me boils. A family to support. Six mouths to fill up with groats and milk. Hate is stuffed into me with my Jewish mother's milk! I want to write the philosophy that will burn down all other philosophies! I want to kill all those who see ideas! Not economy! Yahveh! Economy, the all powerful engine of humanity! Yahveh! Yahveh! Am I right? Yahveh! Yahveh! Give me the weapon! Give me the weapon that will kill! Give me the force! Give me the force! Give me the force . . . to set my teeth on edge and eat fire! Please, please let me be able to sit down like a man should, without pain! Please let me be able to write the book! Please take away the filthy boils! Yahveh! Yahveh! You filthy *Babylonische* bastard—are you powerless to heal?

LEADBELLY: It is the hand of fate! I am here! I am here.

Wonder of wonders! I am here. I am here to make Karl Marx go! Go! I am the force! I am the force to accelerate, to drive Karl Marx on! To drive Karl Marx from inaction to action! Leadbelly is a man with a true purpose. I *ignite* the idea!

(*He puts a flaming torch to Marx's intestines. The others are dumbfounded as Marx, with a surge of superhuman energy, dashes off—to write The Manifesto*)

Curtain

Yale M. Udoff

THE LITTLE GENTLEMAN

A Domestic Fantasy

Yale M. Udoff

Yale M. Udoff was born in 1935 in Brooklyn, New York, and attended Michigan State University where he took a B.A. degree in history. After serving in the U. S. Army, he spent a year at the Georgetown Law School, then returned to New York and joined the staff of the American Broadcasting Company. "I remained there for five years, the last two as Director of New Program Development, which meant that I was one of the men at the network responsible for finding and developing new nighttime program ideas and working with them until they became, hopefully, successful series. Some did. Some didn't."

During his tenure at the network, he started to write and completed two short novels. Though they never were published, Mr. Udoff was undeterred and in 1966, he decided to concentrate on a full-time writing career. To augment his income, he contributed a great deal of film criticism to such publications as *Film Quarterly, Film Comment, Sight and Sound, The Seventh Art* and *Kulchur*. The more he wrote about films, the more intrigued be became with the idea of pulling up roots and heading westward. "I came to Hollywood in 1967 with the hope of becoming a writer-director and, of all places, it was in Hollywood that I found my calling: the theatre. Ironical, sure. Yet, as I've explored the reasons for this irony, it becomes increasingly clear that, to a great extent, knowing less about this art form than, say, the novel or the film, I was in some marvelous way freed. I wasn't intimidated. For the first time, I was arrogant; since I knew nothing, there were no walls to scale. Of course, as I read more and more of what's been written for and about the theatre, that innocent, foolish, wonderful freedom recedes. And so the fight, it seems to me, is to refuse to be afraid. To refuse to be intimidated. To risk being foolish. Not to be intimidated by the past; rather, to accept it, use it and build from it."

Since his arrival in Hollywood, he has written for a number of leading television programs and has worked on several screenplays but, as he admits, "I spend the major part of my writing time on plays, financing it with my television and film work. It comes down to, I guess, doing what one has to do—

making a living—in order to do what one must do—in my case, writing plays."

His initial recognition as a playwright came in 1969 when two of his short plays, *The Little Gentleman* (published here for the first time) and *The Club* won the Stanley Drama Award in the annual play competition sponsored by Wagner College, Staten Island. *The Little Gentleman* and *The Club* were presented at the Off-Broadway Fortune Theatre in January, 1970, and later in that same year, both plays were given staged readings by the Actors Studio West where Mr. Udoff is a member of the Playwright's Unit.

In *The Little Gentleman,* which the author describes as "a domestic fantasy," he "catches the reality of a scene, then bends it slightly into the ridiculous," a technique he also employed in his full-length work, *A Gun Play,* which was given its world premiere in February, 1971, by the Hartford Stage Company. The production drew considerable critical praise, led by Mel Gussow who wrote in *The New York Times,* "The first thing to be said about *A Gun Play* is that its author, Yale M. Udoff, is a discovery. On the strength of this, his first professionally produced play, it is clear that he has a comic vision, verbal facility, and a contemporary consciousness."

In addition to the aforementioned works, Mr. Udoff also has written two other short plays, *Shade* and *Dust to Dust,* the full-length *Magritte Skies,* and a screenplay for producer Roger Corman.

Characters:

MOTHER
RONALD
DORA
SYLVIA
HAROLD'S VOICE

Scene:

The kitchen in an upper middle class apartment building somewhere in a suburb of New York City.

The kitchen is filled with all the latest deluxe gadgetry and extends the width of the stage. Running along the rear wall are the latest model refrigerator, dishwasher, washing machine, dryer, oven, and a long shiny sink with lots of cabinets above and below. Also above the sink, there is a small window that looks out onto a brick wall. In the left wall, a sliding glass door that leads to a large terrace. The door is presently closed, though the drapes that cover it have been pulled open. In the right wall, the hallway leading into the kitchen, and near this wall an oval breakfast table with four chairs. Near the left wall: a baby carriage turned away from the audience. Two telephones, one red and one blue, hang above the sink at either end; they are the sort that both ring and flash. An electric clock is positioned above the sink. It is close to noon.

Mother, a woman in her forties, stands at the sink, her back to the audience. As she sponges down the sink counter, she hums "The Anniversary Song." Suddenly the roar of a jet plane obliterates her voice. She stops working, looks up at the ceiling, angrily following the noise of the plane with her eyes until she is eventually facing the audience. The sound of the plane fades away. She returns to her work, stops abruptly, rushes to the carriage, checks, and smiles in relief.

MOTHER: Good baby. Smart baby. Strong baby. You sleep. Life is long and hard enough. Rest while you can. (*The oven clock rings and she rushes to it, switches alarm off, pulls out a pie. She smells the pie*) A nice apple pie from a pretty oven.

(*She goes to the table, places the pie on it, then tiptoes back to the carriage, peeks into it, again delighted with what she sees. The red phone flashes and rings. She hastens to it*)

MOTHER: Hello, hello!

HAROLD'S VOICE: (*Through phone*) It's me.

MOTHER: Who's me?

HAROLD: Harold.

MOTHER: Harold?

HAROLD: Your husband!

MOTHER: Oh—*that* Harold. The man who supports me, works for me . . . buys me beautiful things.

HAROLD: I'm . . . coming home for lunch.

MOTHER: Oh no, poopie.

HAROLD: What do you mean?

MOTHER: (*Calmly*) I'm sorry, but you just can't . . .

HAROLD: What time is it?

MOTHER: You mean according to the brand new transistorized wall clock you bought me last week? (*Checks wrist*) Or according to the thirty-four carat, sixteen-jewel watch you bought me on our wedding and promised to match with a companion Swiss made pin-watch which you have, as yet, failed to do?

HAROLD: Either.

MOTHER: It's close to noon.

HAROLD: I could be there in twenty minutes.

MOTHER: Not today, dear, please.

HAROLD: But you haven't allowed me home for lunch *once* in the last six months!

MOTHER: Don't I cook you nice dinners? (*Slight pause*) Well, don't I?

HAROLD: Yes.

MOTHER: I promise that next week . . . (*From the carriage: sounds of a child starting to awaken*) Oh my, you've woke little Ronnie. Hold on! (*She rushes to the carriage*) Is my little gentleman up? Has he had a good sleep? Is he refreshed? (*Ronald makes gurgling noises. Mother looks toward the terrace door through which the sun's rays shoot into the carriage*) Is the light bothering you? It's pure fresh sunlight! It is . . . well, we can change that, can't we? (*She turns the carriage so that the open section faces the audience. Ronald still is not seen*) Now it's nice, isn't it, darling?

RONALD: Mmm-hmmm.

MOTHER: Good. (*Returns to the phone*) Are you still there, my husband?

HAROLD: Yes.

MOTHER: You will stay away, won't you?

HAROLD: All right, but this is the last time.

MOTHER: You won't regret it, believe me. I promise.

HAROLD: Tell me one thing—what's so special about to-day?

MOTHER: You really don't know what day today is?

HAROLD: Isn't that what I just asked?

MOTHER: It's your son's birthday. Little Ronnie's day. You didn't even remember . . .

HAROLD: I'm sorry. How old is he?

MOTHER: How old is he?

HAROLD: Is he older than you?

MOTHER: Today, Ronnie is a year-and-a-half old. (*Starts to sob*) How could you forget? How could you?

HAROLD: So why not let me . . . ? I'll wish him a happy birthday.

MOTHER: No, that's out of the question! I've invited Grandmother and Aunt Sylvia. And you know Sylvia has yet to see our beautiful new apartment. (*Ronald clears his throat*) Wait a minute, Harold! (*She rushes to the carriage*) Is my baby up? Ready for his wonderful day?

(*Ronald, a child somewhere between the ages of one and three, sits up. He speaks with a British accent. The fact that he is being portrayed by an adult actor should not be used to burlesque the dramatic situation*)

RONALD: (*Politely*) Be kind enough to clarify what you meant by that, if you will.

MOTHER: Now let's not be difficult, my little one.

RONALD: Mother, why can't you ever define anything? All I ask is for some clarity, a little lucidity of thought. Is that really too much?

MOTHER: (*Slight pause*) Would you like to talk to Daddy?

RONALD: What for?

MOTHER: You will talk to me though, won't you? I am your mother.

RONALD: Do I have any choice?

(*Mother returns to the phone*)

MOTHER: (*Happily*) He's up. Your son is up.

HAROLD: *Your* son is up, not mine.

MOTHER: Sssh! Quiet. (*Lowering her voice*) What a terrible thing to say! Do you want to be responsible for what he'll think? Well, do you?

HAROLD: I'll be home, tonight.

MOTHER: Good. I'll expect you then. In the meantime . . . work, make plenty of money, and please, Harold, make sure you've got enough life insurance.

HAROLD: Yes.

MOTHER: (*Starts to hang up, remembers*) And don't forget to bring me some presents. Any kind. (*She hangs up, moves to the carriage. Ronald plays with a toy*) Your daddy's not well, poor man. A weak heart, bad feet, a touch of lumbago, failing sight, a shrivelled stomach, not to mention a tendency to stoop and cough when in fresh air . . . it's all such a burden to bear. But Harold, my husband, your father, takes it all with a smile. When I think of him, I sometimes think of crying. It's truly a pity, but what can a man expect at his age? At thirty-seven, he's well past his prime, and we were married so late in life anyway. . . . Isn't it a nice pie?

RONALD: I'd appreciate a portion. I'm famished.

MOTHER: (*Correcting him*) *Hungry*. You don't want people to think you're lording it over them. Not *my* little gentleman.

RONALD: I'm hungry, mother. Quite.

MOTHER: Not now, darling. Later, when Grandma Dora and Auntie Sylvia come. By then, the pie will have had a chance to cool to room temperature. And pies at room temperature taste best.

RONALD: Correct me if I'm wrong, mother—but isn't today *my* birthday?

MOTHER: That it is.

RONALD: Then don't you think I should be able to have a slice of my own birthday pie when I want it?

MOTHER: Isn't that being a little selfish, dear?

RONALD: Why is it selfish to ask for something you've prepared *expressly* for me?

MOTHER: Mother is *always* right. Don't argue with her! Mother is *never* wrong. Be a good baby and always obey her. You'll never regret it. Mother promises that.

RONALD: Mother.

MOTHER: Yes.

RONALD: What's your real name? I mean your Christian name. You've never told me.

MOTHER: (*Astonished*) But I'm mummy, mamma—your mother!

RONALD: That I fully understand. All I want to know is what my mother's name is. Is that asking too much? Daddy always calls you things like "idiot" and "stupid" and "don't-bother-me." Grandmother Dora always calls you "my little girl," that is, when she's speaking to you. Most of the time, when people visit, you keep me in the TV room . . . so it's impossible for me to hear any names. And when I'm not in front of the TV you make me sleep. Really, mother, I don't need as much sleep as you think. . . . Please mummy, what's your name?

MOTHER: My! You're a nervy little fellow. (*Proudly*) But then you *are* mummy's child. That's for sure . . . One day mummy will tell you everything you want to know . . . (*The doorbell chimes*) Oh, that must be Auntie Sylvia, or maybe even Grandma . . . or maybe both. (*She starts for the hallway*)

RONALD: But your name!

(*She exits. Ad-libs from the hallway; then Dora, a woman in her middle sixties, enters*)

DORA: There he is! What a boy!

(*Dora jets toward Ronald, who pulls back into the protection—what little there is—of the carriage. Mother remains at the door, smiling happily. Dora looks into the carriage*)

DORA: How is my darling grandson? (*No answer*) Say *gevalt*. Go, say it, darling. (*No answer*) Say *gut-in-himmel*. Come, say it. (*No answer*) Please talk to me. Say things. Tell me, speak my darling grandson. Talk to the one who loves you—most.

(*Mother moves toward Dora*)

MOTHER: Dora!

DORA: He doesn't talk no more?

MOTHER: You scared him.

DORA: *I* scared the most wonderful, beautiful, brilliant baby in the world! I would do such a thing! May He strike me dead if it's so! All I want is to teach him a few words from the old country, so he should know his background, his heritage . . . where he comes from. (*Contemptuously*) From you he'll never learn that! (*Ronald sits up*) There, look! He knows I love him. What a boy! What a beautiful child. Come darling—say, speak, talk to Dora.

(*Ronald looks at his Mother, then Dora*)

RONALD: (*Mispronounces*) Gewalt.

DORA: *V*alt! *V*alt! *Gevalt*. Say again.

RONALD: *Gevalt*.

DORA: Beautiful! Absolutely marvelous! So now say *gut-in-himmel*.

RONALD: *Gut-in-himmel*.

DORA: (*Kisses him*) A genius, that's him. For sure.

MOTHER: That's enough for now, Dora. In fact, it's *already* too much.

DORA: Insulting—you're insulting! I didn't come to be insulted. I'm leaving.

MOTHER: Goodbye

(*Dora starts for the door. Mother doesn't move. Dora halts*)

DORA: All right, I *won't* leave. I'm here to celebrate my grandson's birthday and that's what I'm going to do. I should die on this spot if I don't. (*Returns to carriage*) Who would have thought at two-and-a-half a child would be so big, so smart?

MOTHER: Ronald's a year-and-a-half old.

DORA: He's *two*-and-a-half.

MOTHER: *One*-and-a-half!

DORA: Two-and-a-half!

MOTHER: One-and-a-half and not a day more!

DORA: Two-and-a-half and not a day less!

MOTHER: Sit down and behave yourself!

DORA: I'll do what my little girl says because I love her . . . but not as much as I love my grandson.

(*She sits at the table. Mother moves to the stove and the electric coffee pot*)

MOTHER: I'll make some coffee.

(*Ronald motions Dora to come to him. Mother concerns herself with the coffee*)

RONALD: Grandmother, would you be so kind as to tell me my mother's real name?

DORA: Say again, darling? I didn't understand.

RONALD: What's mother's Christian name?

DORA: *Christian* name! Who's been teaching you such things? Who?

RONALD: (*Urgently*) Is it Ingrid, or maybe Ida, Sandra, Lilly . . . or Daphne?

DORA: *None* of them. Definitely not. I should know.

RONALD: Then what is it?

DORA: She's mommy, like daddy is daddy.

RONALD: But my father has a name. Harold.

DORA: Don't I know!

RONALD: I say, grandmother, won't you please help me out?

(*Mother carries the coffee to the table. Dora crosses to her*)

DORA: You've got to do something about the way he talks. He doesn't sound like he should.

MOTHER: How should he sound?

DORA: Like your son. Like my *grand*son.

MOTHER: (*Proudly*) Am I to be blamed if Ronald, at an early, formative age, happened to have watched a C. Aubrey Smith film festival on the Early Show. It influenced him greatly, changed his way of thinking. Especially when during the following two weeks they ran fourteen Ronald Colman films in a row.

DORA: But he's getting away from his *roots*. He should know where he comes from, what he carries along with him. If only his grandfather was alive there wouldn't be such problems. If only my little girl's father were still here. *There* was a man! He knew. He understood. Generous. A giant! (*Dora sits, starts to sob*)

MOTHER: Really, mother, I don't think there's any problem at all. Why, it's actually a blessing. Think of how it'll help him in the future. An American boy, a darling American boy who happens to talk like an English nobleman. (*To no one in particular*) It fits into my plans . . . my hopes, my dreams! He'll have *everything,* the best, whether he likes it or not. Wall-to-wall carpeting, a college education that'll teach him the value of money, stereo in each room, color TV in home and car, credit cards from only the finest stores . . . in addition to a membership in the Diners, and maybe Carte Blanche, too. That is, if he wants to travel in France. All that and much, much more. . . .

DORA: That I can understand. Who couldn't! But an accent like his is . . .

MOTHER: (*Cuts her off*) He'll be married to a nice girl. He'll be a parent. Then he'll understand and appreciate. He'll live a good productive healthy life. He'll enjoy his children and see them grow and prosper. This will give him great pleasure. Then he'll retire. In old age he'll be honored by his family. He'll have time to think a little . . . but not too much, because then . . . he'll pass away.

(Both women quietly, happily contemplate. Ronald, who has been listening, drops his toys)

DORA: But what will he do? What will he be? Where will he go?

MOTHER: He'll be a doctor or a lawyer, or maybe even, if he wants, a psychiatrist.

DORA: Not bad. Could be worse.

RONALD: But mother, I plan to be a bartender.

MOTHER & DORA: *(Simultaneously)* A bartender!

DORA: You can't be that!

MOTHER: Think of the expensive education I've given you!

RONALD: Admittedly, I haven't taken that into consideration. Well then, I think I'd enjoy being a bum.

MOTHER & DORA: *(To each other)* A bum?

DORA: His grandfather—if only he were here, there wouldn't be such craziness. He knew. A kinder, more learned man there never was—a prince. If only . . .

MOTHER: *(Interrupts)* Calm down, Dora! *(To Ronald)* But darling, you wouldn't enjoy it. It's not *right* for you!

RONALD: *(Ponders)* In that case, and this is absolutely final . . . I'll be an artist.

DORA: Still a bum!

RONALD: I'm sorry, I refuse to discuss the subject any further. My mind's quite made up.

MOTHER: Poopie, darling, what's come over you? What have you been watching on that television? Tell me, tell mother.

RONALD: Mother, those odious endearments—they simply must go. My name is *Ronald* and I'd appreciate it if you addressed me that way.

MOTHER: *(Hard)* I said tell me!

RONALD: I've rather taken a fancy to those late evening interview programs.

DORA: See, that's what you get for letting him stay up so late. A modern mother!

MOTHER: And what have they got to do with what I want for you?

RONALD: To be quite frank, mother, the most interesting people seem to be bartenders and bums, and sometimes even artists. Certainly, they're more interesting than doctors and lawyers and psychiatrists . . . at least on the shows I've observed. Then again, my father's a lawyer, isn't he?

MOTHER: (*Slight pause*) Your father is a lawyer, yes . . . though not as good a one as you'll be . . . if you're not a doctor or psychiatrist.

RONALD: May I please have a slice of pie?

MOTHER: Not until our guest arrives.

DORA: I'm *not* a guest? Let him eat.

MOTHER: Mother, please!

DORA: You want to starve him? Maybe that's why he's like he is. You don't feed him. Stingy! You were *always* stingy! Take after your *father!* Rotten like him. (*Starts for the pie*)

MOTHER: Cut that pie and I'll cut your allowance!

DORA: (*Halts*) Cheap! Cheap! Cheap!

MOTHER: Now, let's have our coffee. When Sylvia comes we'll *all* celebrate Ronnie's birthday . . .

(*The two women sit*)

DORA: I'll bake a cake for Ronnie. (*To Ronald*) He likes the way I bake, doesn't he? (*Dora rises and starts for the stove*)

RONALD: Couldn't I simply have a piece of the pie that's already baked and ready to eat?

MOTHER: Dora! In this apartment *I* bake all cakes and pies.

DORA: It wouldn't hurt anyone. A nice little fruit cake . . . or better yet, a lemon meringue pie.

MOTHER: No!

DORA: A Danish ring then? (*Mother nods "no"*) A few cookies?

MOTHER: Nothing. Not a crumb. (*She finishes her coffee, rises*) More coffee?

DORA: No.

MOTHER: Maybe some tea?

DORA: No!

MOTHER: Apple juice? (*Dora shakes her head "no"*) Apricot juice? (*The answer is "no" and remains so throughout*) Tomato juice? Grapefruit juice? Non-fat milk? Hawaiian punch? (*Desperately*) Tangerine extract? Cucumber juice? Goat's milk? Papaya juice? (*Slight pause*) Straight poison!

DORA: You couldn't get me to have something if you busted!

(*The blue phone flashes and rings*)

MOTHER: Oh, how nice! My blue house phone is ringing. (*She rushes over and answers it*) Hello. Yes . . . Oh, then I'll come right down for it. (*Hangs up; to Dora, excitedly*) The doorman's got a package for Ronnie! The United Parcel man refuses to bring it up. (*As she goes*) I wonder who it's from?

(*Mother exits. Dora moves to Ronald*)

DORA: Tell the truth. She doesn't feed you, eh?

RONALD: Who is she?

DORA: My little girl, your mommy. Admit, admit she doesn't feed you!

RONALD: (*Slight pause*) I wish I could. I'd like to say she doesn't, but that would be patently untrue. Essentially though, it's a question of interpretation. One couldn't say that she, my mother, doesn't take care of my daily requirements. I do get sufficient nourishment. However, as far as *pleasurable* eating is concerned . . . well, that's another matter entirely.

DORA: I knew! I knew!

RONALD: Personally, I don't consider formula, ground spinach, tepid water mixed with sugar, milk-soaked sausage meat, pickled apple sauce, and all the rest as anything to stir one's imagination . . . or excite one's taste buds.

DORA: Wait! For you I'll cook. I'll bake. *Real* food. You'll see.

RONALD: I'd feel considerably better, grandmother, if more attention were paid to what I'd *like* to eat, and less to what the doctor, and all those books mother reads, claims I should be eating.

DORA: I'll bake a big cake with walnuts, and raisins, and pecans, and chestnuts. Also lemon icing with chocolate fudge and plenty of sweets. The best! (*She starts for the cupboard*)

RONALD: No, grandmother . . . please. I didn't mean to mislead you. It's not sweets I'm talking about. I was referring to my daily diet. To breakfast, lunch and dinner. Something simple and tasty, that's all I want. All I need. All I ask.

(*Dora nods, continues going through bins*)

DORA: Maybe she's got a few chocolate covered marshmallows . . . or some cashew nuts.

RONALD: For now, grandmother, the pie will do.

DORA: (*Slight pause*) I'd like . . . but what can I do? My allowance . . . (*Starts to sob*)

RONALD: Don't cry, grandmother. I understand. It's perfectly all right.

(*Dora brightens, attacks the cupboard with renewed energy. Mother returns, carrying a large package*)

MOTHER: I said *no* cooking! (*Dora stops. Mother turns to Ronald*) A present. May I open it?

RONALD: No. . .

(*Mother crosses to the table and violently pulls apart the wrapping paper. Finally, she pulls out a small battery operated phonograph and a record*)

MOTHER: A record player! (*She opens enclosed card, smiles, turns to Dora, who blushes*) But you shouldn't have. You're too kind. (*Hard*) What does he need a record player for? He's already got his own television set.

DORA: For his birthday! The record . . . the record! Pull it out. See! Look! Hear!

MOTHER: (*Pulls the record from the unmarked slip cover, reads*) "Melodies from the Old Country." (*Rummages through the remains of the box*) Nothing for me? (*Dora nods "no"*) Not even the smallest trinket? (*Dora nods "no"*) Selfish, selfish!

DORA: (*Excitedly*) Play the record. Let Ronnie hear!

(*Mother switches on the phonograph. They listen. It is an old scratchy recording. The voice of the singer is that of an old woman who hums a melancholy Yiddish song. As the singing continues, Dora starts a little dance. Mother watches with evident disapproval. Dora halts beside the phonograph*)

DORA: Listen to what else!

(*She moves the arm to another cut. The voices of two young girls bounce into a spirited Yiddish song. Dora dances over to Ronald, does a few steps for him. Suddenly, Mother pulls the needle from the record*)

MOTHER: Enough is enough!

DORA: But from the old country. It took pain and trouble to find such a record. It'll help him know, remember . . .

MOTHER: How can he remember! He's only just been born. He's a baby. An *American* baby.

DORA: I didn't mean that way. It'll help him know what he is, give him a little . . . a little heart.

MOTHER: Ronald will have the best in music as well as in life. I've already ordered, for his birthday, a special five-record set of Beethoven's nine symphonies in full-dimensional sound . . . with an explanatory booklet, and a full color photograph of the conductor, as well as a small plaster bust of Beethoven himself.

DORA: What's Beethoven got to do with the old country?

MOTHER: Now is not the right time for that record! Later on, after Ronald's been properly educated and molded, I'll let him listen to *your* record. . . . He'll be able to properly enjoy it then, and his memories of you.

DORA: She's crazy . . . from what or where I don't know!

MOTHER: You don't really think I'm going to let you destroy what his bearing, his accent will do for him? Compromise the head start he already has?

DORA: (*To Ronald*) Didn't you like? *A little* maybe?

RONALD: Actually, I found the rhythm and lilt of it quite pleasing. (*To Mother*) I'd enjoy hearing it again, if you wouldn't mind.

(*Dora moves toward her record, but before she can reach it, Mother slams the machine shut*)

MOTHER: Sit down! Have some tea. (*Dora sits*) Would you prefer Jasmine or Darjeeling?

DORA: You know what I think of your baking—well, the same I think of your tea.

MOTHER: You drank my coffee.

DORA: Coffee anyone can make. But tea—tea isn't so easy. Tea takes heart.

MOTHER: (*Slight pause*) I wonder where Auntie Sylvia is?

DORA: Let me bake, let me clean—do *something!*

MOTHER: (*Pause*) I will give you something to do.

DORA: What? Tell me!

MOTHER: In the living room, in the bedroom, in the study, and in the bathroom, too, are many matchboxes, all made in Japan, and each a different color. Now, in each of these boxes are small wooden match sticks. That is, there are supposed to be small wooden match sticks in each of the boxes. However, many of the boxes are empty . . . though not all. (*Moves to a bin and takes down a large box*) I'm going to give you this large box of refills. I'd like you to go into the living room, the bedroom, the study, and the bathroom, too . . . and in each room refill the empty match boxes. (*Slight pause*) Will you do it?

DORA: It's something. (*Dora rises. Ronald watches closely*)

MOTHER: I'm not finished yet! (*Dora sits again*) In all these rooms, as I said before, there are many match boxes, each a different color. Now this refill box contains variously colored match sticks—no, that's not exactly true. All the match sticks are the same color, it's the sulphurized tips that are either green, yellow, red or blue. . .

DORA: So?

MOTHER: . . . What you must do is to make sure never to match the color of a box to the color of a tip. Never a blue tip in a blue box. Understand?

DORA: Who wouldn't?

MOTHER: But a green tip in a blue box . . . that's the way it should be. Can you do it?

DORA: I can't bake?

MOTHER: Here are the refills.

(*Dora rises, takes the box, goes to Ronald*)

DORA: (*Indicating phonograph*) It's a nice present, isn't it?

RONALD: It's lovely. Thank you.

DORA: We'll listen to it, don't worry. I'll make sure. Meanwhile, I'll fill up the boxes . . .

RONALD: Please don't work too hard, grandmother.

DORA: When all your life you've been a slave, you don't mind a little extra work.

RONALD: Take care, grandmamma.

DORA: (*Aroused*) Call me by my name! I'm Dora, your mother's mother. (*Calms*) Dora is best, grandmother I don't mind, but, *never,* please, *grandmamma.* The record . . . if we play the record enough . . . you'll understand. (*She starts for the door*)

MOTHER: Remember, never a red tip in a red box!

(*Dora silently exits. Mother goes to the phonograph, opens the machine, lifts the record, and is about to break it*)

RONALD: Don't do that!

MOTHER: (*Turns, sharply*) Do what?

RONALD: Smash grandmother's record.

MOTHER: I have every right! How could you know the childhood I suffered, sweated through? I've given you everything —everything! You could never understand. If only she would have been like that to me . . . It was always the same. (*Little girl's voice*) "Mamma, let me help you. Teach me to bake a cake." And always the answer was, "Later, when you're a big girl." Always later! Days, weeks, years went by and still no cakes, no pies, no cookies . . . nothing. So I'd go out and visit my friends, but they didn't have time for me either. Their mothers had them baking and sewing and cooking and cleaning. Then, one day . . . finally, I met your father. He bought me presents. Your father's always been good at presents. (*Slight pause*) At first they were such lovely little things, but after a while they got bigger, and bigger, and bigger . . . until I couldn't even fit into my own room anymore. In fact, they clogged the entire house from floor to ceiling. Mamma and papa decided it would be best if I moved out. (*Slight pause*) That day, the day I had to move . . . mamma let me bake a pound cake. And the day after that, I married Harold. (*Slight pause*) And I'll kill anyone who'd make you go through that! You're my little boy. My little Ronald. For you, everything will be smooth, clear, quiet, gentle and nice. (*She grips the record as if to break it*)

RONALD: Please, mother! If, as you say, you want it to be quiet and gentle and nice for me you wouldn't want to do anything as violent as smash that record. Particularly a record that doesn't belong to you.

MOTHER: (*Slight pause*) When my little boy's right, he's right. I will control myself. I will not be hotheaded or mean. Today is your birthday. I am your mother and quite a good one at that. (*Puts record back on the phonograph*) There!

RONALD: That's a good sport.

MOTHER: I'll put the pie in the refrigerator. Since it's no longer hot we might as well eat it nice and cold. Cold pies are always so good. The best, I think. (She puts pie in the refriger *ator. The blue phone flashes and rings. She hastens to it*) Yes? (*To Ronald*) Another package! Oh, this is such a good day. (*Into phone*) Will the man bring it up? Fine. Thank you. (*She hangs up*)

RONALD: Mother, may I have a drink of water?

MOTHER: Now do you want to ruin your appetite? Wait, soon Auntie Sylvia will come. Then you'll have the pie. (*Dora returns, puts refill box away*) Finished already?

DORA: It wasn't much, but it's done.

MOTHER: I give her something to do, and still she's not satisfied! When will it end? Will this selfishness ever stop? (*Dora sits, starts to sob. Mother glances toward Ronald, who is watching, then goes to Dora*) All right . . . I didn't mean that. I'm a good girl. Would you like something *else* to do? (*Slight pause*) In the bedroom, the bathroom, in fact in all the rooms in this apartment, except the kitchen, are mirrors of various sizes and shapes. Small ones, large ones, rectangular ones, oval ones, and so on. Each of these mirrors is crystal clear. (*Proudly*) I cleaned them only yesterday! But last night . . . last night I noticed they were maybe . . . too clear. I want you to leave the apartment, go into the hallway corridor, find the incinerator room, scrape up as much grime as you can, come back and spread it on all the mirrors. But—listen closely! The end result of all this must not be to make the mirrors dirty. No, the object is simply to make the mirrors less clean than they actually are. Can you do it? Will you try?

DORA: Only if you let me bake something later.

MOTHER: I can't promise, but I will think it over.

DORA: Fine, that's all I ask. I'm not greedy. No one could say that.

(*The doorbell chimes*)

MOTHER: The package! (*She dashes out of the kitchen*)

RONALD: Grandmother! Why not simply bake a cake, if that's what you want to do?

DORA: Maybe, a long time ago, I could have, when I felt like. For a little while, I . . . I . . .

RONALD: But why? I'm only a baby. In my case there are certain limitations. But you . . .

DORA: (*Interrupts*) No, I can't. I can't . . .

(*Mother returns with a big box as well as a big smile. She puts it on the table and starts to unwrap it.*)

MOTHER: The Beethoven set. (*Pulls a small plaster bust of Beethoven from the box, goes to Ronald*) For you darling. (*He inspects the bust*) Happy birthday! (*Ronald, in the course of inspecting the statue, roughs it up. Mother pulls it quickly away*) We don't want to break it, do we?

RONALD: Can't I hold it?

MOTHER: It's better *I* hold it. Then it'll be around when you're older, which will be very soon, and can appreciate and enjoy it in the proper way. (*To Dora*) Don't you have a job to do, mother? (*Dora exits. Mother returns to the table with the plaster bust*) Now you'll hear some *real* music. (*Pulls out a cellophane wrapped boxed record set, rips off the cellophane, opens the box and reads the instructions*) "In ordering this superb set of records you have demonstrated your superior taste, while at the same time insuring you and yours leisure hours that are both relaxing and productive. These well-spent hours, numberless because each record can be played an infinite amount of times, will make you one of the cultural leaders of your community. Start by selecting any one of the five records, i.e. nine symphonies. You are now ready to experience a cultural experience of the first magnitude. If the particular record, i.e. symphony, you've chosen displeases you, that is, if it makes you feel gloomy or depressed, take it off and put on another record, i.e. symphony, until you find the record, i.e. symphony, that pleases you most. Remember, there are nine symphonies in all and that Beethoven—to rightfully use a word that in our age has been wantonly abused—is a genuine genius. His is a name to remember. We wish you and yours lots of good listening. Thank you. *Note:* Though the symphonies are numbered from one to nine there is absolutely no need to play them in that order. (*She puts down the instructions, turns to Ronald*) What number would you like?

RONALD: (*Indicating bust*) I'd like to have that again, please.

MOTHER: All right, darling.

(*She brings it to him, returns to table, removes "Melodies from the Old Country" from the record player, pulls out a record from the set and puts it on. It is the second movement of the third—Eroica—symphony. Ronald listens with interest. The music depresses Mother. She takes it off*)

MOTHER: It's nice . . . no one could say a word against it. But so depressing. Let's try another one. (*Puts on a particularly bouncy section of the 7th symphony*) That's more like it. (*The doorbell chimes*) Oh, there's Auntie Sylvia! (*She hastens out and a moment or two later returns with Sylvia, a woman in her early forties, dressed in black*)

MOTHER: And this is the kitchen. Pretty, isn't it? (*Sylvia nods*)

SYLVIA: And that's little Ronald! I haven't seen him since you moved. I wonder if he remembers me? (*As she heads for the carriage, Mother turns off the music*) Remember me? Remember Auntie Sylvia? (*He nods*) Say hello. (*Ronald looks to his Mother: she motions "go ahead"*)

RONALD: (*Wearily*) Hello.

SYLVIA: (*To Mother*) Doesn't it touch a mother's heart?

MOTHER: It's little Ronnie's birthday.

SYLVIA: I know.

MOTHER: He's received some beautiful presents.

SYLVIA: Isn't that nice.

MOTHER: It's a greater joy to give than to receive.

SYLVIA: That's what they say.

MOTHER: (*Slight pause*) Why so late?

SYLVIA: A funeral.

MOTHER: Oh . . .

SYLVIA: I didn't want to go, but I had to. Friends of the family. Anyway, I sort of enjoyed it.

MOTHER: You go to a lot of funerals.

SYLVIA: Enough.

MOTHER: It must be tiring.

SYLVIA: No, not really. If, on occasion it is, I recover.

MOTHER: That's good. (*Pause*) Well, now we can have that birthday pie. Everyone's here. (*Calling*) Mother! Mother!

SYLVIA: (*To Ronald*) Aren't you happy to see Auntie Sylvia again?

RONALD: I'm delighted to see you again, Sylvia. But you're not my aunt.

SYLVIA: Little one, how can you say a thing like that?

RONALD: Quite simple . . . you're mother's friend. You lived next door to us in our old apartment. You were a neighbor and are a friend, but never my aunt.

MOTHER: Now Ronald, don't be rude. Take after your mother. Be kind. Sylvia is Aunt Sylvia.

RONALD: Mother, if Sylvia is indeed my aunt, then you can't possibly be my mother. You're not related to her. I know that. I've heard daddy talk about her. He always calls her "that friend of yours" . . . So please stop trying to confuse me, especially on my birthday.

SYLVIA: Very bright for his age.

MOTHER: Yes.

SYLVIA: Just how old is he?

MOTHER: Ronald's a year-and-a-half old today.

SYLVIA: Funny, I thought he was closer to three.

MOTHER: Oh no, never! He's only a baby.

(*Dora enters*)

DORA: Hello, Sylvia!

SYLVIA: How are you, Dora?

DORA: As good as can be expected. More than that no one can ask. (*Sylvia and Dora kiss*)

SYLVIA: It's been a long time. When was it last?

DORA: At Sadie's. After Samuel's funeral.

SYLVIA: A terrible tragedy. Ripped from life in the prime of his time.

MOTHER: But his family was well taken care of.

DORA: True. No one can deny.

SYLVIA: A good man, God rest his soul. And such a well-done funeral. The service was extraordinary. No fluff, everything as it should be. No waste. Very impressive.

MOTHER: Tasteful.

DORA: What are we talking about? It's my grandson's birthday.

(*Mother motions the other two to her, whispers to them. All three go to Ronald and start to sing:*)

MOTHER, DORA, SYLVIA:

"Happy birthday to you, Happy birthday to you, Happy birthday, dear Ronald, Happy birthday to you."

DORA: Again!

MOTHER, DORA, SYLVIA:

"Happy birthday to you, Happy birthday to you, Happy birthday, dear Ronald, Happy birthday to you."

MOTHER: (*To Ronald; happily*) Now we're going to have that birthday pie! (*Mother goes to the refrigerator. The other two seat themselves*)

SYLVIA: Pie! Isn't that inventive. Anyone else would have made a cake, with candles and all. . . . Pie in the refrigerator? Only barbarians eat it that way!

MOTHER: I don't see what's to get upset about. I'll just put the pie in my sparkling new thirty-inch eye-level gas range which features a four-hour signal clock, top burner heat control, oven rotisserie, oven window with light, high-low broiler in addition to many other features—all unavailable in my *old* apartment. (*Ronald starts to sob softly. Mother puts pie on sink, goes to him*) I know, baby. In a few minutes though it'll be so good, so nice and warm. You'll enjoy it more than ever. I promise. Warm pie is best.

(*Mother puts pie in the oven, starts to click dials. Sylvia goes to Ronald*)

SYLVIA: Auntie Sylvia didn't mean to upset her favorite little boy. You're not mad at her, are you?

RONALD: I'm sorry. Forgive me.

SYLVIA: You *will* call me Auntie Sylvia, won't you?

RONALD: I will . . . if you tell me my mother's real name.

SYLVIA: Real name?

RONALD: Her Christian name.

SYLVIA: You mean that woman over there? (*He nods*) Why, that's your mother. Who else could it be?

RONALD: Please . . . all I want to know is her name.

SYLVIA: Why, I've known that woman for years. She's your mother. She's the woman who wears gray dresses in the summer, yellow suits in the winter, orange coats in the fall and green smocks in the spring. (*Lowering her voice*) Ronald, you are feeling well? You're not sick, I hope. It would be a shame to be sick on your own birthday.

(*Dora crosses to Mother*)

MOTHER: Only *she* would want *hot* pie!

DORA: A cake . . . a cake would settle everything.

MOTHER: Maybe so, but it's too late.

DORA: How long would it take? No time. Let me bake!

MOTHER: Just because I've been so busy, don't think I've forgotten the matchsticks and mirrors. You did what I asked?

DORA: Check for yourself.

MOTHER: I will, later.

SYLVIA: (*Examining the phonograph*) Oh, lovely! Why don't we have some music?

MOTHER: It's Dora's birthday gift to Ronald.

DORA: It's European. Made in France. Imported.

MOTHER: And these records, all nine Beethoven symphonies . . . they're *my* birthday present to Ronald.

SYLVIA: He's such a lucky little boy.

MOTHER: That he is.

DORA: (*Picks up her record*) This I also gave.

SYLVIA: (*Inspecting the record*) How long since I heard music like this? Years!

DORA: People don't care anymore.

SYLVIA: Years ago, at a wedding, there was always music like this. It was good heartwarming music. People would cry. On occasion, I did, too.

DORA: True. Such joy!

MOTHER: They still play "The Anniversary Song."

SYLVIA: (*Ignoring her*) Today, at weddings, you don't have music like this. Sure, they got lots of noise, but nothing like this. Nothing as touching, as intimate, as piercing. (*To Dora*) You know what I mean? And I go to a *lot* of weddings. Believe me, I know.

MOTHER: Sylvia, I've never asked because it's always seemed . . . I always thought I might be out of place. But anyway, why spend so much time at weddings and funerals?

SYLVIA: I know a lot of people.

DORA: Why shouldn't she! What else is there? Before and between is heartache.

MOTHER: (*To Sylvia*) Would you like to hear one of Beethoven's symphonies? Any one. There are nine, you know.

SYLVIA: Thank you, no.

DORA: She wants "Melodies from the Old Country."

SYLVIA: No, Dora, I suddenly don't feel like music. (*To Mother*) What I would like is the pie.

MOTHER: I can't overheat the oven or it'll get ruined. Have patience. It'll be ready soon.

RONALD: (*Sits up suddenly*) Mommy, mommy! What's your name? Tell me! Please, tell me?

(*Mother rushes to him, followed by Sylvia. Dora uses the occasion to furtively slip over to the oven and—unobserved—turns the heat up all the way*)

MOTHER: What's wrong, darling? Is my little boy upset? (*Ronald sobs steadily*)

SYLVIA: He looks feverish. (*Touches his forehead*) I'd look into it, if I were his mother.

(*Dora slips back to the group*)

RONALD: How long will I have to *wait,* mommy?

MOTHER: (*To Sylvia*) You think he's sick?

RONALD: (*Desperately*) Your name, mommy—your *name!*

MOTHER: You know, he almost always calls me mother. Sometimes, but not often, mummy. But *mom*my, never. It's so . . . you know. I better take his temperature. (*To Dora*) The thermometer, please. It's in the small bathroom closet behind the large mirror. (*Dora exits*)

RONALD: (*Fearfully*) Ther-mom . . . eter!

MOTHER: Now, there's nothing to be scared about.

RONALD: Please, all I want is your name, and after that, a small piece of my birthday pie.

SYLVIA: I'd like some, too.

MOTHER: Soon. Soon everyone will have what they want. (*Dora returns with the thermometer and hands it to Mother*)

RONALD: It's important. It's urgent! Answer me—*please!* What's your name?

MOTHER: (*Embarrassed*) Ronald . . . Auntie Sylvia is here. Grandmother is here . . . and I'm here, too! You're in the presence of company, of invited guests. How can you behave like this?

SYLVIA: You'd better take his temperature. He's sick, poor dear.

(*Mother unscrews the thermometer, looks to the other two women. Pause*)

MOTHER: Turn over, dear. (*All three women surround the carriage*)

RONALD: Please . . . (*The women turn him over. Mother inserts the rectal thermometer*)

MOTHER: (*To Sylvia*) I'm sorry. I'm embarrassed. I don't know what's gotten into him. He's never acted like this before.

DORA: Don't lie.

MOTHER: Oh well, once or twice maybe, but only recently. Then again, he *is* growing older, starting to formulate things for himself. Maybe it's only natural. But I won't let him get away with it! He's really such a good boy.

DORA: My grandson is a darling boy. No one could say different.

SYLVIA: You know, in a way, Ronald reminds me of my older sister's boy, Sidney.

MOTHER: I remember your mentioning him once.

SYLVIA: I haven't seen her in years. She moved away, quite suddenly. We haven't kept in touch. It's sad the way families drift apart. But time and circumstances are to blame, I guess.

DORA: It's not a good thing. Families should stay together.

SYLVIA: My sister and her husband had a habit of referring to their child, to their little boy, to Sidney, as Young Sidney. They liked to call him that. Yes, they called him that all the time.

DORA: So?

SYLVIA: Well, Sidney like Ronald, talked at a very early age. He was a bright child. Quite intelligent and very sensitive. In fact, everyone who met Young Sidney was awed by him . . . and I must say that in our family—at least as far as I know—there never had been one like him. We all enjoyed him so much . . . his warmth, his intelligence, his . . . niceness. I spent a lot of time at my sister's . . . maybe too much. I don't think he liked being surrounded by all of us. In a way, I guess it was unfair. I always felt that Sidney, though he was too much of a lovely little gentleman to say anything, felt that we . . . that we cramped him. Sometimes I even thought, looking at him there in his little crib, that he was suffocating. But he was a healthy baby—the family doctor said one of the healthiest he had ever known—so there was no reason, I knew, to think that way. (*Slight pause*) But though Sidney was an exemplary baby, he did have a problem . . .

MOTHER: What?

DORA: Tell us?

SYLVIA: He would ask the most difficult questions . . . all the time. There was no stopping him. It grew to be a problem. My sister and her husband were hardly able to get a decent night's sleep. It could happen anytime. At midnight, at two-thirty in the morning, at five a.m. And during the day, well, during the day—mind you, only after a certain point had been reached—it hardly stopped. Questions, questions and more questions. (*Directly to Mother and Dora*) Who could answer such questions? "Mother, what's this and why is that?" And "Mother, how come?" And "Why not?" And "Must you?" Occasionally, even things like, "Have you really thought it over?" Or, "Is there another, better way to do it?" Well . . . when a baby asks questions like that, what's a mother and father to do? I mean, it's a bit too much. Don't you think?

DORA: Absolutely.

MOTHER: Without a doubt.

SYLVIA: I'm glad you agree because something had to be done . . . and was done. Sidney was upsetting everyone. Things just couldn't go on that way. No ma'am, not on your life! It would never have ended—the "Why is that?" . . . "What's this?" and "How come?", would've gone on and on and on. So, instead of having to think out the answers—you'll admit, that's the part that can be fatiguing, so much work—my sister and her husband . . . guess what they did? Go ahead, guess! (*Pause*) They worked out a system. A simple system. Afterwards we all laughed at how simple it was. But simple doesn't mean it wasn't effective. Suppose Sidney asked his father, "Why is it this way?" . . . *it* being whatever-have-you. Well, the simple answer was, "That is this way because it's this way." (*Slight pause*) Or say Sidney asked, "Why is that?" The answer, using the system, was a simple "This is that way because it's that way and for no other reason whatsoever." You can see that with their system even the most difficult questions were easy to answer. And the best part— once you memorized the few answers, they covered *all* the questions. Every one of them! At least the ones Sidney was asking at the time.

MOTHER: Did the system work?

SYLVIA: Didn't I just say so?

MOTHER: He didn't ask any more questions . . . especially difficult ones?

SYLVIA: It took a little time. Miracles don't happen overnight. But after awhile he stopped asking the difficult ones . . . and after that, he hardly ever asked any questions at all.

MOTHER: Have you seen him . . . Sidney, recently?

SYLVIA: (*Sits*) No.

MOTHER: Oh . . .

SYLVIA: (*Uncomfortably*) My sister moved away. I told you that!

MOTHER: Quite suddenly?

SYLVIA: Yes . . . suddenly.

(*The carriage starts to shake gently. Dora rushes to it*)

DORA: (*To Ronald*) Stop! Don't touch. Leave in.

MOTHER: (*Checks watch*) It's time to take out. (*She goes to the carriage, pulls the thermometer out*) Why, the dear doesn't have any temperature at all. (*Turns him over, smiles*) My boy is a healthy boy. Thank God! (*Ronald sits up, looks at all of them as if sizing them up*)

SYLVIA: (*Pause*) What's behind the drapes?

MOTHER: Our terrace. It has a beautiful view. Quite picturesque.

SYLVIA: (*Rises*) May I see it?

MOTHER: Of course.

SYLVIA: Why cover the view if it's so beautiful?

MOTHER: The sun was hurting Ronald's eyes. Anyway, it's so filthy outside. (*She draws the curtains*) We hardly ever use the terrace. Air pollution, dust, slime, dirt, disease . . . it's so uninviting. Actually, we moved in during the winter and that's about the only time we've been able to use it. (*She pushes open the sliding door*)

SYLVIA: During the winter? Outside . . . in the cold?

MOTHER: Yes. It's the cleanest, safest time. Harold builds a nice little fire in our portable fireplace. We bundle up real snug and warm, and then we have a good steak dinner and a beautiful view. One evening it even snowed during the salad.

SYLVIA: I see.

MOTHER: I wish we could use it more often. Want to step out and take a look?

(*The two step out onto the terrace. Dora rocks the carriage, humming a melancholy Yiddish song. After a moment or two, Mother and Sylvia come back in without closing the terrace door*)

SYLVIA: It certainly is an *interesting* view.

MOTHER: Didn't I tell you? Have you ever known me to lie? This is a very fine luxury apartment building, not like where we lived before. And don't think every apartment—even in this building—has a three-sided terrace. Some only have two views. We have three. We overlook things.

DORA: (*To Sylvia*) It's a sight to look out onto, isn't it?

SYLVIA: Yes . . . especially the side that faces the city dumps. And, of course, there's the other side, too. The one that faces, forgive me . . . overlooks the polluted river. (*To Mother*) We never had anything like that . . .

DORA: Before, where you two used to live, you had a beautiful side. Remember, the one that faced the Gardens of Moses . . . where entire families are buried together, as is right and proper? In life divided, in death united.

MOTHER: (*Pause*) It's time my baby had his birthday pie . . . which he already would have had, had Sylvia been generous enough to eat it cold. (*She goes to oven. Ronald sits up*) Who did it! *Who?* (*She turns off oven, opens it. Out comes smoke and the burnt pie*)

DORA: (*To Sylvia*) I . . . have . . . to finish . . . some work. (*Starts out*)

MOTHER: You! How dare you! (*Starts to cry*) How could you? My little boy's birthday pie. How could you!

(*Dora starts to sob*)

DORA: (*To Ronald*) I'm sorry . . . I'm sorry! I didn't think. (*She tries to embrace Ronald; he pulls away*) What am I going to do? Forgive me, darling. Forgive me. (*To Mother*) It's my fault. I'm sorry. Let me bake a cake. I'll do it quick. He'll have a cake that will make the pie look like nothing.

MOTHER: *Look* like nothing—it *is* nothing!

(*Dora, nervous and shaken, rushes to the cupboard containing the baking equipment*)

MOTHER: Stop that!

DORA: Please! Please. . .

MOTHER: Put your coat on, take the elevator down, walk to the corner bakery, and buy a cake.

DORA: Buy?!

MOTHER: (*Spells*) B-U-Y. Do what I tell you! Do it now! (*Dora, in defeat, starts to put back the pots and pans. Ronald watches*)

SYLVIA: Maybe . . . while we're waiting, you can show me the rest of the apartment.

MOTHER: Come. (*They start toward the door. Mother stops, turns to Dora*) Well?

DORA: (*Sits*) Let me rest a second.

MOTHER: Have the cake here in ten minutes! And close the terrace door before you leave.

(*Mother and Sylvia exit. Dora sits for a few moments, her strength ebbing back. She stands, notices the small plaster bust of Beethoven, grabs it and hurls it to the floor: it smashes to bits. Ronald watches without saying a word. Dora realizes she's destroyed something that belongs to her grandson. She looks at him guiltily, as if to say "I'm sorry," but is unable to utter those words. She starts to leave*)

RONALD: (*Calling*) Grandmother! Before you go, push me out onto the terrace, please.

DORA: But your mother wouldn't . . . (*She glances at the broken statue, then looks at Ronald*) Yes, darling. Yes.

RONALD: Will you buy a nice cake?

DORA: The best one. The best. Don't worry.

RONALD: With lots of icing and chocolate . . . and everything?

DORA: Everything!

(*She wheels the carriage onto the terrace. Eventually, she comes back into the kitchen, waves to Ronald*)

DORA: Enjoy. I'll be back soon.

(*She exits. Silence. From the terrace: sound of the carriage jerking forward, followed by a banging sound, then a heavy thud. A long silence. Mother and Sylvia enter*)

SYLVIA: Well, it's big. No one can deny that.

MOTHER: I told you so.

SYLVIA: You certainly did.

MOTHER: I hope she buys a decent cake. (*Notices that the carriage is no longer in the room*) Where's Ronald? Where's the carriage? (*Spots the open terrace door*) I told her to close that door. (*Notices the broken statue, glances from it to where Ronald used to be, to the open door*) Where's my baby! Where is he! *Where!*

(*She rushes onto the terrace, screams. Sylvia moves to the door, stands tight, watches. Mother is heard sobbing. Sylvia cups her hand over her mouth, turns and slowly drags herself to the table. She sits, lowers her veil, puts her head into her hands and starts to gently rock and sob*)

Curtain

John Mortimer

DESMOND

John Mortimer

One of Britain's leading contemporary writers, John Mortimer has divided his professional career into four equally successful component parts: dramatist, novelist, scenarist, and barrister. The son of a barrister, he was born in Hampstead, London, in 1923, and was educated at Harrow and Brasenose College, Oxford. While working at the bar he wrote a number of novels and a play for radio, *The Dock Brief* (1957), which won for him the Prix Italia and brought him to the theatre when, in the following year, it opened on a double bill with his domestic comedy, *What Shall We Tell Caroline?* at the Lyric Theatre, Hammersmith, and later transferred to the Garrick on the West End. (The 1957–58 London season was a notable one for having introduced six important new dramatists to the theatre: Harold Pinter, Robert Bolt, N. F. Simpson, Ann Jellicoe, William Golding and Mr. Mortimer.)

The Dock Brief, a study of the underside of the law, went on to international success and was performed in dozens of countries, including the United States (on stage and television), Italy, France, Yugoslavia, Germany, Poland, Sweden, Spain and Belgium. As the author himself has noted, *"The Dock Brief* was first written as a play for sound radio. It was later performed on television, then in the theatre and was made into a film. It has not been danced or done on ice. It has, I think, been performed in most countries of the world and I last heard of it being done by two men under life sentence in San Quentin jail in America. I don't know why it has met with such a universal response, unless it expresses some feeling deep in everyone. I believe that we all hold the law in some contempt, and realize, in our hearts, that barristers, judges, and all the elaborate pageantry of the law, are dependent on the hardworking criminal for their existence. In a sense, the lawyers are the criminal's servants. . . . As King Lear said, 'Handy-dandy, which is the Justice, which the thief?' That is the feeling I hope this short play releases."

The Dock Brief was followed by a full-length work, *The Wrong Side of the Park* (Cambridge Theatre, 1960) and in 1961, the author returned to the short play form with *Lunch Hour* in the triple bill, *Three,* that also included plays by Harold

Pinter and N. F. Simpson. The production originated at the Arts Theatre and subsequently moved to the West End with a cast headed by Emlyn Williams, Wendy Craig and Alison Leggatt.

In 1962, Mr. Mortimer was represented on the London stage by *Two Stars for Comfort,* and in 1966, he scored an enormous success with his adaptation of Georges Feydeau's French comedy, *A Flea in Her Ear,* mounted by Britain's National Theatre Company with Albert Finney and Geraldine McEwan at the helm of a sparkling troupe.

"Comedy," Mr. Mortimer has said, "is, to my mind, the only thing worth writing in this despairing age, providing it is comedy on the side of the lonely, the neglected and unsuccessful."

His "elegant, witty dialogue and as sharp an eye as any in the theatre for manners, morals, and pleasures of modern Britain" again were manifested in *Come As You Are!,* a quartet of short plays dealing with a common theme, extramarital relationships, and set in four different districts of London. Starring Glynis Johns and Denholm Elliott, *Come As You Are!* opened in January, 1970, at the New Theatre, ran for almost a year and presently is scheduled for Broadway presentation.

It engendered much praise from the press. In his coverage for *The Manchester Guardian,* Philip Hope-Wallace wrote, "The plays are genuinely theatrical in their trick of exciting surprise: with the wit of the dialogue and the deftly managed stroke of sentiment, they earn their time on the stage and keep us amused and involved." Herbert Kretzmer (*Daily Express*) described the plays as "not only funny, but witty and caring as well," a pronouncement echoed by the *London Evening Standard*'s Milton Shulman who concluded that "they are replete with acute comic observation and sharp, witty lines."

John Mortimer's most recent works for the theatre are: *A Voyage Around My Father* (Greenwich Theatre, 1970), a reconstruction of incidents in the author's early life and memories of his father who suddenly went blind in middle age; and a new version of Carl Zuckmayer's 1931 satire, *The Captain of*

Köpenick, created for Paul Scofield's first appearance with the National Theatre Company and opening in March, 1971.

Desmond, originally written for television and produced on the B.B.C. with Rachel Roberts as the wife of the philandering title character who never is seen, yet whose presence constantly is felt, proves anew that "bereft of his barrister wig, John Mortimer, QC, is not a man to demand serious damages for moral misdemeanor." The comedy appears in print for the first time anywhere in *The Best Short Plays 1971*

In addition to his plays, the author has written and published six novels, a book on travel, and numerous screenplays.

Characters:

EMMA GRANT

Scene:

A large dining room in a London house with a hatch through to the kitchen. Modern furniture. Slab-of-marble table. Abstract paintings. All over the place are photographs of Desmond—Desmond, perhaps thirty but looking younger and more boyish; Desmond skiing; Desmond diving; Desmond on a horse; Desmond in a white dinner jacket caught in a flash of light. Desmond on water-skis, skin-diving or just looking beautiful.

The table is laid for lunch for two. At one end, a full battery of knives and forks, decanters, glasses—at the other, a plate on which there are two biscuits and a glass full of some cloudy chemical substance. The places are laid at each end of the table so that there is a long space of cold marble between them.

Emma Grant is fussing round the room, opening cigarette boxes. She finds a cigarette, searches for a match. She is very thin and elegant and in her forties, though dressed as if she were younger. She is in an extremely nervous state. She finds a lighter. Then, picks up a card from the mantelpiece, holds it close to read it. Feels for her glasses; puts them on to read.

EMMA GRANT: "Joanna Waterhouse, 2 Appleby Court. Kensington 7568. I love you, rabbit." (*She puts down the card, goes to the phone, starts to dial, thinks better of it and puts the phone down again*) No, Miss Waterhouse, I'm not going to put you off, much as you'd be relieved to hear from me that lunch is unavoidably postponed because I've run out of courage. I mean, it's got to be *faced up to*. We've got to discuss this whole thing like a couple of civilized people . . . well, one-and-a-half civilized people. I'm not all that civilized this morning. No sleep. That's the real trouble . . . no sleep. (*She yawns*) It's all

been like a sort of dream . . . (*She moves away from the phone*)
Well, we've done quite well so far. A calm and controlled phone
call after breakfast. "Is that Miss Waterhouse? Oh, this is Emma
Grant. Desmond's wife. Yes, the one whose weekly articles are
standing in the way of his being a genius. Didn't he tell you
that? He usually does. No, I don't think we've met. In fact,
you've been rather kept from me; even to the extent of being
whisked down the fire escape when I got back early from the
paper. Desmond found that a very flattering incident. It made
him feel like Casanova's memoirs." "Look," I said, "Why don't
you come to lunch, Miss Waterhouse—I mean, if you really
want to marry my husband why don't we discuss this like two
civilized people?" And she said, "How lovely! Thanks for asking me." Such nice party manners. Now I wonder what Mrs.
Mac's dreamt up for you to eat? I mean, what would be really
suitable. (*She goes to the hatch, pulls it open and shouts through
it*) Mrs. Mac! What are we giving our little visitor to eat?
(*Without waiting for a reply, she bangs the hatch shut again and
says very angrily:*) You know what I think you need? Nursery
cooking! Builds up the puppy fat! Polishes up the little white
milk teeth! Something inoffensive. Bread and butter, macaroni
and cheese, frozen peas, tapioca in a brown overcoat and eat it
up and help the poor soldiers at the front! That's a thought, Miss
Waterhouse. When you were being made to eat up your tapioca,
I was a poor soldier at the front. A poor bloody lieutenant with
khaki bloomers and portable typewriter, sending home human
interest stories about our brave boys in battle dress. And you
ate up your tapioca pudding. Just to help me! Dear little Miss
Watermouse! Thank you so much. (*She opens the lid of a dish
and sniffs*) Steak and kidney pie! Yellow crust and thick gravy
and . . . (*She lifts up another lid*) . . . new potatoes. Butter
and parsley. (*She puts down the lid. Then, goes to the mantle-
piece, stubs out her cigarette in an ashtray; coughs*) What's for
afters? Wait and see, Miss Watermouse dear! Treacle tart with
Devonshire cream, bread and Stilton and Irish coffee. You're going to do a great job today for the poor soldiers! (*She takes a
cigarette out of the box and puts it in her mouth*) Steak and

kidney pie! You live dangerously, don't you little Miss. . . . All right! I know your name. Miss Waterhouse. Miss Joanna Waterhouse. (*She lights her cigarette*) Watermouse is what I *choose* to call you! (*A clock over the mirror chimes*) I'd better collect my thoughts. Collect my poor, bloody scattered thoughts! (*She looks at herself critically in the mirror, feels her neck, puts down her cigarette and takes off her glasses*) I bet *you* don't wear glasses. They're a sign of surrender, according to Desmond. Like gray hair and wrinkles 'round the neck and taking off your shoes in the cinema and going to bed at eight-thirty with a poached egg and *Panorama*. And neither Desmond nor I *could* surrender. Not while our war was on. (*She looks in the mirror again and straightens up. Starts to address herself in the manner of a general addressing his troops on the field of battle*) Well, this is it. I'm very much afraid that at 00.10 hours the enemy's going to hit us with all he's got, which is a nineteen-year-old blonde, with a daddy in the Stock Exchange and a frightfully sweet pony and a really super flat just off Ken. High Street in which the enemy has now established his temporary headquarters . . . (*Her voice changes, becomes serious*) Oh, it's not funny . . . it's not funny. All the same, better have a plan! (*She picks up her cigarette, goes to her place at the table, sits down, leans her elbow on the table and talks as if her guest were at the other end*) I shall say . . . I think I shall say . . . (*Serious, intense*) Dear Joanna—do you mind if I call you Miss Waterhouse? (*She smiles for a moment, then goes on seriously*) I shall talk to her seriously. I shall say . . . Seriously, Miss Waterhouse. Seriously, Joanna. Look here, love, I shall say, with all due respect . . . What the hell, I mean what the *hell* do you know about life? Shall I tell you something, darling? Let me tell you, at your sort of age I'd risen from being a cub reporter on the old Derby Echo, which I'd joined at fifteen-and-a-half, covering murders and garden parties, to be put in sole charge of the best women's page in Fleet Street, and I had the finest editor in the world die in my own divan bed in The Boltons on a night when he was meant to be in Morocco with Mister Winston Churchill, no less. Could I now tell you that I've built up a readership so world-

wide that I get approximately fifty letters a day, and am syndi-
cated in the North American continent simply because I see life
through eyes clear and disillusioned, without fear or favor . . .
that is, on any occasion when I haven't lost my damned glasses!
And may I say that I've been through four wars, not counting
marriage with Desmond, and have on my left breast the scar
caused by the fragments of a bottle of Pernod shot out of my
hands in the old Bar Neptune in Algiers! And what have *you*
been through Miss Waterhouse, dear, apart from chickenpox
and a nasty toss at the gym? So what do *you* know about *life!*
(*Pause*) And don't think *he's* averse from any of all that either,
will you? Don't think Desmond actually turns his nose up at
the free champagne, and Presidential Class Trans-Atlantic Air
Lines, or he doesn't enjoy mentioning that we were at Kensington Palace in the course of conversation. And what can *you*
offer him to take the place of all that? The Richmond Horse
Show? Miss Waterhouse. Dear, dear Miss Waterhouse—do you
happen to know what you're taking on? I mean . . . now at this
present moment he may be all, being very gentle and sweet; he
may be remembering your birthday and sending you red roses
on *my* account and bringing you back a bottle of perfume he
crept out and bought in Paris when I was in the Manager's
office, adding up the bill. But it won't last. It can't possibly last!
I shall say . . . (*Pause. She is thoughtful; becomes less angry*)
I shan't say *any* of that. Sounds revolting, my life story in the
Ladies' Home Journal as told to Joanna Watermouse. Miss
Waterhouse. Miss Waterhouse, *may* I call you Joanna? Joanna,
you look like a sensible and sensitive girl—that's how you look
to me. I mean, that's what's so very marvelous about today.
Everyone gets to know so much more so quickly. I bet nothing
shocks you, does it? Undoubtedly you've seen it all—in your
area of Surrey? Death and drugs all 'round Guildford as we
read in the papers. Nothing shocks you—not even what you
may be doing to me. I mean, you mature so young nowadays. To
be totally honest with you—I lost my virginity at the age of
twenty-three. And even then it was a kind of mistake. A man
came up to me at a dance and he said "You're Hermione, aren't

you? Come out to the Humber. I understand you do that sort of thing . . ." Well, I wasn't Hermione, and I didn't, but—can you believe it?—I didn't even have the courage to tell him, and so I went. It was appalling! I never really knew what it was like, not till I met Desmond. Honestly, I didn't ask you to lunch to get your sympathy. Nothing like that. I asked you . . . (*Pause; she frowns*) I asked you because naturally *he* wouldn't come. Oh, he'll leave all that sort of thing to you, sacking the char, ringing up the bank manager. I tell you . . . if a washer comes off the tap he'll leave home and not come back until you've had a man to fix it. So . . . this is a message for him really. Oh love, you see it's the *War!* Tell him *that's* what he's going to miss. Will you tell him that? Life's going to be very dull and un-eventful for him without it. Desmond was never much of a reporter. When I first met him he was at Queen Charlotte's Ball for the *Diary,* and he was sitting on the stairs surrounded by a lot of stupid girls like—oh not like you in the least, except they all had puppy fat and baby blue eyes, and teeth just out of braces —and he was saying, "This is the sort of occasion that keeps England great." And I was coming down the stairs with a per-fectly nice osteopath, whom I might just've well've married, come to think of it, and I happened to say, "What a bloody silly remark that was." And Desmond looked up at me and said, "Move over girls, here comes my Mother." We danced then. And arranged our future battles. Look, why don't you have a drink? (*She gets up and goes to the sideboard, pours gin from a decanter*) Why don't you have a nice, great big gin and oh . . . an enormous gin and tonic! (*When she has poured it, she looks at it*) I can't, you see. In this sort of war you've got to keep your wits about you. Besides, if I drank this it'd land me with great big impossible calories which Desmond would object to. In fact, he'd probably . . . that sounds funny, I was going to say in fact, he'd probably leave home . . . You think you know what's happening, don't you? You think he's fallen in love with you. I tell you. It's part of the campaign. It's what he enjoys. Part of the battle with me. You know how I found out, don't you? Your name and address written on his membership card to Dolly's with "I love you, rabbit" written underneath it. Well, the point is, he left it on the table by my bed. Oh, he pretended to have forgotten it. He pretended he'd made an awful mistake—but that's what you are in our lives. His secret weapon. "Rabbit!" What a thing to call anyone! "Rabbit!" We keep each other going you see, we keep each other up to the mark. If it weren't for him . . . God knows what'd happen to me. I think . . . I think I'd become old quite suddenly. I think . . . well, I'd just let myself go, wouldn't I? I'd put on calories. I'd go out to lunch and say, "Forget the cottage cheese salad—I'll have the joint and two vegs, with apple tart to follow." I'd start the day with bacon and eggs and muffins! I don't know . . . can you *still* get muffins? Desmond saved me from that. Of course he's younger than I am, and so beautiful. He keeps me up to the mark. I mean, because of him when I get back from the paper we go to all these places. Last night we went to one. (*She yawns*) The Electric Current. Psychedelic lighting and a group dressed as corpses. I'd never really know about life . . . (*She yawns again*) . . . if it weren't for Desmond. I tell you, I'd be propped up in bed with a tray full of eggs and toast, watching Robin Day on the problems of Ethiopia. (*She yawns*) I'm afraid I'm not making much sense. . . . We didn't get back till five and then he carefully dropped the information on his way to the bathroom. So we fought till nine, and then he left banging the door, and I went to the paper and rang you and ordered lunch. What I want to know is—are you strong enough for it, Miss Waterhouse? You can't relax, you see . . . you can't relax at all! (*She picks up the drink and looks at it*) "One gin," he'll tell you, "is as good as a three-course meal and if you want to go about looking like a prolapsed district nurse, don't blame me, darling." So you'll have to be careful now; I should warn you, Joanna. You'll be on guard all the time with Desmond. (*She picks up the drink and suddenly finishes it*) You'll never be able to drink things like that. (*She goes to her place and sits down disconsolately*) Swedish slimming biscuits, that's what you'll live on! A whole day's meal packed in a nourishing square inch. (*She bites*) With the flavor of medicated sawdust! And to wash it down . . . sugar-free, slimline, vitamin souped-up, health-kick barley water! We must keep ourselves beautiful for Desmond. Desmond's is a world without a stomach. . . . He's flat, of course. Flat as an ironing board! Kept like that by lifting dumbbells in the garage, and water-skiing on Ruislip reservoir and . . . oh, he's taken you, hasn't he? He took care to tell me that, just because I'm afraid of drowning and I feel ridiculous in a rubber suit. But there's more treats in store for you, Joanna. Great long workouts in private gyms with Bach on the Hi-Fi and cups of coffee and gray-haired inquisitors tanned from the sunray lamp, saying, "Only another quarter-of-an-hour on the rack for you, Mrs. Grant. We don't want to waste your fifty-guinea subscription, do we?" You know what they're trying to stamp out in that little torture chamber, don't you? The heresy we might any of us grow old! (*She pours herself another drink and knocks it back*) That was the calorie equivalent of three enormous Christmas dinners! (*She goes back to the mantelpiece and picks up her glasses and puts them on. She goes back to the dishes on the heater, lifts the lid off the steak and kidney pie and sniffs*) I'd forgotten the experience of steak and kidney! (*She breaks off a bit of crust, starts to nibble at it*) Thank God, Desmond's kept me away from any such temptations! You know what I am? Forty-four at the very best is what I am, and if it wasn't for Desmond I'd know nothing about contemporary life, I'd never have been jumping up and down all night with my head split in two with psychedelic music. I'd have been alone and lonely, all last evening, eating sausages and mash and turning the pages of my library book over with a fork. (*Almost absent-mindedly, she picks up a plate from the sideboard and begins to spoon steak and kidney pie onto it*) I'd've stretched out all across the bed at night and in the morning I'd've gone down in my dressing gown, covered in cigarette ash, to make scrambled eggs and come back and eat them and listen to House-wives' Choice with crumbs all over the eiderdown. You know what? Without Desmond there'd be no obligation . . . no obligation at all. (*She takes the plate of food with her and goes back to her place at the table. She takes a big greedy bite of pie-*

crust and pours a glass of wine to wash it down) Look here,
Miss Waterhouse. Look here, Joanna . . . Desmond's part of my
life, of course. I've kept up with him man and boy now for ten
years, fighting and dieting and seeing he got all the sun he deserved, and changed his motorcar regularly, and every year we've
got younger . . . and thinner . . . and smaller it seems to me.
And now we're just slips of things, just a couple of kids trem-
bling on the brink of middle age . . . and of course it's been
wonderful, but . . . (*She tears off a bit of bread, starts to butter
it lavishly*) This is what I'm trying to say . . . (*She bites into
the bread*) If you *really* care about Desmond . . . look here, I've
thought this over very carefully and if you really want to take
him on . . . *I'm not going to stand in your way.* I wouldn't be
so selfish. (*She wipes her mouth, then raises her glass*) Good
afternoon, Miss Waterhouse! Good luck, Desmond! Give my
love to everyone at the gym. I shan't be seeing them any more.
(*She kicks off her shoes, leans back in her chair. She seems, for
a moment, entirely happy. The phone on the sideboard rings.
For a moment, she sits still, smiling, not answering it. Then, she
gets up, and still smiling happily, picks up the phone*) Yes . . .
yes, this is Emma Grant. Who? Joanna . . . Well, it's a good
thing you rang as a matter of fact. I feel . . . I feel I can save us
a lot of trouble. I've been thinking and honestly, this morning
I was really being dreadfully turgid, wasn't I? I mean, there
wasn't any reason to ring you up as if you'd committed some
crime. I really think the way you and Desmond feel about each
other is a hundred-percent understandable. Given the fact that
for all practical purposes he's still about *eighteen,* and you're the
extremely bright and attractive character that I'm willing to bet
you are. So . . . there's honestly no need for you to come over
here and for us to thrash 'round and 'round just as if we really
hated each other, when all I want to say is, be happy because you
deserve it. (*She looks round guiltily at the table*) Also, something seems to have happened to your lunch. (*She listens to the
telephone. Her smile fades*) Desmond feels *what? Guilty!* Well,
that's ridiculous. I mean, I've got the paper and oh . . . all sorts
of things I'm going to have time for that I never did before. . . .

Well, like cooking. I said like . . . sleep and library books and the study of British Regional Food and. . . . No, tell him he's not to feel guilty! Let me . . . let me speak to him. Of course he's there! Oh, I know. The number of times I've told people on the telephone he's just gone out while he's stood beside the instrument making signals. (*Pause. She's appalled*) He's *what?* He's on his way back here. . . . You decided you couldn't do a thing like that to me . . . you couldn't ruin . . . a wonderful relationship! Joanna . . . Miss Waterhouse . . . Don't ring off! No! Listen to me! Listen to me! Please. . . . (*She stands for a moment and listens to the dead phone*) She's gone. Miss Watermouse has left us. Desmond. Poor old Desmond. We're left with each other. (*She looks round the room and then goes to the doors of the hatch, opens them and shouts through*) Mrs. Mac! Mrs. Mac! Come and take away all this food. For God's sake, Mrs. Mac, please come and remove the steak and kidney pie! (*She moves away from the hatch and looks, almost bewildered at the room*) What have I eaten . . . oh, whatever have I eaten? I must've gone mad! From tomorrow . . . We'll do it *together*. From tomorrow, nothing but hot water . . . with a little lemon juice. (*She goes to the mirror, pulls off her glasses, looks at her face*) The district nurse! I was getting quite fond of her. All right, Desmond. All right, you bastard! I know, she'll have to go! (*She pulls a lipstick out of her handbag and quickly starts to redo her make-up*) Won't we *ever* rest? (*She pauses a moment at the sound of a door opening somewhere in the house. She starts to speak, brightly, as if she were ten years younger*) Not that I'm tired, darling. I'm *not* tired, honestly! (*Her lips are on now. She turns towards the opening door of the room, smiles brilliantly and apparently with perpetual inexhaustible youth*) Welcome home!

Curtain

William Packard

SANDRA AND THE JANITOR

Since 1957, when he received a Robert Frost poetry award, William Packard has distinguished himself both as poet and dramatist. Born in New York City in 1933, and a graduate of Stanford University, he also teaches poetry and drama at various metropolitan schools and universities and at present is an assistant professor at New York University where he conducts classes in creative writing.

In 1963, he was chosen to be the first playwright-in-residence at the Institute for Advanced Studies in the Theatre Arts, New York, an educational organization dedicated to the enrichment of the American theatre through greater knowledge of world theatre, past and present. The experience intensified his interest in international drama and, subsequently, he wrote an English verse adaptation of a classical Japanese Noh play, *Ikkaku Sennin,* that was performed at the Institute. In the fall, 1971, the same organization will stage his version of a Peking Opera staple, *The White Snake.*

In 1965, Mr. Packard completed a new English Alexandrine translation of Jean Racine's tragedy, *Phèdre.* Directed by Paul-Émile Deiber of the Comédie-Française and co-starring Beatrice Straight and Mildred Dunnock, it opened at the Off-Broadway Greenwich Mews Theatre in February, 1966. The production ran for one hundred performances, a record-breaking engagement for an English-language presentation of the play, and won an Outer Circle Award, voted by critics of out-of-town periodicals for distinctive achievement in the New York theatre. In 1970, he resumed his affiliation with *Phèdre* by providing the English subtitles for the French film based on the play. It starred France's leading tragedienne, Marie Bell, whose frequent stage appearances in the role inspired the late Jean Cocteau to rhapsodize, "One would like to see her immobilized, turned into a statue, so that one could go on painting her beauty for the rest of his life."

An artist who accepts and even welcomes challenges, Mr. Packard has dipped into many languages in pursuit of source material for his translations and adaptations. Among these: French, Italian, Chinese, Japanese, Burmese and Babylonian.

A collection of his poetry, *To Peel An Apple,* was published in 1963, and his own plays include: *In the First Place; Once and for All; On the Other Hand; From Now On; The Funeral;* and *Sandra and the Janitor,* which originally was presented at the Herbert Berghof Playwrights Foundation, New York, and is published here for the first time.

A vice president of the Poetry Society of America, William Packard has recorded his own poetry and excerpts from his plays for the Library of Congress, Washington, D. C. In 1970, he spread his creative wings a bit further when he assumed the editorship of *The New York Quarterly,* a national publication devoted to poetry—"a magazine of pure craft, designed to be a toolbook for the practicing poet"—and whose advisory board is composed of W. H. Auden, Robert Lowell, Anne Sexton, Stanley Kunitz and Paul Blackburn.

Characters:

THE JANITOR

SANDRA

Scene:

*A basement apartment filled with a potpourri of junk.
There is an enormous stuffed owl with great wise eyes;
a fire extinguisher; an old tattered mannikin; stacks and
stacks of old yellow newspapers and magazines, piled two
and three and four feet high. An old iron cot, a plain
wooden chair, a hot plate, teakettle, mugs. Shirts and
socks strewn here and there, dirt and dust.*

The apartment is lit by a single standing lamp.

*The Janitor enters through door, carrying a pail and mop
and muttering to himself. He is dirty and unshaven and
badly in need of a haircut. He shuffles around in bedroom
slippers, deposits the mop and pail. Gradually, his mutterings become audible and tumble out erratically, accompanied by jerky gestures.*

JANITOR: Look at me—cold panic, all sweaty, desperate
to figure what is what and why am I cooped in with all this
goddamn stuff! No, no, no, no, no good trying not to notice,
cover it all over and you only get sick at the pit of your stomach.
Whatever it is inside the head keeps coming back and back, so
there's no knowing what to do with it . . .

*(He kicks the chair and collapses on cot, drops off his
bedroom slippers and breathes a deep sigh of rest and
resignation. Occasional mutterings arise from the cot,
then silence. The door slowly swings open, soundlessly,
but there is no one there. Then, after a moment, a figure
appears, dressed in an ancient black silk ankle-length dress.
A black silk scarf is draped over the head, masking the
face. A lighted candle in its hand. An awesome sight.
Slowly, the figure comes forward into the room, moving*

*in a dream-like ritual, one foot forward, pause, then the
other. A hollow voice begins chanting a curious litany,
a benediction over every part of the room, which the
figure visits slowly, systematically*)

FIGURE: Bless this mop and bless this broom, bless this
fire extinguisher and bless these newspapers strewn all over
everywhere, bless this old stuffed owl, bless this manni-nanni-
mannikin, and especially bless this junky bum, this germ-ridden
old trashcan janitor, lying here so popeyed and maggoty on his
old army cot. (*The figure is standing over the cot, looking directly down at the Janitor, who lies petrified for a moment, completely uncomprehending*)

JANITOR: Aw, what the hell, what the hell, what the
hell . . .

*(Suddenly, he regains his senses, leaps to his feet, snatches
the black silk scarf from off the head of Sandra. She is seventeen, high-strung, shy)*

JANITOR: (*Viciously*) Aw, you goddamn woman! Ain't
you got better to do than get yourself all dressed up crazy like
so, like the inside of your head, and come down here to scare
me! Now you go on and get hell back outa here right now!

SANDRA: (*Timidly*) No, no, don't make me go. I *had* to
come down to see you. There's no light upstairs in my apartment, none at all, no light inside the icebox and the TV won't
work and I've been groping around up there all night by candle-
light . . . (*She sets the candle down on floor*)

JANITOR: Yeah, well why didn't you go to bed and get
some sleep or something, insteada you had to come down here
trying to scare hell outa me. Go on now, get!

SANDRA: (*Desperate*) No, no, please! Don't you see, this
time it's *urgent*. This time it's an *emergency!*

JANITOR: Yeah, I know with you is always urgent, is *always* an emergency.

SANDRA: But it is, I tell you this time it *is,* it really *is.*

JANITOR: Yeah, well maybe my needing a little peace and
quiet is maybe also an emergency, you ever think of that? Go on
now, go, scram hell out of here!

SANDRA: But I told you, I blew a fuse or something, and I didn't want to bother you, and I tried staying up there all alone in my dark apartment because I remember you said to me I should never under any circumstances ever come down here and see you again ever, but I got scared and I couldn't stand it any more up there, and so I decided to get dressed up funny and maybe if I could make you laugh, you'd forget all about everything that happened last time and we'd be friends again, and you could maybe let me have a new fuse or something.

JANITOR: I ain't got no new fuses down here and so you gotta wait 'til morning when the stores open, and that is that. So go on now, get out of here.

SANDRA: Okay, but could I maybe stay here for just one more moment? You could maybe give me a cup of tea like you used to do . . .

JANITOR: There ain't no hot water heated.

SANDRA: Oh, I'll do it, I'd be glad to do it. You never used to let me do it, but I watched and now I know where everything is.

(*Sandra moves over to hot plate, fills teakettle, plugs cord into outlet and in the process knocks over a stack of newspapers in her way*)

JANITOR: (*Erupting*) Goddamn it, you get hell away from there! Can't you see, you can't do anything the way it should be done and so go on, get away, get out!

SANDRA: I had to see you.

JANITOR: Okay, so you see me, now go.

SANDRA: No, I mean I had to talk to you.

JANITOR: *Absolutely no,* absolutely not! Not after all them things what you said to me last time about how I was a dirty smelly trashcan janitor and about how my head was a dead-end and all like so, and you expect me to give over and forgive as easy as that, you got another thing coming! (*He goes over and rearranges stack of newspapers*)

SANDRA: Listen, last time I had huge bruises when I got back upstairs because you threw me down on the floor.

JANITOR: Yeah, well you had it coming to you—how you

threatened to tell Mrs. Schultz and get me thrown out of here and all that stuff, so I'd end up on that damned Bowery or something.

SANDRA: I didn't tell Mrs. Schultz anything. Do you think I could have done a thing like that? Ha ha, that's funny! I can just see me up there now, knocking at Mrs. Schultz's door, and she opens it . . . (*She begins to imitate Mrs. Schultz, a honey voice with a crass hard edge to it*) Why hello there, honey, come in there, honey, where you been there, honey? Huh? Oh, you been downstairs in the smelly basement in that nasty janitor's pigsty, huh? Honey, you tell me now, has he ever tried to *do* anything to you, huh? I mean, has he ever tried to take *advantage* of you or anything, huh? You tell me, honey, it's okay, you tell me if he has and I'll fix him good. I'll telephone the landlord and let him know what kind of *animal* he has down there in the basement, that's what I'll do!

JANITOR: *Okay!* Now okay, you cut that out! I'm here, see, and I'm gonna *stay* here, see, and ain't no screwball rich kid gonna throw me outa here, you understand what I am saying to you?

SANDRA: I'm sorry.

JANITOR: Bad enough I gotta be always fussing, always stuck with all this goddamn stuff without you come down here and torment me like so.

(*Sandra moves over to mannikin and drapes her black silk scarf over it, to represent Mrs. Schultz; then she slowly begins to unbutton her own black silk dress, voluptuously slips out of it to reveal that underneath she is wearing a man's white shirt and Levis. This is all done to the following speech, in imitation of Mrs. Schultz*)

SANDRA: Honey, come on, honey, you just unbutton your little old clothes for me now. That's it, you just undress right here and now and let me see what happened to you. Oh God, honey, just look at all the great huge bruises all over your beautiful two boobs! Just look! Why, honey, they're so black and blue! Why, that ugly grubby janitor man must have molested you, the way your poor body looks. Ah, God, just wait 'til I get my hands on him, just wait, I'll fix him good!

JANITOR: I bet you did! I bet you would! Strip down like
so in front of that witch-bitch up there. Unnatural stuff!—to let
her see you like so, all naked and looking over you with her
hands and eyes. Goddamn, doing such disgusting stuff, in front
of someone else! You just plain no good, you never was!

(*Sandra throws herself down on cot, sobbing, broken. The
Janitor stands above her, momentarily perplexed*)

SANDRA: You hate me, I can tell, you hate me! I knew it,
upstairs there in my dark apartment, I said to myself, the janitor
hates me! I know he has all the answers, he really does, and he
could help me *find* all the answers to everything, if only he didn't
hate me so much.

JANITOR: I don't love or hate nothing, I'm just tired.

SANDRA: Me too! I'm tired, and you know what I'm most
tired of, of all? I'm tired of *people*. People are what's wrong with
things. People, people, people, people, people! *All* people. People
appall me.

JANITOR: Yeah, well, people ain't so bad.

SANDRA: You don't know, you just don't know. Do you
know what that new doorman said to me just yesterday? He
asked me to go to bed with him. Just like that. He came right
out and said it. What do you think of that?

JANITOR: You probably led him on.

SANDRA: I didn't, I swear I didn't. I was just sitting outside there on the steps, smoking and looking at him like I usually
do, and he was standing over by the curb for about a half-hour
with his hands in his pockets and suddenly he came right back
over to me and he didn't even try to make conversation or anything, he just came right out and said it.

JANITOR: And what did you say?

SANDRA: Say, my God, I didn't say anything! I spit in his
face and shot my cigarette into his crotch and then I kept on
sitting there, looking at him and laughing at the top of my lungs.

JANITOR: You crazy!

SANDRA: Don't say that!

JANITOR: You crazy, I'll say it.

SANDRA: I'll go upstairs and tell Mrs. Schultz about the
time I saw you up on the roof of the building, standing there

and looking down on everyone in the street. (*She imitates Mrs. Schultz*) I'm glad you came up and told me about that, honey, because you know what he was doing? He wasn't only *looking*. I can tell with these creeps, most likely he also had his hands in his pockets and he was *playing* with himself—making himself happy over all the little old ladies down there in the street. That ugly disgusting dump of a bum!

JANITOR: (*Erupting*) You cut that out, you hear me, you hear what I am telling you?

SANDRA: (*Herself again*) You're the most important person in my life.

JANITOR: Listen, you got problems, you should go get help.

SANDRA: But you help me, you do, you really do. Every time I come down here, it helps me, it gives me something to hold onto, so I can make it through the next day.

JANITOR: Listen to what I am saying to you. You got something sick and twisted in you, you understand, you hear what I am saying to you?

SANDRA: (*Not having listened, not having heard*) All evening long up there, sitting upstairs in my dark apartment, I say to myself, the janitor has all the answers, the janitor really does, he has all the answers to *everything*.

JANITOR: I ain't got no answers to nothing.

SANDRA: Yes you do, and I know how it is. Sometimes, I can feel as if I know all there is to know, I see everything, on rare days all I have to do is close my eyes and I can see it all so clearly . . . (*She sits upright on the cot, her eyes very wide and staring straight ahead, intense, terrified, held in her vision*) Oh God, oh God, I can see, I can see. . .

JANITOR: (*Taken aback*) Okay, so you can see. Okay.

SANDRA: God! God!

JANITOR: What's what?

SANDRA: It *is!*

JANITOR: What is?

SANDRA: *It* is!

JANITOR: Yeah, well what's *it?*

(Sandra suddenly turns the full intensity of her attention on the Janitor, thoroughly intimidating him)

SANDRA: You know.

JANITOR: Naw, I don't know.

SANDRA: Yes, you *do* know.

JANITOR: *Naw, I don't know!*

SANDRA: *Yes, you do know!*

(Silence)

JANITOR: Naw, I don't know what hell you talking about, so cut out playing games on me like so, please.

SANDRA: *(Brightly, chattering)* You know the first thing I'm aware of in the morning when I wake up is I can hear the garbage being taken away outside my door, and then I wait awhile and finally the mail arrives. I hear the postman downstairs unlocking the box and dropping the letters into all the slots plop plop, and then after awhile, I hear you come along mopping the floors, and then the people begin to walk in and out and the elevators going up and down, and then the doorman comes around delivering packages to everyone and about that time I decide to get up.

JANITOR: You got things too easy.

SANDRA: You remember the doorman that was here last year, his name was Harry and we were very close friends, extraordinarily close. You see, we understood each other. Harry had his problems because I don't suppose he ever really had anyone to care about him. He had some very strange ideas, Harry did . . . *(She is up on her feet with her hands behind her back, imitating Harry)* Ya-know, once I was out there in California and ya-know, it gets pretty hot out there. Oh yeah, because ya-know they got that there Sahara Desert there right next door in Texas and all that warm hot air what blows all heat across the sands of the desert into California and if it weren't for the cool air comes down from Alaska and up from the Gulf of Mexico, it's hot as hell.

JANITOR: *(Laughing)* Yeah, Harry was pretty stupid all right.

SANDRA: There! I made you laugh, I made you laugh!

That's what I wanted, that's why I came down to see you, because I said to myself, if only I can make the Janitor laugh, perhaps it will cheer up his life a little bit, and make it easier for him to get through the day.

JANITOR: Go on about Harry.

SANDRA: But then one day Harry went away. He didn't even say goodbye to me, I who had been his close bosom friend, and it almost broke my heart. I stayed alone and lay on my bed long days knowing that now there was no one, no no now there was no one, and that was when I began riding the elevators all day long. I'd get in and push the buttons to the different floors and finally I came down here to the basement and I remember your door was open, so I looked in and you were lying right there on the cot . . .

JANITOR: Yeah.

SANDRA: And I knocked on the door and asked if I could come in and sit and visit with you, and you made an ugly face and motioned for me to go away, but I came in anyway and sat down and started to talk to you.

JANITOR: Yeah. (*Bored, he picks up old newspaper and begins to read*)

SANDRA: Listen, promise we'll always be friends, won't we, no matter what happens, you'll never go away and leave me, will you, and we'll always be friends?

JANITOR: Yeah, okay.

SANDRA: I don't have that many friends.

JANITOR: It's good to have friends.

SANDRA: As a matter of fact, I don't have any friends at all.

JANITOR: You should have friends.

SANDRA: I wasn't even that good friends with Harry. I only thought I was. (*She suddenly grabs newspaper from Janitor*) You don't have any friends at all either, do you? (*Janitor grabs the newspaper back*)

JANITOR: I got friends okay.

(*Sandra grabs newspaper, crumples it, sits on it*)

SANDRA: Well then, where are they? I never see them,

when do they ever come to visit you, these friends of yours?

JANITOR: Listen, goddamn you, just quit dumping all your junk problems on top of me and leave me be, you hear what I am saying to you? Sure I got my problems. I been kicked around plenty in my lifetime, without I listen to you always pestering me and trying to get me upset.

SANDRA: But all I want is to get close to you so I can be your friend.

JANITOR: I don't need you as no friend! I got enough to do around here by myself. I got to go up and down the stairs all day and mop the floors and do all sorts of chores, collect the ashcans and empty out the trash and take care of the incinerator and then clean outside where all the damned women out walking their dogs, letting them drop their dirty turds all over the sidewalk . . . (*He collapses on cot*) And then come back down here and try to take care of myself because I got a bad case of pain and a queer creaking in my joints all through my body parts and a wheezing when I breathe and sometimes I get a fungus in between my toes.

SANDRA: Poor old trashcan janitor, you've really got it rough. (*While Janitor sits musing on cot, she goes over to broom and begins sweeping around the room, imitating Janitor*) I got to go up and down the stairs and I got to take care of everything and I got to sweep out all the halls so I can be a goddamn good janitor so Mrs. Schultz won't throw me out of here, so I won't end up on no damned Bowery where I'm nothing but a stumble-bum . . .

(*Janitor leaps to his feet and grabs the broom from Sandra*)

JANITOR: Listen, you cut that out, you hear what I am saying to you?

SANDRA: (*Still as the Janitor*) Okay, I hear what you are saying to me.

JANITOR: You hear what I am saying to you, you got no right!

SANDRA: (*Still as the Janitor*) That's right, I got no right.

JANITOR: (*Totally mocked and speechless at this imita-*

tion) *You goddamn coming down here trying to get me all up-set!* (*He shrieks in pain and throws himself onto cot*)

SANDRA: (*Sadly, still as the Janitor*) Yeah, goddamn my coming down here trying to get you all upset.

(*Silence*)

JANITOR: You no good. You crazy!

SANDRA: (*As herself again*) I shouldn't have come down. I should have stayed upstairs, up there in my dark apartment all by myself, giving a little tea party for all of my imaginary friends. You should see me. I seat everyone around the room and I serve them all imaginary tea.

JANITOR: (*Baffled at this new madness*) Aw come on now, that's *really* crazy.

(*Sandra is on her feet, welcoming imaginary guests to her tea party, playing the pert hostess*)

SANDRA: Yes, who is it?—Oh, it's the janitor, how lovely that you could come. Won't you sit over here, my, you're look-ing filthy today, no, you're not at all early, I was just straighten-ing up a little bit before . . . Oh, excuse me, there's the doorbell again. Yes, who is it? Why, it's Harry the doorman, fresh from the Sahara Desert, do come in and sit down and shake out all the sand from your clothes . . . excuse me, la, it's the doorbell again. Oh, hello, it's Mrs. Schultz, do come in, you can sit right over here right next to the trashy ashcan janitor man. . . .

JANITOR: Hey, wait a minute!

SANDRA: Now does everyone have a tea cup?

JANITOR: I said wait a minute, hold your goddamn horses!

SANDRA: Is there something wrong? Didn't I give you any tea, la, of course not, silly me, I get so carried away with all the excitement and all, but here you are, now try tasting it and see if it needs a bit more spicing. . .

JANITOR: I said wait a minute, I ain't sitting next to no Mrs. Schultz at no stupid tea party, do you hear? I am telling you she ain't at any tea party what I'm at!

SANDRA: Oh, but my dear Mr. Janitor, it *is* up to me, you

know. I mean, after all, it's *my* tea party and I *do* decide who comes and who doesn't come.

JANITOR: Yeah, well if that's the way things are then maybe you better damn well scram-ass outa here back upstairs where you came from and play your crazy games all by yourself. I got things to do down here and don't think I don't!

SANDRA: (*Quickly*) Oh, no, not yet, please not yet. Let me stay just a little longer, please. . .

JANITOR: (*Swatting at her with a newspaper*) The hell, back upstairs to your damn tea party and Mrs. Schultz and the rest of it!

SANDRA: (*As hostess again*) Oh, on second thought, Mr. Janitor, perhaps I forgot to tell you, I distinctly remember Mrs. Schultz saying she couldn't come to my tea party after all, something had come up at the last minute.

JANITOR: Yeah? What came up?

SANDRA: I believe she said she had to shampoo her cat or something *silly* like that. (*She leans forward, becomes confidential*) You know, so long as there are only the three of us here now, and I know I can trust you both, I've been wanting to say that I've been noticing Mrs. Schultz for some time now and, well, she's not exactly "right."

JANITOR: Damned right she's not exactly right!

SANDRA: (*Suddenly herself again, dreamily*) I remember the very first time I went out to get something to give you, I spent the whole afternoon rummaging through old junk shops until I finally found something I wanted to buy, and then I saw it, that old stuffed owl over there, and I remember I came back and gave it to you so it could sit and stare at you while you were lying there on your cot.

JANITOR: Yeah.

SANDRA: And you seemed glad.

JANITOR: I liked it okay.

(*Sandra goes over to stuffed owl, strokes it*)

SANDRA: Nice old owl, sweet old owl.

JANITOR: Listen don't kid yourself, them old owls ain't

so damned nice and sweet, you should see the way they kill field mice. They catch them in their claws, like so, and tear their flesh apart and rip them into tiny shreds, and then they eat them with their beaks, and you should hear the way the field mice shriek.

SANDRA: (*Shivering*) I didn't know. (*The water in the kettle begins to boil*) The water's boiling.

JANITOR: Yeah. (*Janitor sighs, gets up, fixes tea*)

SANDRA: (*Watching him*) You make good tea.

JANITOR: Yeah.

SANDRA: No, I mean it. You make really good tea, you do, you make very good tea.

JANITOR: (*With self-satisfaction*) I know how to make a cup of tea.

SANDRA: God, I've been so bored!

JANITOR: How come you never go out, you ain't got no boy friends or like that, it ain't right.

SANDRA: If you must know, I'm recuperating.

JANITOR: Which is what?

SANDRA: I'm getting over a major breakdown, an illness.

JANITOR: Yeah, well you still got a ways to go if you ask me. Right now, you ain't nothing but a pain in the ass, is what you are.

SANDRA: That's because you don't give me half a chance to be anything else. (*She roams around the room*) Listen, if you like, I could come down here sometime when you're not here, and I could sort of straighten up. You know, pull all these old papers away, because you know they're really not doing you any good, all these old papers, full of news that isn't really news any more . . . (*She appraises the piles of newspapers by kicking against them as she talks, and several of them spill all over the floor*) I'm sorry, I didn't mean to do that.

JANITOR: (*Frantic, racing to save the piles of newspapers*) Aw goddamn, all the time making problems on me, *goddamn, goddamn!*

SANDRA: You know, you'd make a good juke box, all someone would have to do would be to put a penny in you and listen to you make a lot of fuss. (*She rummages around in an imaginary purse*) Now let me see if I have a penny in here somewhere . . . yes, of course, here we are . . . (*She mimes putting coin into Janitor*)

JANITOR: (*Shrieking with pain*) Aw goddamn witch-bitch woman you cut that out!

SANDRA: Oh, my, that was such fun! Wait, let me see if I have another penny in here somewhere . . . (*The telephone rings and they both fall silent*) Aren't you going to answer it?

JANITOR: No.

SANDRA: I think you should, I really think you should. It might be Mrs. Schultz calling to tell you she has cockroaches under her linoleum and wants you should come up and shout at them.

JANITOR: I got no time to listen to her slop of gossip.

SANDRA: Maybe she is trying to inquire after your welfare.

JANITOR: Welfare hell!

SANDRA: Maybe her toilet is overflowing.

JANITOR: Listen, she's got a damn good toilet, she's got a hell of a lot better toilet than she deserves.

SANDRA: Then maybe you should just answer the phone and tell her to stop bothering you.

JANITOR: That's *exactly* what she wants, listen, that's exactly what she wants! She wants I should tell her off, see, then she can report me to the super for being disrespectful or something like so, and I get canned—aw, I'm wise to her!

SANDRA: Maybe she was calling to tell you you'd *already* been fired, she just wanted to be the *first* to tell you. (*She imitates Mrs. Schultz*) Hello there, you smelly old honey, I just called to tell you that you're going to end up on that Bowery after all, that's right, that's where you'll be, isn't it marvelous! You'll be totally alone, a dirty, filthy nobody, and we'll all come by and laugh at you, you lying in doorways with sores all over your legs and bloody stubble on your chin and upchuck stuck all over all your clothes. Oh, it will be such fun, you there sitting and staring straight ahead, so ghastly sad and no way back for you at all, won't that be marvelous?

JANITOR: Oh God, you just shut up!

SANDRA: (*Coolly assessing him*) You know, I think you'd make a pretty good bum. If you really set yourself to it.

JANITOR: (*Moaning*) Oh God, oh God, why can't you shut up, why can't you leave me alone?

SANDRA: (*Brightly*) Listen! I've got a great idea, you could always get away from here.

JANITOR: How's that?

SANDRA: Easy!

JANITOR: You mean all that stuff about your family so rich, what owns a big apartment house down there in Florida? That's a lot of junk!

SANDRA: Well, they do, they really do, and it's all nice and new, and who knows, maybe they may need a janitor for it, or else maybe you could dress up as a doorman and stand all day blowing your little tin whistle at taxicabs, and anyway, you'd have a large apartment all to yourself, you could have tons of old crummy yellow newspapers piled up to the ceiling and dozens of silly manni-nanni-mannikins and carloads of dirty shirts and wastebaskets full of junk and dust and crap all your very own, and you could go out and spend the day just lying on the beach, listening to the great waves break on the sand, and maybe you'd be lying next to some millionaire who wouldn't even have to know you're really nothing but a crummy filthy trashcan janitor.

JANITOR: Now listen, you cut out that rotten talk about me being so dirty and all, you hear, you ain't got no right coming down here talking to me like so.

(*Silence*)

SANDRA: Actually the truth of the matter is, my family is sick and so is all of Florida sick and so am I sick, sick, sick, sick.

JANITOR: Yeah, you sick all right.

SANDRA: I'm sick all right. Some days all I have to do is lie down and close my eyes, and I go wading in great waves of rage, and other days I am mostly floating, coasting, nothing but a lot of lapses, naps, occasional good days when I may break free briefly, but the rest is just the great gray shade, the haze, as I go plodding, plodding, plodding. Ah God, you don't know what it's like, all the crazy chaos in my brain, sometimes I'm fogged out of my groggy mind, and I go around gassing everyone with my half-assed sadness, ah God, I'm so incomplete, I'm just a sappy fraction of the person that I ought to be. (*Silence*) Maybe it is and maybe it isn't.

JANITOR: Maybe what is?

SANDRA: Maybe it is. But maybe it isn't.

JANITOR: Maybe it is.

SANDRA: But maybe it isn't.

(*Silence*)

JANITOR: Like I say, you got problems, you should go get help.

SANDRA: There isn't any help for a person like me. Sometimes I think I need some sort of total surgery or something, an entire amputation of the mind. Christ, if I could only break out of the icy silence of my life!

JANITOR: You should go get help.

SANDRA: I did go, lots of times. They tried analyzing all of my anxieties, but always the bug doctors just kept sitting there staring at me and wouldn't say anything, and I had to talk and talk and talk and it never got anyone anywhere.

JANITOR: And so you come down here and dump all your junk on top of me.

SANDRA: But you're something different, you really are. You're the first person I could ever really talk to, and you do truly listen to me, don't you? Yes, I know you do, and you know all about me. Tell me, why do I feel so inferior? Is it because I really am?

JANITOR: God knows.

SANDRA: Sometimes I wonder what would it be like to jump out of a window, to feel myself falling down, down, through the air down, and the wind whistling through my hair and me shrieking to see the dead instant of landing ahead of me, a dull thud, and then the last vague thought as I lie dying on the sidewalk.

JANITOR: You sick okay.

SANDRA: I'll gradually get better.

JANITOR: You'd better get better.

SANDRA: Don't you think I'll make it?

JANITOR: God knows.

SANDRA: Tell me how I should do it.

JANITOR: I can't tell you nothing.

SANDRA: Yes, you can, I know you can, because you know all the answers.

JANITOR: I don't know nothing. You gotta figure it all out for yourself.

(*Sandra collapses on cot, sobbing. Janitor is dumbfounded, stands a good distance from her, looking at her*)

JANITOR: Come on now, come on, quit it, quit crying like so. (*Sandra continues sobbing; he gestures frantically*) Listen, look, what hell you want me to do about it? I mean, I can't tell you nothing. You want I should talk to you? About something? About what? I don't know what to talk to you. (*Sandra raises her head, lets out a loud wail*) Oh, for crying out loud, listen, look here, you want I should show you something, maybe like how they make it in a baseball game or something? (*Sandra stops sobbing, looks up curious*) Okay, okay, so watch here. Say the baseball player takes his place at the plate, like so, and see how he adjusts his cap and swings his bat like so across the plate to find the strike zone, see, and then, he settles in and stares at the opposing pitcher, like so, and see the way he waves his bat behind his back, like so, and patiently until the ball comes racing fast across the plate, and suddenly he swings and watch out, *Pow—eee!*

SANDRA: *Pow—eee!*

JANITOR: Like so, the ball goes up and up and up, higher and higher in the sky, and he is off and on his way, racing racing racing all around the bases.

SANDRA: I want to try it!

JANITOR: Okay you do like so.

(*Sandra assumes appropriate position and goes through all the motions, and hits a home run*)

SANDRA: *Pow—eee!*

JANITOR: That's right, like so.

SANDRA: It's wonderful! *You're* wonderful! (*She hugs Janitor*) You're wonderful to teach me something so wonderful!

JANITOR: Okay, okay, take it easy.

SANDRA: No, no I mean it, you *are* wonderful! Do you know just *how* wonderful you are? No, of course you couldn't, that's all a part of your being so wonderful!

JANITOR: Calm down now, huh?

SANDRA: Do you know what I think you are? Sometimes when I'm sitting upstairs in my dark apartment, I say to myself, the janitor is God Almighty, he really is, and he knows all the answers to everything!

JANITOR: Okay, come on now, cut that.

SANDRA: As a matter of fact! Do you know what I dreamt last night? Honestly, I'm not making it up—last night I dreamt you were Almighty God away up high above me, and I was standing somewhere small in front of you and you began to frown down clouds of disapproval on me. Oh, your eyes were angry and you said I was a phoney and an awful fraud, you said that you could see deceit in every part of me, and then you reached down and hit me and it felt as if I was being thrown out into the great waste of space, into the unknown, and I had to stay there forever all alone, there in the silence of the skies. . .

JANITOR: That's crazy stuff.

SANDRA: Listen, I know you *do* know all the answers, I know you *are* Almighty God, and so tell me, what else do I have to do in order to make it?

JANITOR: How the hell should I know? I don't even know nothing about all that stuff.

SANDRA: But you do, I know you do, and if you really truly do care about me then you'll tell me what is what.

JANITOR: That's sure as hell one thing you don't know, what's what.

SANDRA: I can't tell the difference between what's what and what's not what.

JANITOR: Well, you got to be able to tell, like that crazy tea party what you say you have upstairs all alone in your dark apartment, that's an example of what's not what.

SANDRA: But it is!

JANITOR: No it ain't, it's crazy and insane and it tells me you got something haywire going on inside your head.

SANDRA: Don't say that, don't say I'm crazy!

JANITOR: You don't know what's what.

SANDRA: Okay, so tell me. I need to know, so please, tell me as much as you can!

JANITOR: Goddamn, it's simple. Listen, this is this and that is that, okay?

SANDRA: Okay.

JANITOR: Okay. Like, the sun is the sun.

SANDRA: The sun is the sun.

JANITOR: The sun is the sun. And things is things.

SANDRA: Things is things.

JANITOR: And the dark is the dark, and the truth is the truth, and like so, and you can't get all this stuff mixed up together with other stuff because otherwise you won't know what is what.

(*Silence*)

SANDRA: You know something, you'd make an awfully good fortune cookie.

JANITOR: (*Enraged*) Aw, what the hell, I thought you was interested in learning about what was what.

SANDRA: But I am, I swear I am! Let me see if I can remember everything—the sun is the sun, right, and things is things, right, and the dark is the dark, right, and the truth is the truth—how am I doing?

JANITOR: (*Exasperated*) Aw, skip it!

SANDRA: No, don't you see, I *can't* skip it, because I have to have it, right here, right in my hands, right out in the open, so there's no more not knowing! (*She reaches up and switches off the standing lamp, so now there is only the flickering light of the candle on the floor*) Can't you say anything? Can't you think anything? (*She leans over and blows out the candle, and now there is total darkness*) Go ahead, whatever you want to say, don't be afraid, I'm here.

JANITOR: I . . .

SANDRA: Yes, go on, say it.

JANITOR: You . . .

SANDRA: Yes, it's all right, say it!

JANITOR: (*Close to tears*) It takes a lot of guts, is all I got to say, I got to face it all alone, be on my own, because I never had no one . . . (*Sandra turns on standing lamp again*)

SANDRA: (*Very efficiently*) Okay, now we're getting somewhere, you're lonely, well, my God, no wonder you're lonely! Listen, what do you do for love?

JANITOR: (*Baffled*) Huh?

SANDRA: For love, what do you do for love?

JANITOR: I do what I do.

SANDRA: I just bet you do, ha ha, I just bet you do! I can see you now, coming down here when you're all alone. How do I know you haven't got a lot of nylon stockings and stuff hidden away somewhere here, and maybe you get all dressed up like a woman and put on high heels and promenade up and down in front of that old stuffed owl?

JANITOR: Naw, I don't do like so.

SANDRA: (*Closing in on him*) Or maybe you make love to the manni-nanni-mannikin over there, is that it? Because that funny dummy never says anything, it just stands and stares at you, and maybe you go up to it and put your arm around it and maybe you unbutton your trousers and take *it* out and press it up against the mannikin? And then maybe you dance over and lie down on your cot and stretch your legs and release all your germs all over the bedsheets and blankets and dirty shirts and everything, is that what you do?

JANITOR: Come on now, cut it out. I do what I do, and you got no right to be coming down here making fun of me, you hear what I am saying to you?

SANDRA: (*Imitating Janitor, strolling around the room,*

stroking an imaginary penis) You hear what I am saying to you? That's right, I gave it to old owl last time and I am going to give it to the manni-nanni-mannikin this time, and maybe I might give it to that nice dirty pile of newspapers over there next time . . .

(*Janitor leaps at Sandra and strikes her so she falls onto cot, sobbing*)

JANITOR: *I told you!* You shouldn't go at me like so.

SANDRA: (*Very lucid*) You know, all the times I've come down here you could have taken advantage of me very easily, I mean here I am, all sick and twisted like you say, and lying right in front of you on your old cot, and you could make me do just about *anything,* whatever you want, and so why don't you? Don't you want me, don't you find me at all attractive?

(*Sandra begins to unbutton her blouse, takes out a breast and holds it towards the Janitor*)

JANITOR: Put it back!

SANDRA: It's for you, it wants you, it wants to feel your wet mouth on its nipple, it wants to feel you breathing hard all over it.

JANITOR: Listen, how do I know you ain't already done all this stuff before, maybe with Harry, the doorman. How do I know you didn't do all this stuff with him and that's why he had to go away, because you made trouble on him, the same as how you're trying to cause trouble on me now, so I'll have to go away and end up on that Bowery!

SANDRA: If that's what you think! Then I might as well go upstairs and throw myself out the window, I can just feel myself drop dead weight down, down, down to the ground, lie there all broken open on the pavement, and you come out with your broom and sweep me up and dump me into the incinerator. (*She starts for the door*)

JANITOR: No, don't do that, goddamn, you wait, come back . . .

SANDRA: No, I'm going to show you . . .

JANITOR: You listen, please, you leave me be, can't you,

stop making trouble on me! (*He grabs Sandra, shakes her roughly*) I am asking it of you, as one person to another, yes, don't do these things to me, don't do it, don't ever come down here no more ever, you hear what I am saying to you?

(*Sandra spits in Janitor's face*)

SANDRA: You think I care anything about a dirty trashcan janitor?

(*Janitor strikes her, she falls to floor*)

JANITOR: You think you so extra special! You think you the cat's ass! You think you the inside of the light bulb!

SANDRA: That's right!

JANITOR: Okay, go ahead, get outa here, go upstairs and report me to Mrs. Schultz, tell her I tried to rape you, she'll believe you. You can take off all your clothes in front of her and show her all the goddamn bruises, only get the hell out of here and leave me be in peace!

SANDRA: I will, and I'll say you made me do all sorts of unnatural stuff and it was *horrible!*

JANITOR: You . . . you . . . you . . . !

SANDRA: Me . . . me . . . me . . . !

(*Silence*)

SANDRA: Light.

JANITOR: Huh?

(*Sandra is suddenly intense, staring straight ahead*)

SANDRA: Light.

JANITOR: Where?

SANDRA: Light, light, light—I see it, I feel it, oh God, it's too much, I can't face it, make it go away, please, make it go away!

JANITOR: What the hell you looking at?

SANDRA: Yes, I see it now, I see everything!

JANITOR: You don't see nothing.

SANDRA: I see you, out there, on the Bowery, a bum, dirty and stinking and shivering, your clothes all torn apart and horrible sores all over your stomach and your penis hanging out all ugly and covered with fungus, and you reaching out to me, weeping and pleading, saying please, please, help me out of this hell, please, and me there laughing at you, laughing, ha ha ha ha. . . .

JANITOR: God, I got no words for you!

(*Janitor seizes Sandra, throws her towards door. She picks up her candle, black silk scarf, dress, and stands in doorway shaking with rage*)

SANDRA: This time I'm *really* going to tell on you, this time I'm really going to go through with it, I swear to God this time I'm going to make you good and sorry!

(*Sandra exits slamming door. Janitor collapses on cot, muttering to himself*)

JANITOR: So go ahead, so see if I care, so goddamn make up your lies, go goddamn do anything you want to do, say anything you want to say, only leave me be.

Curtain

The Editor

In his review of *The Best Short Plays 1970,* Bill Edwards wrote in *Daily Variety,* "The myth grown up around the frequent cry that 'nothing is being written for the theatre' has become almost a byword amongst producers . . . but as long as there is a Stanley Richards to ferret out new plays and compile them for *The Best Short Plays* series, the plaint will be nothing more than empty words. In his selections for this anthology, Richards has presented some brilliantly conceived and executed short works by authors who, whether proven to be major writers or promising novices, reflect the temperament of the times and the tastes of contemporary audiences . . . works that successfully hold up under close scrutiny and retain the authority that a valid theater piece must have. . . . His selections are meticulously picked and arranged in a sensible order. It is a book that should be on the shelf of anyone and everyone connected with—or remotely interested in—theatre today."

Within the comparatively short span of three years, Stanley Richards has become one of our leading editors and play anthologists, earning rare encomiums from the nation's press, and the admiration of his colleagues as exemplified by William Saroyan's comment, "It may just be that you are going to do more for the theatre than the money and arty and subsidized producers and theatrical groups. Something large is really shaping up. In short, you're doing a very important work with a lot of style and class. And the consequences are going to do something very special and right for both the United States and, therefore, the world theatre."

Mr. Richards has edited the following anthologies and series: *The Best Short Plays 1971; The Best Short Plays 1970; The Best Short Plays 1969; The Best Short Plays 1968; Best Mystery and Suspense Plays of the Modern Theatre; Best Plays of the Sixties* (the latter two, *Fireside Theatre-Literary Guild* selections); *Best Short Plays of the World Theatre: 1958–1967; Modern Short Comedies from Broadway and London;* and *Canada on Stage.*

An established playwright as well, Mr. Richards has written twenty-five plays, twelve of which (including *Through A*

Glass, Darkly, Tunnel of Love, August Heat, Sun Deck, O Distant Land, and *District of Columbia*) originally were published in earlier volumes of *The Best One-Act Plays* and *The Best Short Plays* annuals. His television play *Mr. Bell's Creation* holds a record: it has had more live television productions (both here and abroad) than any other play.

Journey to Bahia, which he adapted from a prize-winning Brazilian play and film, *O Pagador de Promessas,* premiered at The Berkshire Playhouse, Massachusetts, and later was produced in Washington, D. C. under the auspices of the Brazilian Ambassador and the Brazilian American Cultural Institute. The play also had a successful engagement at the Off-Broadway Henry Street Playhouse during the summer of 1970 and is currently in the 1971 repertory season of the New York Theatre of the Americas.

Mr. Richards' plays have been translated for production and publication abroad into Portuguese, Afrikaans, Dutch, Tagalog, French, German, Korean, Spanish and Italian.

In addition, he has been the New York theatre critic for *Players Magazine* and a frequent contributor to *Playbill, Theatre Arts, Writer's Digest, Writer's Yearbook, The Theatre, Actors' Equity Magazine,* and *The Dramatists Guild Quarterly.*

As an American Theatre Specialist, Mr. Richards has been awarded three successive grants by the United States Department of State's International Cultural Exchange Program to teach playwriting and directing in Chile and Brazil. He taught playwriting in Canada for over ten years and in 1966 was appointed Visiting Professor of Drama at the University of Guelph, Ontario. He has produced and directed plays and has lectured extensively on theatre at universities in the United States, Canada and South America.

Mr. Richards, a New York City resident, is now at work on a collection of *Best Short Plays of the World Theatre: 1968–1973;* and *The Best Short Plays 1972.*